PIPE, BIBLE, AND PEYOTE

AMONG THE OGLALA LAKOTA

A Study in Religious Identity

Paul B. Steinmetz, S.J.

The University of Tennessee Press ■ Knoxville

Library of Congress Cataloging in Publication Data

Steinmetz, Paul B.
  Pipe, Bible, and peyote among the Oglala Lakota : a study in
religious identity / Paul B. Steinmetz. —Rev. ed.
    p. cm.
  Bibliography: p.
  Includes index.
  ISBN 0–87049–623–9 (cloth: alk. paper) :
    I. Oglala Indians—Religion and mythology. 2. Native American
  Church of North America. 3. Indians of North America—
  South Dakota—Religion and mythology. 4. Teton Indians—
  Religion and mythology. I. Title.
  E99.O3S83 1990   89–33829 CIP

CONTENTS

ILLUSTRATIONS

PREFACE

The author of this book is a remarkable man, out of the ordinary, and occupies a unique position in American Indian religious studies.

For a couple of decades Father Paul Steinmetz, S.J., served as a dedicated missionary among the Oglala Lakota in South Dakota. It was during this time that he launched the startling Christian reinterpretation of Lakota religion based upon the inspiration that the Sacred Pipe, the most holy of Lakota religious sacramentals, could be transformed into a symbol of Christ. Not unexpectedly, this innovation in ritual theology created mostly favorable reactions among the Indians concerned, served as a model of missionary adaptation, and provoked an engaging debate among anthropologists. It was also during this time that Paul Steinmetz himself took on the role of the anthropologist and conducted field research among the Oglala, with great reward, for the Oglala evidently put much trust in him. So Father Paul finally turned out as both missionary and scholar in the anthropology of religion, a subject in which he finally earned his Ph.D. As a man of high intellectual ability and deep human kindness, he has managed to make weighty achievements in both these activities.

His connections with American Indian religion are two-dimensional. I know of no other person in modern times who, to the same extent, has been both a subject in and an object of scholarly research on North American Indian religion. He has engaged himself deeply in such research, but he is also himself part and parcel of recent Native American religious history.

This is a book about the religion of Red Cloud's people as it appears today. The once warlike Oglala Lakota have, like other Indians, been known for the way in which religion has guided and penetrated their everyday life. In the old days they were famous for their spectacular Sun Dance, with self-sacrifices of a stunning intensity. Their holy men made lofty speculations on the Godhead and the spiritual world, their medicine men divined the secrets of the future in dramatic seances, and their young men experienced encounters with spirits in fasting visions. Memories of old religious expressions have been told by former warriors and medicine men like Black Elk and Lame Deer.

The present Oglala religion is, however, not just a relic of the past. As this book shows, the essential, traditional religious creed and many of the great ceremonies live on, although, of course, some changes in the general religious picture have taken place. The ancient military overtones are gone; probably they were never as strong as we may imagine. We face a spiritual faith emphasizing peace, harmony, and well-being, and stressing good relations between people. Such values were certainly shared in the old Oglala religion, but they come better to the fore in today's setting. Also, we are confronted with a new acculturative situation, where the influence from both other Indian religions (including Pan-Indian movements) and Christianity have expanded the religious perspectives. Oglala Lakota religion implies today not only the heritage from traditional religion, it includes, as this book demonstrates, new religious movements such as Peyotism—the Native American Church-and a modified Indian form of Christianity, the Body of Christ Independent Church.

No other monograph on the Oglala Lakota gives such an extended and searching presentation of their religious life today. This book shows the Indian attitudes in the matter of religious pluralism, their combination of traditional and new religious values. Paul Steinmetz is uniquely competent to describe Oglala religious life as he experienced it. During his long stay with the Oglala, he became thoroughly acquainted with all sides of their religious activities. He created fine relationships with them and had no difficulties in winning the hearts of people who followed another faith. The secret of this success lies no doubt in his congenial personality.

ÅKE HULTKRANTZ

ACKNOWLEDGMENTS

This study is the result of having been deeply associated as a Catholic priest between 1961 and 1981 with the religious ferment that is taking place among the Oglala Lakota on the Pine Ridge Reservation in South Dakota and of a scholarly reflection on my experience. My main involvement began when I prayed with the Sacred Pipe at the funeral of Rex Long Visitor on November 6, 1965, in the Slim Butte community on the reservation. My taking up the Sacred Pipe led me to an intimate relationship with medicine men and others deeply involved in Lakota religion. I share with you the sacred knowledge which they have shared with me, since I feel that the contribution the Lakota are making to the history of religion should be more widely known.

I am indebted to the many Oglala Lakota people who have accepted me not only as a Catholic priest but also as a "holy man" in their own religious tradition. I must confess that Lakota religion has added a new depth to my priestly life. My special appreciation goes to four medicine men: John Iron Rope, who first accepted my praying with the Sacred Pipe; George Plenty Wolf, who also considered the priest as one worthy to handle the Sacred Pipe; Pete Catches, Sr., who put me on the hill and directed my Pipe Fast; Frank Fools Crow, who asked me to participate in the most sacred of Lakota ceremonies, the Sun Dance. I am grateful to Edgar Red Cloud and the entire Red Cloud community for wholeheartedly accepting me during my first years among them. Others deserve appreciation. Lawrence Hunter introduced me to Stanley Looking Horse at Green Grass on the Cheyenne River Reservation in South Dakota, where the Sacred Calf Pipe is kept. John and Beatrice Weasel Bear accepted me as one of their own family and have honored me in many Native American Church ceremonies. Phillip Eagle Bear conducted the two Half Moon Peyote meetings for my safe journey to Europe and back. Emerson Spider, High Priest of the Native American Church for the State of South Dakota, has extended me a deep friendship and made valuable contributions. Eugene Rowland of the Body of Christ Church has shared his religious experiences with me. Richard White Calf was my faithful interpreter. Other Lakota have contributed. Without all of these friends, this study would have been impossible.

My Jesuit superiors continually supported me in my work among the Lakota, particularly in my efforts to form a bridge between Christianity and Lakota religion: William K. Powers is completely misinformed when he states that "Steinmetz began participating in local native ceremonies much to the consternation of his superiors" (1977: 116), and Patricia Kaiser continues this same misinformation in stating that "Father Steinmetz began to use the pipe in Mass, an act which greatly angered his superiors" (1984: 19). Dr. George Morgan, who was an Honorary Research Fellow at the Botanical Museum at Harvard University and a close friend for many years until his untimely death, gave me valuable insights into the Native American Church. Father William Stolzman, S.J., author of *The Pipe and Christ*, helped me develop the model of religious identity. Dr. Wilcomb E. Washburn of the Smithsonian Institution has expressed appreciation for my involvement in Lakota religion (1975: 264). Dr. Harold Turner, formerly of the University of Aberdeen in Scotland has given me an appreciation of the typology of new religious movements in primal societies. Dr. Carl Hallencreutz, Professor of the Department of Missiology at the University of Uppsala, has been helpful in the discussion of religious symbolism. Dr. Åke Hultkrantz of the University of Stockholm recognized the importance of the Christian influence on Oglala Lakota religion and felt that I had a contribution to make in this relationship. I may add that I feel privileged to have been directed in my doctoral dissertation by one recognized as an international authority on the Native American Indian.

I am grateful that Dabney Otis Collins (1969), J. S. Smith (1970: 91–93) and Christopher Vecsey (1987: 347) have all given me recognition of my work with the Lakota as a priest who appreciated the validity of the Lakota religious tradition.

This book was first published in the Stockholm Studies of Comparative Religion monograph series (Steinmetz 1980). However, it is out of print. For this new publication, extensive revision has been made in the introduction. Books that have appeared since its first publication have been included. The argumentation, especially on the relationship between Christianity and Lakota religion, has been expanded. Despite these improvements, the major documentation has remained the same.

Cante waste ya napeciyuza pi. I shake hands with a good heart with each and every one of them.

PIPE, BIBLE, AND PEYOTE
among the Oglala Lakota

INTRODUCTION

A study of contemporary Lakota religion is very impor-
tant for a number of reasons. No one has ever treated the total religious
activity among the Oglala Lakota, bringing out the complexity of the
religious situation to achieve a better understanding of what is actually happening on the Pine Ridge Reservation in South Dakota. Fur-
thermore, because Oglala religion is in a state of transition and the
religious identity of these people may be undergoing more rapid change
today than at any other time, the preservation of the historical process is a vital concern. Very little has been written on its religious
history. Among the extensive literature on Peyote, for example, there
are only a few passing references to the Oglala Lakota in the latest
edition of Weston LaBarre's *The Peyote Cult* (1975). To my knowledge,
the Body of Christ Independent Church has not even been mentioned
in any literature. Consequently, this study is an original contribution
to ethnographic research. Finally, I hope that the investigation into
the interdynamics of Pipe, Bible, and Peyote will be a contribution
to the theoretical knowledge of religious acculturation by showing
for the first time the effect all three religious traditions have had on
the Oglala Lakota religious identity. This research provides the basis
for an important conclusion: namely, that Indians need not necessarily
acculturate to white culture but they may also acculturate to nontraditional Native American culture. This conclusion eliminates the
false assumption that Joseph G. Jorgensen and Richard Clemmer make
in claiming that acculturation analysis "assumes that Indians acculturate to white culture" (1978:39). This study also shows that acculturation is a most crucial social factor in Indian-to-Indian relations as
well as in Indian-to-White ones.

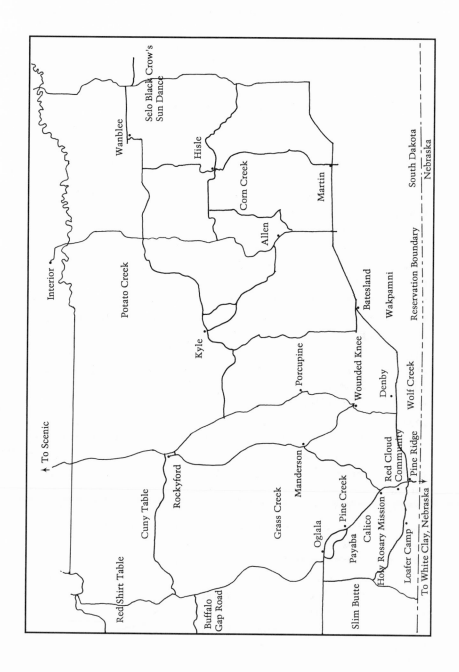

A few historical remarks are necessary for the reader to know who the Oglala Lakota are.[1] The Sioux, speaking the dialects of Lakota, Dakota, and Nakota, were first mentioned by white explorers around 1640 in the western Great Lakes region. They lived off hunting, fishing, and the gathering of lake and forest products. Partly due to pressure from the Ojibwa or Chippewa, the Teton tribe, speaking Lakota, moved westward into the Northern Plains in the early 1700s and filtered into the Black Hills region sometime after 1750. During this period they acquired the horse (McGee 1897:173–174; Haines 1938:434) and became the well-known buffalo hunters and warbonnet warriors. However, the first recorded notice of the Oglala as a distinct subtribe of the Tetons is that of Lewis and Clark, who in 1806 found them living on the Missouri River between the Cheyenne and Bad Rivers in the present South Dakota (Hodge 1907/1910:109). The Oglala Teton or Lakota were confined to the Pine Ridge Reservation in 1878 (Hyde 1937:23). The reservation, a 4,350-square-mile area measuring approximately fifty miles north to south and one hundred miles east to west, is located in semi-arid country in the southwestern corner of South Dakota, near Rapid City and directly below the Badlands National Monument.

The Lakota Sioux are related to a linguistic group called Siouan including the Assiniboin, Omaha, Ponca, Osage, Kansas, Iowa, Oto, Missouri, Winnebago, Mandan, Hidatsa, Crow and other tribes. (Dorsey, 1894:361).

In one sense we are dealing with a religious tradition that goes back into the prehistoric past and in another sense with one that has a very short history. The Lakota used the Sacred Pipe perhaps for several thousand years. However, the Pipe with the particular meaning given it by the Legend of the Buffalo Calf Woman dates most likely from around 1785. Elements of their most important ceremony, the Sun Dance, may have originated in world renewal and other ceremonies in distant parts of the world and in distant times. But the best evidence indicates that the Sun Dance as it is practiced today goes no further back than the beginning of the eighteenth century. These two claims will be substantiated later.

The definitions of religion are numerous and the debates over them are lengthy. In employing the term *religion* I am referring to a transcendent relationship to a superhuman power or personal being. Because of religion's transcendence it cannot be completely understood through history, anthropology, and sociology, although these disciplines give us important insights into its nature. I feel that religion as religious experience—that is, in its transcendence—can only be understood through the phenomenological investigation of its symbols. Phenomenology, "the systematic study of the forms of religion" (Hultkrantz 1970:74), is the discipline which allows religious experience to speak to one without being prejudiced by predetermined definitions or theories.

Perhaps the most notable scholar to use this approach was the late Mircea Eliade, in his classic treatment of primal religion, *Patterns in Comparative Religion* (1958). There is a large body of literature evaluating the strengths and weaknesses of Eliade's method (Allen 1978, Altizer 1975, Dudley 1977, Girardot and Ricketts 1982, Saliba 1976, Silva 1982). However, Eliade's approach to the nature of symbolism can be understood without entering into this controversy.

In his essay, "Methodological Remarks on the Study of Religious Symbolism," Eliade discusses the nature of religious symbolism:

> Since man is a *homo symbolicus*, and all his activities involve symbolism, it follows that all religious facts have a symbolic character. This is certainly true if we realize that every religious act and every cult object aims at a meta-empirical reality. When a tree becomes a cult object, it is not as a *tree* that it is venerated, but as a *hierophany*, that is, a manifestation of the sacred. And every religious act, by the simple fact that it is *religious*, is endowed with a meaning which, in the last instance, is "symbolic," since it refers to supernatural values or beings (1959:95).

His method of understanding a religious symbol such as the Cosmic Tree will be presented in the last chapter.

Eliade compares his method to that of the depth psychologist (1959: 95). And I do find that his method is similar to Carl Jung's understanding of symbols by means of amplification. My discovery is confirmed in an exhaustive study of Eliade in which the claim is made that his "comparative method is a type of Jung's amplificatory method" (Silva 1982:227).[2]

Marie Louise von Franz, in commenting on Jung's method, writes:

A still living symbol can never be "resolved" (that is analyzed, understood) by a rational interpretation, but can only be circumscribed and amplified by conscious associations; its nucleus, which is pregnant with meaning, remains unconscious as long as it is living and can only be divined. If one interprets it intellectually, one "kills" the symbol, thus preventing any further unfolding of its content ... The more significantly a symbol expresses an unconscious component that is common to a large number of people, the greater its effect on society (1980:83).

This is the approach that will be used here to understand the religious symbolism found in the Oglala Lakota religion.

In discovering what this religion is, I do not start with a definition, but rather I look at what the Oglala Lakota people are practicing and what they consider Lakota. I discovered that Oglala Lakota religion includes the traditional Lakota religion of the Sacred Pipe, the Native American Church, which has gone beyond its pan-Indian identity and acquired a Lakota one, and the Body of Christ Independent Church, whose members regard it as a Lakota (in contrast to a white man's) church. Pipe, Bible, and Peyote are being used to symbolize these three religious traditions. The Bible also symbolizes the influence the traditional Christian churches have had on Oglala Lakota religion.

I believe that the ultimate source of personal identity is religious. Carl Jung said that no one came to him for psychotherapy in the second half of life whose problem was not ultimately religious. This is why I use an investigation into the Oglala Lakota religious identity as a means of pulling together all the diverse data contained in this study. I am using the term *identity* as defined by Erik Erikson: "At one time, then, it will appear to refer to a conscious sense of individual identity; at another to an unconscious striving for a continuity of personal character; at a third, as a criterion for the silent doings of ego synthesis; and finally as a maintenance of an inner solidarity with a group's ideals and identity" (1959: 102).

Identity involves the concept of full-blood and mixed-blood. Racially this designates the degree of blood, but sociologically it refers to the receptive values being lived, regardless of blood quantum, a distinction which MacGregor brought out (1946:25). Thus a person of quarter-Indian blood may be a sociological full-blood.

This study involves several very distinguishable groups among the

Oglala Lakota. The first one is the American Indian Movement. This is a pan-Indian movement which originated in the Minneapolis–St. Paul urban area and has become established on various reservations throughout the United States. It is a militant group that engages in political activity and urges Indians to return to their "original" Indian religions.[3]

The second and third are groups of Lakota who are seeing a relationship between Oglala Lakota religion and Christianity. Native American religions have been significantly influenced by their encounter with Christianity. This is a fact that has only recently been recognized by American anthropologists. I use the terms *Ecumenist I* and *Ecumenist II* for these groups in an extended sense, wider than the relationships between Christian Churches.[4] Ecumenist I designates those Lakota Christians who separately practice their traditional and Christian religions but see common religious forms between the two traditions. Ecumenist II designates those Lakota Christians who see the Christian religion as a fulfillment of the Lakota religion through the symbolic identifications they made. Although they are a small minority of Lakota, the medicine men and more serious thinkers, they have influenced a large number of Lakota, and their contribution to the history of Lakota religion is important.

The fourth and fifth groups are the Cross Fire and Half Moon fireplaces in the Native American Church. This church is a pan-Indian religious institution first incorporated with a state charter in Oklahoma in 1918, followed by incorporation in other states, and later with a national charter in Oklahoma in 1934. According to J.S. Slotkin, the main purpose of incorporation was to legalize Peyote, (a small, spineless, carrot-shaped cactus growing in the lower Rio Grande Valley of Texas and southward into Mexico) as a sacrament (1956:58, 62.). The Half Moon and Cross Fire fireplaces are two divisions within the church but do not appear in any of the N.A.C. charters examined. This group offers one a most remarkable opportunity to understand the nature of religious acculturation by showing what happens in the encounter not only of traditional and Christian religion but also of traditional and nontraditional Indian religion.

The sixth group is the Body of Christ Independent Church. This is a Pentecostal-type fundamentalist church which is an offspring of the encounter between Lakota and Christian religious traditions. The effect this group's position has on the Oglala Lakota religious identity is most instructive.

Harold Turner's treatment of new tribal religious movements in primal societies is valuable for understanding all these groups (1980).

I use the term *primal religion*, instead of *primitive*, which has been frequently used in the past. *Primitive religion* has inappropriate derogatory connotations. *Nonliterate religion* seems to be too narrow a characterization. *Tribal religion* was considered but the pan-Indian aspects of Lakota religion makes this term inaccurate. Instead, primal religion in the sense of original, being the origin of man's religious aspirations, is used. Primal religion is closer to man's basic religious feelings and instincts than the so-called "universal religions."

In addition to the phenomenological approach, my own research in the field has been influenced by a cultural historical method based on Paul Radin's "Reconstruction from internal evidence" (1932:183–252).

Radin's *Method and Theory of Ethnology* received a mixed reception from his colleagues, R. R. Marett being very critical (1934:116–18) and Alfred Kroeber sympathetic (1933:765–66). However, it contains, in my opinion, some excellent observations and a valuable method on understanding religion in the field. Radin insists on the importance of being a part of the cultural scene and not standing outside of it, as is done in a scientific approach:

In science we stand beside or, if you will, above the facts. We are not a part of them. But we are a part of the cultural facts we are describing in a very real way. The moment we stand beside or above them, we do them injury; we transvaluate them or make them facts of another order. In short, they are reduced to facts of the physical world. "The disadvantages attendant upon being an integral part of the phenomena we are describing must seem a fatal defect to the scientific mind. Unquestionably it is. But it is inherent in cultural phenomena and nothing can very well be done about it. This defect is not being corrected by treating them as physical facts. Objectivity, in the sense in which it exists in the natural and physical sciences, is impossible for culture history, except, perhaps, in the domain of material culture. For culture, the ideal of permanency and durability towards which a description of the physical world inevitably strives is unattainable. The more culture historians and ethnologists attempt it, the more suspect their descriptions become. There are too many *imponderabilia*, and these are too intimately connected with its very life blood. (1933:11–12).

I was a Catholic priest on the Pine Ridge Reservation from 1961 to 1981. Ever since I prayed with the Sacred Pipe in 1965, I have developed deep personal relationships with many Lakota, in which they shared their lives with me. At times this knowledge has become so intimate that names and details have been omitted. While remaining sensitive to the confidence they have placed in me, I share a part of this experience, hoping that it will benefit Indian and White alike. I have made every effort to be aware of any disadvantages this relationship may have had. My acceptance of the Lakota and their religion at least minimized their need to please me. Some Lakota expressed beliefs which they held for many years. As we will see below, Fools Crow formed many of his Lakota Christian beliefs on his own, without the assistance of a Catholic priest. Some of my observations were confirmed by Luis Kemnitzer while he was doing field work on the reservation and by Omer Stewart in his research. One young medicine man told me that Christ was not God but merely a powerful medicine man. Finally, the Lakota I spoke with had characters above deception. This is at least some indication that the opinions that the Lakota expressed were not adversely influenced by their awareness of my being a priest. Rather, my praying with the Sacred Pipe as a priest established an intimate relationship with some medicine men which was impossible for nonclerical anthropologists.

There is a second reason why my being a priest was an asset in my field work rather than a liability. Robin Horton in his "Ritual Man in Africa" writes:

A first step in the analysis of an alien religious system must always be the search for an area of discourse in one's own language which can appropriately serve as a translation instrument. And in so far as he is thoroughly at home in the religious discourse of his own culture, the Christian would seem to be at an advantage over the agnostic in this matter. The reasonableness of this argument receives support from the defects of most of the religious analysis carried out by agnostic anthropologists (Horton 1971:353).

Gottfried Oosterwal takes the same position in being critical of Weston LaBarre's treatment of crisis cults:

LaBarre's statement that "anthropologists should grasp at each and every theory that they can find from whatever discipline" (p. 26) is refreshing. It strikes me, however, that LaBarre himself has left out the recent contributions made by theology, missiology and the history of religion on the phenomenon of crisis cults. Why should such studies be more biased than the ones written by a Marxist economist or an "unbelieving" psychologist? Whatever our presuppositions, we cannot deny the depth of thought in modern theological and religious-historical studies. And there may well be another dimension to these cults than those the anthropologist and psychologist have detected. Modern anthropological studies on religion suffer from an "accomplishment complex": we draw our concepts from too narrow a tradition. It is time for us to broaden our horizons and take into consideration what recent philosophical, theological and religious-historical studies have contributed (Oosterwal 1971:32).

One purpose of this study is to broaden the anthropological study of Native American religions and to show that a person with a Christian perspective is in a privileged position to understand them. It is the Christian, and especially the Catholic, who has a sense of sacramentalism, which I believe, along with the presence of spirits in nature, is the basic foundation of all primal religion. Recognizing the sacramental nature of Lakota religion, Vine Deloria, Sr., a Lakota Episcopal priest, raised a challenging question to the Christian churches: "When an Indian prays over a stone and says he's made it holy, that's superstition and practicing magic. Why isn't it superstition when we pray over water for baptism and the water suddenly becomes possessed of special qualities? The two things are exactly alike" (1987: 109). And W. E. H. Stanner uses sacramentalism as a means of understanding Australian Aboriginal religion (1960).

However, as Deloria's question indicates, a fundamentalism which results in a too literal interpretation of the Bible, and a religious imperialism, which fails to recognize valid religious forms in non-Christian religions, made it impossible in some cases for this sense of sacramentalism to be recognized.

However, I am involved in contemporary Oglala Lakota religion in a deeper dimension than even Radin had in mind. At certain times, which will be clearly indicated, my participation in their religion as a Catholic priest has been an influence on their attitudes and even on their ceremonies. Consequently, at times my own personal beliefs are a part of the history of Lakota religion. At times I am not an outside observer projecting my ideas on ethnographic data but, instead, part of the history influencing it.

Radin lays down several other requirements:

The failure to [specify the qualifications of informants] together with the very frequent failure to distinguish carefully between the record as obtained and the discussion of it, constitutes one of the most glaring and inexcusable defects of the majority of all monographs on aboriginal peoples. No introduction on the method of field work or in the critical controls to be observed, such as Malinowski and Mead indulge in, can make amends for this offense against the elementary requirement that others have an opportunity of scrutinizing the record as it was obtained (1932: 115–16). . . .

[There is need for] an adequate body of texts; and this can be accomplished only if we realize, once and for all, that we are dealing with specific, not generalized men and women, and with specific, not generalized, events. But the recognition of specific men and women should bring with it the realization that there are all types of individuals and that it is not, for instance, a Crow Indian who has made such and such a statement, uttered such and such a prayer, but a particular Crow Indian. It is this particularity that is the essence of all history and it is precisely this that ethnology has hitherto balked at doing. It is a mistake to believe that it cannot be done any more. (184–85).

Consequently, I have included not only ample documentation and the qualifications of my principal informants but have also maintained a separation of record and discussion. This approach allows credit to be given to exceptional individuals who have had a substantial influence on Oglala Lakota religion, a point Radin insists on (1933:7). A large amount of the material was obtained on a tape recorder and translated. Replaying of the material allowed me to check it with accuracy. This study, then, is primarily the contribution of Lakota people, whose qualifications are presented now.

For the traditional religion of the Sacred Pipe, the principal sources are:

Pete Catches, Sr., at one time a Catholic catechist, who became a medicine man through witnessing the healing power of the Pipe. He conducts his own Sun Dance and Pipe Fasts.

Lawrence Hunter (deceased), who was originally from the Cheyenne River Reservation in northern South Dakota. He grew up near Green Grass, where the Calf Pipe is kept, and heard about the tradition of the Sacred Pipe in his early years. He sang for the ceremonies of various medicine men and was a practicing Catholic.

John Iron Rope (deceased), a respected medicine man in the Slim Butte Community and a practicing Catholic.

Frank Fools Crow, the oldest living medicine man on the Pine Ridge Reservation and influential in the Lakota religious world. He has conducted most of the official Sun Dances on the reservation throughout the years. He is a practicing Catholic who insists on the Christian influence on Lakota Religion. Thomas E. Mails published his biography (1979).

Lucy Looks Twice (deceased), the daughter of the famous Black Elk about whom John G. Neihardt (1932) and Joseph Epes Brown (1953) wrote. At the time of her interview with Michael Steltenkamp, S.J., she was the last remaining member of that immediate family, the most authoritative living source on the Black Elk tradition.

Richard Moves Camp, a young medicine man highly respected in the Wanblee Community and a descendent of the Chips family, which has a long tradition of being medicine men.

Dawson No Horse (deceased), who acquired influence as a medicine man, especially among young Lakota. He received some of his power from Fools Crow and was his principal assistant in the Sun Dance. He was also an active Episcopal lay reader.

George Plenty Wolf (deceased), a medicine man in the Red Cloud Community and a practicing Catholic. As an old man he knew Lakota tradition well.

Edgar Red Cloud (deceased), a great grandson of Chief Red Cloud. He was a Sun Dance singer for fifty years and a leader of the singers for twenty-five of those years. He lived in the traditional Lakota world and was a practicing Catholic.

Pete Swift Bird, from a family deeply involved in traditional Lakota religion. His mother was a medicine woman.

For the Native American Church there are the following sources:

Phillip Eagle Bear (deceased), the State Secretary of the Native American Church in South Dakota. He was a Half Moon roadman (conductor of meetings) on the Rosebud Reservation for many years.

Ira Elk Boy (deceased), a roadman on the Pine Ridge Reservation.

Lawrence Hunter (deceased), who attended meetings in the 1930s and 1940s and knew many of the old-time Peyote men. He was a practicing Catholic.

Bernard Ice (deceased), who was blind for many years but developed a remarkable spiritual vision through Peyote. He had a very beautiful religious imagination.

Bernard Red Cloud, a descendent of Chief Red Cloud. His family is the only Red Cloud family in the Native American Church. He grew up with Silas Yellow Boy, one of the original members of the Half Moon fireplace. He is a roadman. His wife, Christine, is also an active member.

Emerson Spider, of a family with a Peyote tradition from its very introduction into the reservation. As State High Priest of the Native American Church in South Dakota, he has authority over all spiritual matters. He conducts both Cross Fire and Half Moon meetings. He is a dedicated Christian and has brought an evangelical spirit to the Native American Church.

John (deceased) *and Beatrice Weasel Bear.* John was a roadman, and Beatrice is still active in both the traditional Lakota religion and the Native American Church.

For the Body of Christ Independent Church, the sources are:

Garfield Good Plume, who has been in the Church since it started and is a prominent member.

Eugene Rowland (deceased), who was the principal minister. A personal conversion experience is the basis of his ministry.

The religious experience which these Lakota have shared with me has enriched my life. My own reflection on their experience has given me new insights into the nature of religious experience.

Finally, after presenting all the documentation, in the last chapter I develop a model of religious identity in order to interpret the diverse data contained in this study. Through this phenomenological comparison of religious symbols, one can gain insight into their fundamental meaning.

1

THE TRADITIONAL LAKOTA RELIGION

The treatment of the traditional Lakota Religion will be divided into its history, contemporary beliefs and ceremonies.

HISTORY OF THE CALF PIPE

According to the Lakota, their traditional religion as it is practiced today began with the bringing of the Sacred Calf Pipe by the White Buffalo Woman. This is a legendary tradition which most Lakota know and consider as an historical event. Since the elaborate Pipes of the Hopewellian Mound Builders in the Ohio Valley are of great age (Kroeber 1948:478) and the Sioux came into contact with straggling herds of buffalo east of the Mississippi River (McGee 1897: 187), the essential components of contemporary Lakota religion were present before their hunting days on the Plains. These facts confirm the dates for the bringing of the Calf Pipe which Garrick Mallery derives from two picture writings, namely, 901–930 and 931–1000 A.D. (1893: plate 1). However, after a thorough examination of all available winter counts, John L. Smith concludes: "It is the writer's firm belief that the legend was started some time between 1785 and 1800" (1967:6).

The Sacred Pipe venerated as the original one is kept at Green Grass on the Cheyenne River Reservation in northern South Dakota.[1] In my own personal experience I discovered that medicine men journey to Green Grass to touch their Pipe to the Calf Pipe bundle. Stanley Looking Horse, father of Orval, the present keeper, told me that the bundle is opened on special occasions only, the last being several years ago. It is through this ceremony that the Keeper receives his power.[2] Stanley Looking Horse also told me that Green Grass is a place where all the spirits of all the medicine men who pray through the Pipe are present, since all their Pipes are related to the Calf Pipe.

Green Grass has become a place of pilgrimage. One interesting pilgrim I observed was a mixed-blood Lakota who was making video tapes of the Longest Walk from San Francisco to Washington, D.C., a march taking over three months to demonstrate the plight of the American Indian. He came to Green Grass to participate in the sweat lodge ceremony one night I was there before going back to the march. Looking Horse told me that there is now a continuous stream of visitors, many of them young. American Indian Movement leaders have various meetings there. In October of 1976, I requested to pray in the presence of the Calf Pipe. Looking Horse conducted a sweat lodge ceremony for me and late at night opened the small house where the Calf Pipe is kept. He told me that this was the first time a priest or minister had made this request and that he was pleased. During the summer of 1977 on the first day of the Sun Dance, the bundle was brought outside for a public ceremony. Sidney Keith, a prominent member of the tribe, defended my presence there against the complaint of a Lakota woman. He said that the Calf Pipe is open to everybody regardless of race and that is the way they do it there. Without doubt, Green Grass is the religious center of the Sioux world.

HISTORY OF FEDERAL LEGISLATION

Throughout the years and even to the present day, American Indians have been deprived of their basic right of freedom of religion. On March 30, 1883, the Secretary of the Interior, H. M. Teller, wrote the Commissioner of Indian Affairs, Hiram Price, that the Sun Dance was an old, heathenish dance which hindered the civilization of the Indians and stimulated the warlike passions of the young warriors, that the medicine men, always found in the anti-progressive party, used their conjurers' arts to prevent people from abandoning their heathenish rites and customs and that the destroying and distributing of property at a person's death prevented the Indians from appreciating the value of property as an agent of civilization (U.S. Government 1883a). In response, Price wrote Teller that Indian ceremonial dances, practices of medicine men and giving and destroying of property at funeral rites would be declared Indian offenses and that a Court of Indian Offenses would be established to pass judgment and punish all violaters (U.S. Government 1883b). Although Teller's letter brings out cultural prejudice, in all fairness it should be pointed out that one of his accusations had some validity. According to George Sword, one of James Walker's most important informants, the Scalp-Staff Dance was performed among the Oglala on the last day of the Sun Dance: during this time the musicians sang a scalp song and the conductor waved "the scalp on his staff down and up in front of each warrior" who expressed intense satisfaction (Walker, 1917:119–20). [Frances Densmore confirms Sword's position in her many references to war-related practices in the Sun Dance (1918: 100, 104, 107, 113, 125, 127, 142 and 149).] However, this was no justification for suppressing the entire ceremony. One medicine man related to me in a sad voice that after the 1883 suppression Indian religion went underground: "But the Indian police found out who the medicine men were. The medicine bundles were destroyed; the Pipe bowls broken and the stems burned. The Pipes could not be renewed. Very few medicine men survived this period. Their knowledge was lost." This prohibition officially lasted until John Collier's Circular on Indian Religious Freedom and Indian Culture of 1934, which stated: "No interference with Indian religious life or ceremonial expression will hereafter be tolerated. The cultural liberty of Indians in all respects is to be considered equal to that of any non-Indian groups. [They shoud be] fluent in their vital, beautiful and efficient native languages. . . . [No punishment should] be so administered as to constitute an interference with, or to imply a censorship over the religious or cultural life, Indian or other (U.S. Government 1934a).[3]

Despite this policy directive, the need to guarantee religious freedom still existed in 1978, as can be seen from the resolution passed by the U.S. Congress in that year. The need to guarantee the practice of Indian religion in federal correctional institutions, the accessibility to sacred sites on public land for ceremonial purposes, the possession of federally prohibited objects such as eagle feathers and the right not to have sacred medicine bundles opened for inspection on the U.S.–Canadian border were the primary concerns of the bill (U.S. Government 1978:80–85).

HISTORY OF YUWIPI

During the reservation period the most frequently performed traditional Lakota ceremony is the one called *yuwipi*, "they bind up." During this ceremony held in the dark, the yuwipi man is bound in a blanket. According to Lakota belief, he calls in the spirits he acquired through visions to untie him and in the process communicates with them. The Lakota also believe that it is through the spirits that the yuwipi man heals, finds lost objects, and receives answers to prayers. However, according to Eugene Buechel, S.J., *yuwipi* is also a noun meaning "transparent stones, usually found in ant hills and used in the wakan wicohan [holy work] called yuwipi, which consists in one being tied all around and being loosed by magic" (1970: 656). The word for *stone* in the sacred language is *tunkan*, said to be an abbreviation of *tunkasilia*, "grandfather" (Densmore 1918:205). Buechel states that *tunkan* "is also called the yuwipi wasicu [literally "stone men"] which he defines as "a sacred hard round stone that is supposed to have power in the hands of those who have dreamed" (1970:656). Densmore comments on a healing ceremony: "During a demonstration for the curing of the sick it is said that the stones, flying through the air in the darkened tent sometimes strike those who have refused to believe in them" (1918:205). The association of yuwipi with the sacred stones draws attention to a much neglected aspect of the ceremony.

Powers states that "the number of Yuwipi and Yuwipi-like rituals has increased since the mid-sixties, and it is in these rituals that we see the dynamics of Oglala Religion, even more so than in the sun dance" (1977:207). MacGregor claims that the "only continuing cult of the old Dakota religion is the Yuwipi meeting" (1946:98). In my opinion, these statements are misleading. On examining the chart on pages 25–26, even assuming I may have missed a few practitioners, one notices the large number of deceased yuwipi men as compared to a few practitioners today. What makes this significant is that the population of the reservation was so much smaller in the early days. But it was a period when an overwhelming sense of powerlessness engulfed the Lakota people and they had no other alternatives but to rely upon this ceremony. Leo American Horse comments that "there were more yuwipi men in the early days a long time ago than there are now since there was no hospital like there is now and people really depended upon it." We will see Bernard Red Cloud making the same comment about reliance upon Peyote. I see the mid-sixties as a period of yuwipi revival in the post–World War II period, but it would not even be close to the level of activity during the early reservation days.

Åke Hultkrantz reviews the literature on the shamanistic complex to which yuwipi is related, distinguishing between a "general shamanism" as found in North America and a limited "Arctic Shamanism" (1967:35). Andreas Lommel presents a psychological interpretation (1967), evaluated by seventeen scholars (Lommel 1970). William K. Powers gives us the Lakota classifications of shamans. (1986:179–95). Although there is a general agreement that the various conjuring ceremonies, including yuwipi, are a result of diffusion of the Shaking Tent rite of the Woodland Algonkians, as described by A. Irving Hallowell (1942) and John M. Cooper (1944), there is insignificant data for any definite historical reconstruction. Verne Ray suggests the Plains Cree as the transmitters of the complex to the Plains and Plateau (1941:214). However, Claude Schaeffer concurs with Donald Collier's position (Collier 1944:48) in stating that "both the Northern Plains and Plateau versions of the conjuring rite were sufficiently different from the Woodlands pattern to indicate that the complex was of some antiquity in the west and probably existed prior to the migration of the Cree" (Schaeffer 1969:33). Schaeffer suggests that the earliest diffusion westward was from the Blackfoot and Arapaho without implying any diffusion to the Lakota (1969:34).

Some consider the old man Chips to be the source of yuwipi on the Pine Ridge Reservation. The history of this family will be traced because it demonstrates how power is transferred by a combination of heredity and personal vision. A family tree is given here to make the discussion easier to follow. Arrows indicate the ways the powers were handed down and the dotted lines are generation lines.

According to Bernard Moves Camp, the great-grandson of the old man Chips, when the famous Crazy Horse was about eleven years old, his father either died or left his wife. His mother remarried and Crazy Horse was unable to get along with his stepfather, so he went fifty miles to the camp of his uncle, with whom the old man Chips was living. The uncle made Crazy Horse and Chips brothers through

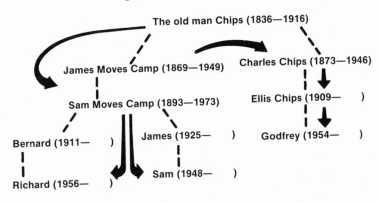

a ceremony of smoking the Pipe. It should be noted that according to Eagle Elk, Chips taught Crazy Horse how to protect himself in battle (DeMallie 1984:157) The old man Chips, who had a father who was a medicine man but perhaps not yuwipi (a distinction that will be treated later), was the first one to practice on the Pine Ridge Reservation.

His son, James, changed his name to Moves Camp. He did not receive his powers from his father but from his own personal vision. James helped his brother, Charles, get power through a vision Charles had. The old man Chips passed his power on to his grandson, Sam Moves Camp, who in turn passed it on to his two grandsons, Richard and Sam. Charles passed his power on to his son, Ellis, who passed it on to his son, Godfrey. However, it should be noted that personal visions always accompanied the hereditary reception of power. This one family has dominated yuwipi practice not only in the Wanblee District but in the eastern half of the reservation.

Lawrence Hunter stated that the old man Chips was highly esteemed on the Cheyenne River Reservation because he was able to tell through the spirits where to find the bodies of Palmer Horse Shoe's sons in a blizzard and the body of a drowned boy beneath the ice on the Cheyenne River.

A full-blood man in his middle sixties related two incidents from Charlie Chips' practice. "I had a friend who had to have part of his leg amputated. We went to a meeting conducted by Chips. My companion brought a flashlight into the meeting. There were not many of them around at the time. He told me that he would poke me in the ribs when he decided to turn it on. After the lights were turned out and the singing was going on, he poked me in the ribs and just as fast a sharp crack was heard just in front of him. Then Charles Chips stopped and told how he was disappointed that one of the relatives of the man who was putting on the meeting wanted to expose what was going on. He asked that the lights be turned on and the flashlight was by the Pipe resting near the altar. The crack was the flashlight hitting the wooden part of his leg and in some way it got placed next to the Pipe. That made a believer out of me.

"At another meeting a person was coming on horseback to the meeting. There were three drop fence sections used instead of gates. At the third one near the house where the meeting was taking place, the horse would not go through but instead had to be taken way around to another gate. When the man entered the room, Chips told how a horse refused to go through the last drop gate because the spirits were present there. The man had not told Chips about the incident and he had no way [i.e., normal] of knowing what happened."

Some personal accounts of Richard Moves Camp are of interest. He stated that "a white doctor told my mother that she could not have children. But my grandfather, Sam Moves Camp, told her that it would be all right and so I was born safely. The Indians believe that some men are born to be medicine men through a prophecy or sign." Moves Camp is not alone in this claim. Leonard Crow Dog, a spiritual leader on the Rosebud Reservation, claims that spiritual power was given to him on the day he was born (Ortiz 1977:36). Moves Camp continues by telling the place of a dream in receiving power from his grandfather: "One gets called through a dream like I did. Or else a medicine man passes his power on to someone. The spirits tell the medicine man whom to pass the powers to. A dream comes from the spirit of man, that part that lives on after the body is dead. When I was eleven years old, I had a dream that I was facing the west on a hill. There was lightning. I looked down and I was holding a Pipe. The dream bothered me. I dreamt it twice in one week. I went to Sam Moves Camp and he put me in a sweat lodge with water and no food since I was only eleven. When I was fourteen, Sam put me on the hill for a vision quest."

Garfield Good Plume mentions Fred Ashly as a yuwipi man who was from Norris, South Dakota, near Wanblee. We will see that, according to Good Plume, he had a son, Eddie Rich, who turned away from yuwipi to establish the Body of Christ Church.

Cherry Seed seems to have been the first yuwipi man in the Kyle District. He had a daughter who was a medicine woman. His son, named Black Fox, was a powerful medicine man, but he became an Episcopal minister and gave up his medicine practices (Steltenkamp, n.d.). So Cherry Seed passed his power on to Frank Fools Crow. He told Fools Crow: "What I mention is really *wakan*; it is holy. But there are many strings attached to the kind of Pipe I am giving you. You will meet a lot of difficulties in your life with this Pipe. In everyday living, people will come to you with things that disturb you and rumors against you. You will have to withstand all these trials. I want you to remember that I told you about this holy house with all those strings attached to it. But to keep you working in this ministry I will tell you about the holiness of this Pipe." Fools Crow continues: "I was told this when I was thirteen years old. A few years later I went to Bear Butte [near the Black Hills] and I stayed up there four days and four nights. The man who put me on Bear Butte was Stirrup, the father of James Black Bull's wife."[4] Fools Crow passed his powers on to Dawson No Horse of Wakpamni District.

Other districts also had yuwipi men. Steve Red Elk mentions Thunder Bear, Living Bear, and Hollow Horn as very early yuwipi men in the Manderson District. Little Warrior is also mentioned there. He is the one that Brown refers to (1967:xii, 60). Good Lance succeeded him. (Pete Catches describes his healing powers below.) Good Lance passed the power of his Eagle Spirit to Pete Catches and Charles Hard Heart. Charles Kills Ree, who received some of his power from Mark Red Star, also practiced in the Manderson District. Mark Big Road lives at Manderson. In former times he practiced regularly in the Red Cloud Community just outside the town of Pine Ridge, but now he conducts most of his meetings on other reservations. Hultkrantz attended one of these in Wyoming and has given a classic description (1967). George Plenty Wolf was the resident yuwipi man of the Red Cloud Community, and John Iron Rope practiced at Slim Butte. Some years ago George Poor Thunder practiced near Allen. Robert H. Ruby describes one of his ceremonies (1955:62–66). According to Plenty Wolf, Poor Thunder accepted money to teach a young Lakota to use the Pipe and died shortly after. This is similar to the cases of *wakunza* or "supernatural retribution," which Elizabeth Grobsmith cites (1973: 131).

John Fast Wolf was an old yuwipi man mentioned for the Oglala District, and William Good Voice Elk practices there today. Pete Swift Bird mentioned two yuwipi men, Eagle Horse and Holy Bird, who practiced years ago in the Wolf Creek area. Holy Bird had a medicine bundle from which two screech owls would fly out—a person could see it. He would doctor only if the birds flew out. When he finished doctoring, the owls would return and he would wrap them up in his medicine bundle. Red Star practiced in the Wounded Knee District. Once he was conducting a meeting on a dirt floor to doctor a girl with tuberculosis. The girl was inside a circle of war paint which was painted on the dirt. Red Star was told by the spirits that if the spirit helpers missed the circle, the girl would die, but if they were within, she would live. During the singing there were vibrations in the ground and a gopher threw dirt out in the middle of the circle. The gopher came out and went back into the ground. Selo Black Crow states that Robert Steed from Rosebud has an altar made from gopher ground because the gopher can travel underneath the ground and see everything. Pete Swift Bird continues in saying that yuwipi used to be strong in the Grass Creek area. Three yuwipi men from there were Weasel, White Plume, and Blue Legs. Sam Moves Camp has moved into that area since he is married into the New Holy family living there.

Leo American Horse states that "on his mother's side Black Whirlwind was a family with a long tradition of yuwipi men. My grandmother told me that when her father died, he told them not to bury him right away but that something would happen about twenty-four hours after he died. This was during a period when there was no embalming. When the time arrived, he made a noise and they rushed over to him and a bird flew out of his body, and then he turned over finally and was quiet. Her father used a bird in his yuwipi meetings to heal. Another old yuwipi man would build a mound in the shape of an anthill. When he was doctoring someone, if an ant did not come out of the mound, the person would die. But if one did, he would get well. Because of that I have great respect for ants." People in the Allen District had a yuwipi man from the Rosebud Reservation, George Eagle Elk, conduct meetings for them until his recent death. This is by no means a complete history of yuwipi among the Oglala Lakota, but there is sufficient detail to indicate that this developed into a common practice throughout the reservation.

However, praying through yuwipi spirits does not receive the approval of all the Lakota people. One Lakota relates a vision his maternal grandfather had. "He took sick and he saw the yuwipi. He saw a dark cloud coming from the east across towards the west. All the time the cloud was men. There was a hairy man with horns, sharp ears, and a tail. He came and sat on his chest and said: 'These are all my helpers. If you bow down and worship me, I will give you whatever helpers you want to use. These are all my helpers. I will give them, all of them.' So he said, 'No, I believe in Christ.' These disappeared and the Holy Ghost came in the form of a dove and so he saw a vision of Christ with a cane and he said to my grandfather to feed his sheep. But my grandfather could have been the most powerful yuwipi man around if he would have accepted the devil's invitation." A young educated full-blood man made this comment: "Today yuwipi is being used in a bad way. It is being used for misused power. People are praying against others. They are using it for political ends. They are seeking to contact spirits for information. This is not the old religion of the Pipe. Yuwipi is making the Christian churches weak. People will be back to the churches someday."

A full-blood Lakota woman tells about a dream. "I had so many problems that I could not handle them. So I went to yuwipi meetings but it did not help. Then I had a dream that I was buried in soft dirt just like a grave and I was trying to get out. I heard people talking above me and so I hollered for help. But no one seemed to hear me so I was in a panic and kept hollering for help. Finally an aunt heard me and scooped away the dirt so my head was visible and she pulled me up by my chin. Then I understood that I must follow Jesus and put all my burdens on Him. Ever since I did that I am all right. I went down on my knees and bowed my head so that it touched the floor and prayed."

Her following Jesus involved praying with the Pipe. On a Good Friday march, a group of people carried a large cross four miles as a manifestation of their Christian faith. During one of the stops for prayer she prayed with her Pipe. It is not belief in the Pipe or even in the world of the spirits but the practice of yuwipi that this group rejects. Yuwipi is a practice that does divide the Lakota people.

Yet more and more young Lakota are seeking information and power from the spirits. This has created a demand for new yuwipi men.

Several years ago one educated full-blood told me that "yuwipi is an inseparable element of Indian religion. If Indian religion is going to survive, it will be through yuwipi ceremonies. Some young men tried to become yuwipi men but the people did not accept them. In the years just ahead you will see many young yuwipi men." However, his prediction has not come true. And one medicine man warns: "Now with AIM and interest in Indian religion young people don't have sufficient respect. They think they can learn about the Pipe and how to handle it in a short time. But it takes a man until middle age or more to learn this. The young people will have to find out."

The same concern is expressed among the Arapaho on the Wind River Reservation in Wyoming. "The AIM members, 'young people,' in their twenties, spoke at meetings in violation of customs, and they criticized council leadership and the strategies in Indian-white relations used by 'elders' in the past. Ceremonial Elders were particularly anxious about the youth's noncomformity; some had reportedly been fasting for 'medicine power,' which alarmed the elders as in their view young men did not have the ability to use this 'power' wisely or well" (Fowler 1978:760).

Table of Yuwipi Men

We will summarize this section with a table of the yuwipi men mentioned according to their districts. "Dec." stands for deceased. There is a great divergence in the number of yuwipi men in each district. Some areas are smaller than others, such as Wolf Creek, Slim Butte, Red Cloud community, and Calico. In other areas such as Kyle, Wakpamni, Porcupine, Wounded Knee, and Allen, I may have missed a considerable number of names for these areas. Fools Crow, for example, mentions additional names of people, probably all yuwipi: Red Shield, Running Shield, High Wolf, Drum Carrier, Spotted Horse, and Small Eagle (Mails 1979:53). So definitive conclusions of the relative strength of yuwipi in the various districts cannot be drawn.

Wanblee

old man Chips, dec.	Sam Moves Camp, Sr. dec.	Ellis Chips
James Moves Camp, dec.	Fred Ashly, dec.	Godfrey Chips
Charles Chips, dec.		Richard Moves Camp

Manderson
Thunder Bear, dec.
Living Bear, dec.
Hollow Horn, dec.

Little Warrior, dec.
Frank Good Lance, dec.

Charles Kills Ree, dec.
Mark Big Road, dec.

Kyle
Cherry Seed, dec.

Black Fox, dec.

Frank Fools Crow

Grass Creek
Weasel, dec.
White Plume, dec.

Blue Legs, dec.

Sam Moves Camp, Jr.

Calico
Black Whirlwind, dec.

Pete Catches*

Charles Hard Heart, dec.

Wakpamni
Dawson No Horse, dec.

Porcupine
Charles Mexican

Wounded Knee
Mark Red Star, dec.

Wolf Creek
Eagle Horse, dec.

Holy Bird, dec.

Pine Ridge Community
George Plenty Wolf, dec.

Slim Butte
John Iron Rope, dec.

Oglala
John Fast Wolf, dec.

Allen
George Poor Thunder, dec.

*not yuwipi but lowanpi, a distinction in the kind of spirits used.

HISTORY OF THE SUN DANCE

From the descriptions of Deloria (1929), Densmore (1918: 84–150), Dorsey (1894:450–466) and Walker (1917:92–121), I will present a composite picture.

There was a three- or four-day period of preparation, during which time many appointments were made: ceremonial officers, children to form a procession to the Sacred Tree, men to scout the tree and to carry it back, virgins to cut the tree, musicians, women to stand behind the men during the Sun Dance for encouragement, men to pierce the children's ears. During this time feasts and dances were held which lasted far into the night. A large group charged the grounds on horses to drive away the evil spirits. During the next four days, the cottonwood tree was scouted, cut down, brought to the Sun Dance grounds, decorated, and raised. Rawhide effigies of a buffalo and a man were hung from the top of the tree. (The significance of these will be discussed in the last chapter.) The Sun Dance lodge was built and tipis pitched in a circle around the dance grounds. J.B. Walker places the dancing itself on the last day, during which there was the

Buffalo Dance, the piercing of children's ears, the sun-gazing dance, and the scalp-staff dance (1917:120). Densmore gives two days for the dancing. On the second day the men danced until they fell unconscious from exhaustion and were carried off to regain consciousness, after which they spent time in the sweat lodge and were given water and food. In James Owen Dorsey's account, Bushotter said that on the first dance day men danced through the night resting at midnight. At sunrise on the second day they stopped dancing (1895:462). Deloria states that they danced two days and two nights (1929:400). During the Sun Dance there was a great deal of feasting and socializing. Densmore writes: "Meantime many incidents were taking place in the great tribal gathering. Those who rejoiced were asking others to rejoice with them, while still others joined their friends in lamenting chiefs who had died during the year or warriors who had been slain by the enemy. The relatives of those who took part in the Sun Dance provided feasts, and little groups were seen feasting here and there in the camp while at the same time songs of lamentation could be heard" (1918:136).

Although the age of the Sun Dance is unknown, Hultkrantz does have a meticulous reconstruction of its history (n.d. 223–43). He states that "In a Yanktonai Dakota winter count, named after John K. Bear, we are informed that they danced a Sun Dance in 1713. James Howard states that this is 'the earliest accurately dated mention of the Sun Dance anywhere in the anthropological literature so far as we are aware'" (Howard 1976:26, quoted in Hultkrantz, n.d.:236). After examining an abundance of historical data, Hultkrantz concludes that the "Sun Dance thus seems to have spread over the northern plains not earlier than the first half of the eighteenth century" (238).

Deloria mentions a Rosebud and Pine Ridge joint ceremony in the 1870s, where there were forty groups of from six to twelve dancers, each with a holy man. "The diameter of the encampment was four miles, so large and so crowded that it was difficult to see the ceremony" (1929:358). Riggs describes a Sun Dance held in June of 1880 by the Teton under Red Cloud. Although seven hundred lodges were pitched in a circle about six miles in circumference, there were only seventeen dancers pierced. Four of the dancers "were young and inexperienced, so they could not break their bonds. Consequently they gave away three horses each and were cut loose" (1893:231–32).

Although Indian religion was prohibited in 1883, there is evidence that Sun Dances were held almost every year during the prohibition era. Harry W. Paige cites testimony indicating this (1970:102) and Mails gives an interview with Fools Crow (1978:197). I am supplementing this claim with information given me. Pete Swift Bird states that Bernard Grabbing Bear, born about 1870, was a seasoned singer in the 1920s and had been doing it for at least twenty years. Black Horse and Sam Back were seasoned singers in 1934. Fools Crow told me that there were three Sun Dances performed before large crowds of people, twice in Kyle in 1917 and 1918 to pray for the ending of World War I, and one held in Porcupine the next year as a victory celebration. Four men were pierced in 1917. Al Adams partially confirms this in saying that as a small boy he attended a Sun Dance at Kyle during the middle of the second decade of this century and there were about a thousand people there. There were about eight dancers pierced. Matthew Two Bulls saw a Sun Dance at Oglala and Noah Kills Enemy saw one conducted by Spotted Crow near White Clay, around the late 1920s. According to Fools Crow, 1929 is the date from which the Sun Dance was continuously held in public with official Government approval but without the piercing. This brought medicine men together and started a revival of Indian religion. Hunter was present near a Sun Dance at Manderson in the early 1930s. He did not actually see the dancing, since young people were not allowed close by. It was the old men that danced. Maybe one young man did occasionally. "They offered their lives because they were old and they wanted the younger generation to be blessed. Occasionally they had a heyoka, a clown. He tried to tempt the dancers with food and water. But they danced and looked at the sun and had visions." Opposition to the Sun Dance was voiced by Rev. Lawler, an Episcopal priest and later bishop, in 1934 because of the preparations being made for one at Wolf Creek in connection with a rodeo (U.S. Government 1934b). Pete Swift Bird confirms this date. Richard White Calf saw a Sun Dance near White Clay, Nebraska, in the late 1940s in which one dancer was pierced. Although all the dates may not be completely accurate, it is significant that people remember Sun Dances throughout the entire reservation.

One medicine man told me that there was not much activity in Indian religion during the 1940s because so many of the young Lakota were away during World War II. However, the 1950s are important.

Stephen Feraca describes one day of the 1954 Sun Dance. The procession consisted of Fools Crow carrying a buffalo skull in a bed of sage, four dancers (three from Cheyenne and one Lakota, one being a Korean War veteran on crutches), and the director, George Poor Thunder. Ben American Horse addressed the people, saying that he "considered it something of a disgrace that only one tribal member could be found who was willing to undergo the sacrifice" (1963:9). Feraca states that few contemporary Sioux Sun Dances lasted more than two days.

Sometime during this period, permission was obtained from the BIA in Washington, D.C., for piercing the Sun Dancers. Schweigman, also known as Eagle Feather, was the first one officially pierced. After consulting the literature (Feraca 1963: 68; Mails 1978: 46; Nurge 1966: 108) and having a personal conversation with Fools Crow, one finds that the most likely date is between 1958 and 1960.

The 1960s would be a decade of more development. Nurge observed a four-day Sun Dance in 1962 (1966:106), and I observed three-day Sun Dances from 1965 to 1968 and four-day ones from 1969 to 1971. Concerning the Sun Dance during this time, Thomas Lewis writes: "The Sun Dance provides an example of enforced change in the acculturation process" (1972:44). He gives a number of examples from interviewing dancers and observation:

Although some described fasting, vision-seeking, or other preparations, the descriptions often indicated a perfunctory or even purely verbal procedure. . . . Several members participate yearly and receive a payment from the tribal council. Several others presented themselves as candidates on the night before the fourth (last) day. One of these was partially inebriated. One aspiring political figure danced the last day only, with attendant self generated publicity. . . . The days selected are suitable for a 4 (or 3) day powwow, often associated with a rodeo, a small carnival and ball games. A festal atmosphere is surely retained, but without temporal separation from the religious days. The number of arrests for intoxication soars during the Sun Dance. . . . Ceremonial procedures are conducted in the early morning with a small audience and do not interfere with the busy Omaha (Grass) dancing and popular entertainments of the afternoons and evening (1972: 46).

Two observations should be made. Not only was there a commercial atmosphere, with a Ferris wheel and other carnival equipment, but admission fees and additional fees for tape recorders and cameras were charged for the ceremony itself. Secondly, the Sun Dance was of secondary importance in relation to the powwow.

Nurge has some important observations on the third day of the 1962 Sun Dance:

At 5:00 [in the morning] one began blaring religious music from popular records, e.g. 'It is no secret what God can do'. . . . At 5:20 a man began to pray in the Lakota language over the public address system. He reverted to English to paraphrase the eighteenth verse from the sixteenth chapter of Matthew 'Thou are Peter and on this rock I will build my church and the forces of evil [will not prevail against it]. . . . Sun Dancing is the work of the devil and should not be taken to heart. These dancers should be in church tomorrow not parading around showing themselves. I know the machine (i.e., microphone) may be taken from me tomorrow but you're not praying to Him when you pray in the Sun Dance (Nurge 1966:106, 108).

Out of the eight men and two women dancers, only Schweigman was pierced. During part of the ceremony a young boy danced.

The public protest against the Sun Dance which Nurge observed was most unusual. This shows the conflict that existed among the Lakota people themselves over the relation between traditional Lakota religion and Christianity. During the Sun Dances I observed and participated in, there was a harmony between the two religious traditions. Jake Herman, considered a "tribal historian," helped to foster this harmony. He was influential in the decision to have Mass celebrated on the Sun Dance grounds. I was asked to do this from 1965 to 1970. Since the piercing was done on the third day, a Saturday, for the first three years, the celebration of Mass was by itself. One of the Sun Dance committee women told me that they wanted to keep Sunday open for a Christian service, reflecting the attitude of the people in charge. During the next two years, Mass followed the piercing ceremony. Approximately three hundred people attended Mass each year, probably about the same number as the Sun Dance. In 1969, Edgar Red Cloud, the leader of the Sun Dance singers, sang a Sun Dance song, holding the Sacred Pipe during the distribution of Holy Communion. I prayed with the same Pipe during the prayers of petition. Red Cloud, Plenty

Wolf, and Fools Crow all received Holy Communion on the Sun Dance Grounds, making a public profession of their Catholic faith. Fools Crow had just conducted the Sun Dance ceremonies and performed the piercing a few minutes before. In 1970, I planned to make the scheduled Mass a memorial celebration for Jake Herman, who had died during the year, because of his many years of service in the Sun Dance. However, due to the opposition of a young militant, I was unable to do so.

The next year Fools Crow asked me to help him pray in the Sun Dance, since he knew I prayed with the Sacred Pipe as a priest. On Sunday morning he painted my face with red paint and put me into the Sun Dance with my Pipe along side three militants. He did this to show that a Catholic priest had a right to participate in the Sun Dance and to pray with the Pipe. He made a public manifestation of what he had repeatedly told me: that the Indian religion and the Catholic Church are one. This was his way of expressing common religious forms on the phenomenological level. When one of the militants threatened to throw me out, Fools Crow told me to take a long rest. He had proven his point.

The militant then proceeded to deliver a long and bitter attack against Holy Rosary Mission and the Catholic Church. During the next rest period I presented my credentials: "When I prayed with the Pipe at the funeral of Rex Long Visitor, the people asked the medicine man of their community, John Iron Rope, if it were proper for a priest and a non-Indian to pray with the Pipe. He answered that anyone can pray with the Pipe if he does it sincerely from the heart. When I buried the sons of Edgar Red Cloud, the leader of the Sun Dance singers, he requested that I pray with the Pipe on both occasions. Finally, Frank Fools Crow had asked me to help him pray in the Sun Dance and I did not feel I could turn down a request to pray." Afterwards, Lakota people remarked to me that the militant person knew nothing about Indian tradition. Otherwise he would not have criticized anyone while the Pipe was in ceremony. This Lakota Christian confirmation was a complete reversal of the condemnation Nurge observed in 1962.

Completely ignorant of the circumstances of my involvement, Jorgensen and Clemmer expressed unwarranted false assumptions: "Father Paul Steinmetz . . . entered the Sun Dance under the guidance of Frank Fools Crow in 1971 so as to 'fulfill, not destroy, the Indian spiritual vision.' This seems to be a mixture of one part fatuousness and one part insidiousness. From all the details Washburn avoids (1975:264), it appears that Steinmetz sought to accommodate Christian acts with Sioux traditions so as to transform the Sun Dance to Steinmetz' image of the Godhead. Perhaps Washburn did not recognize his authoritative theme as the denigration of the Sun Dance as a variable of Christianity" (Jorgensen and Clemmer (1978:43). What they should ask themselves is why Fools Crow, for whom they have the highest praises, should completely on his own initiative have asked a Catholic priest to participate in the Sun Dance. Fools Crow was the one transforming the Sun Dance to his own image. Apparently, this is a "denigration" in the minds of Jorgensen and Clemmer and not in the mind of Fools Crow.

In 1972 there was a strong presence of the American Indian Movement in the Sun Dance. As a result, the mixed-blood Dick Wilson Administration banned the Sun Dance for the next two years, claiming that AIM had taken it over for their own political purposes. In 1975, under the Tribal Administration of Al Trimble, the Sun Dance was once more reinstated. For four years it was held at Porcupine, a full-blood stronghold of AIM, away from the Bureau of Indian Affairs in the predominately mixed-blood town of Pine Ridge. Fools Crow was still in charge.

A number of characteristics should be noted about the present-day Sun Dance. It is no longer primarily a ceremony of tribal unity, although this element is not entirely lacking. It is pan-Indian in participation, and the seeking of individual Indian identity seems more important than a tribal one. Moreover, there is more than one Sun Dance taking place on the reservation each year despite Fools Crow's claim to the contrary (Mails 1978:199). For about five years, Selo Black Crow has sponsored a Sun Dance east of Wanblee, which is especially pan-Indian in participation. In 1978 there were a dozen young European visitors whom Black Crow met on a European lecture tour the preceding year. In 1978 and 1979, Pete Catches conducted a Sun Dance mostly for mixed-bloods near Holy Rosary Mission. Reuben Fire Thunder also conducted a Sun Dance during the same two years near Allen. I was told that some people considered the first one a learning experience, since they felt that a number of mistakes were made.

According to a reliable observer, the family sponsoring the Sun Dance did so, at least partially, to establish their *tiospaye* or "extended family" as the most important one in the Allen area, indicating how complex the dynamics of the Sun Dance can become. And the trend towards multiple Sun Dances seems to grow each year. Marie Red Cloud told me that during the summer of 1987 there were at least fourteen Sun Dances on the Pine Ridge Reservation: Richard Moves Camp and Celo Black Crow in Wanblee, John Around Him in Kyle, Frank Fools Crow with DuBray helping in Three Mile Creek, Reuben Fire Thunder and Reno Richards in Allen, Ricky Two Dogs and Sarah Thunder Hawk in Porcupine, Pat Janis in Wolf Creek, Pete Catches near Holy Rosary Mission, Billy Good Voice and Richard Broken Nose in Oglala, and one in the Yellow Camp and one north of Calico. An increasing pan-Indianism, the stress on discovering personal identity, and multiple Sun Dances all show in a dramatic way the process of acculturation that has taken place in the Sun Dance as documented by Spier (1921).

There is a greater participation of a larger number of Indian people. There are personal celebrations taking place, such as the piercing of children's ears, memorial give-aways[6] for the deceased and for dancers, and other thanksgiving prayers. During the 1978 Porcupine Sun Dance, a prayer of thanksgiving was offered for a baby who was allegedly cured through a yuwipi ceremony after the hospital had failed to do anything. The woman had the child in a traditional Lakota cradle, which she touched to the Sun Dance tree. Some sharp criticism was directed towards the Public Health Service.

These celebrations provide the Sun Dancers with long rest periods during the afternoons, especially for the last two days. During the piercing, which takes place every day, relatives and friends stand behind the man pierced, within the sacred area, dancing in rhythm with the drumbeat and shouting encouragement as he runs back to pull himself free. Or else they follow the pierced man as he drags buffalo skulls around in a circle. When a dancer was suspended from the tree at Porcupine in 1978, all the people present were asked to stand up, remain silent, and pray for the success in his efforts.

The age of the dancers is getting younger. Most of the dancers are in their upper teens or twenties. The presence of small children is also growing. The number of woman dancers has increased, sometimes equaling the men.

The forms of torture are getting more severe. All men dancers are pierced, most of them in two places, and wood skewers attached to the rope leading to the center tree. The women take flesh offerings from their arms. However, the practice of piercing women is developing. During the 1978 Black Crow Sun Dance, a teenage boy and girl, twins, were pierced and tied to the tree. They both dreamt when they were about eight years old of hanging from a tree. They interpreted this to mean that they should be pierced at a Sun Dance. So the girl was pierced on the left arm and the boy on the right side of the chest. They pulled free together in a dance in which they were the only ones pierced.

We will see below that two women and a girl were pierced in the 1979 Porcupine Sun Dance. During a Sun Dance at Allen, Reuben Fire Thunder was pierced all four days. The one suspended from the tree, just mentioned above, hung holding on to the rope for several minutes. When he did release himself, he fell to the ground unconscious, taking about five minutes to be revived. Another dancer was pierced in four places in his back, and tied to six large buffalo skulls. He was unable to pull these or to tear himself free. A group of dancers carried the skulls behind him as he circled the dance area. Finally, they dropped the skulls and two dancers took him by each arm and ran him forward to tear him free. The same method is used by those attached to the tree. In these recent celebrations, dancers become exhausted from four days of dancing from sunrise to late afternoon.

Finally, there is, at times, an element of confrontation. In 1978 at Porcupine, a white man wanted to dance. The dancers were divided, and after discussion the group against it won out. The announcer commented that the white man had destroyed his own religion and they did not want him destroying the Indian religion. At Black Crow's Sun Dance some dancers refused to have white people make flesh offerings on the Sun Dance grounds. So Black Crow told his group of European visitors that they could make their offerings in a sweat lodge away from the dance grounds. The day before Pete Catches' Sun Dance in 1978, a few young mixed-blood militants demanded that no white people be present. Although he had invited Allen, a friend visiting from Hawaii, and me to be there, he gave in to the pressure but wrote a note to me: "Please, Father, don't come to the Sun Dance at all as friction here is strong against any form of white man coming here. Even Allen is not allowed to be present to look on. And I am personally very hurt by this. And I told the opposing party that if we cannot approach the Sun Dance with an open mind, then this will be the last Sun Dance here at our place. Yours Sincerely and Respectfully, Pete Catches, Sr." This short letter perhaps best dramatizes the confrontation developing between the militants entering Lakota religion and most of the established medicine men. In 1979, the next year, Catches's Sun Dance was open to everyone to attend with the exception of any militant. It should also be noted that militant influence at the 1979 Porcupine Sun Dance was also noticeably absent. Two women wore crosses around their necks and several men told me they thought of Christ as they danced, one being a Half Moon member of the Native American Church.

HISTORY OF THE AUTHOR'S INVOLVEMENT

As has been noted, the present Pine Ridge Reservation was established in 1878 (Hyde 1956:23). According to President Grant's policy, each reservation was given to a particular Christian denomination. The Pine Ridge Reservation was allotted to the Episcopal Church despite "the fact that in 1876 the Sioux Indians publicly and unanimously declared their desire that their clergymen be exclusively Catholic priests. They were bent on that kind of clergymen who remonstrate, who refuse their aid to treaties made in violation of the rights of the people and solely to satisfy speculation" (New York Freeman's Journal, Jan. 27, 1877, quoted in Duratschek 1943:48). Red Cloud had gone to Washington, D.C., no fewer then three times to ask for Catholic missionaries (Indian Sentinel, April 1919, quoted in Duratschek 1943:60). The Catholic missionaries "labored under difficulties, since it was territory allotted to the Protestant Episcopal Church. From 1879 to 1881, the priests remained just outside the reservation limits and ministered to the Indians who came to them, as the Indian country was closed to them. When this restriction was removed in 1881, conversions were numerous. Father Buschman reported 800 baptisms from October 1883 to April 1884, among them the famous Indian chief Red Cloud, his family, and five other chiefs. Red Cloud promised to commit his children to the care of the missionaries as soon as churches and schools were built" (Duratschek 1943: 97). Holy Rosary Mission, also known as Red Cloud Indian School, was established in 1888.

My involvement began in 1961 when Lakota Catholics decorated their church under my supervision. The heart of the church is a mural expressing the Christian Trinity in Lakota religious symbols. The work of creation, contained within a tipi, uses the mythological theme of the water bird diving into the watery depths to bring up a part of the earth so that the Great Spirit could breathe a soul into it and make man. The work of redemption is expressed by an Indian-featured Christ on the Cross. The work of sanctification is shown by an eagle with twelve tongues of fire, representing the Holy Spirit descending on the apostles on Pentecost day. Beneath the crucifix, the Pipe represents man's offering of himself to the Trinity. As a dedication, the patronage of the parish was changed from St. Elizabeth to Our Lady of the Sioux. This was a symbolic expression of the rationale of my relationship as a priest to the traditional Lakota Religion (Collins 1969:15–19; Paige 1970:123–25).

On November 6, 1965, I prayed with the Sacred Pipe as a priest for the first time at the funeral of Rex Long Visitor at Slim Butte. The night before the funeral I had an inspiration that seized me emotionally, an intuition of the relationship between the Pipe and Christ. A ceremony came to me that I used at that funeral and others on the Pine Ridge Reservation. I held up a Pipe filled with tobacco, and taking the stem and bowl apart, I said: "Remember, man, that the Pipe of your life some day will be broken." I then laid the separated Pipe on the coffin. After the ritual prayers I took up the two separated pieces, and putting them together, I said: "Through the Resurrection of Christ the life of Rex Long Visitor and all of us will be brought together into eternal happiness." Then repeating in the four directions, I prayed: "I am the Living and Eternal Pipe, the Resurrection and the Life; whoever believes in Me and dies shall live, and whoever lives and believes in Me shall never suffer eternal death." After the fourth direction I touched the bowl of the Pipe to the earth in silence. It was after this funeral that Lakota people went to John Iron Rope, the yuwipi man of the community, and asked him if this were proper. He gave his approval.

However, Stolzman objects to the identification of the Pipe with

Christ because there are "many ways in which the Pipe and Christ functioned differently. . . . By similar reasoning it could be said that Christ is the air, Christ is the tree, Christ is you" (Stolzman 1986:208). Intuition expressed through symbolic identification implies similarities and differences without spelling them out (something that must be accomplished through analysis). Nonetheless, the symbol touches the depths of a person's psyche, giving it numinous power.

This is why St. Paul said that Christ is the rock that Moses struck in the desert so that waters flowed from it (I Cor. 10:4). This statement cannot be taken literally. Instead, it contains an intuition that Christ is the source of life but it expresses the truth in an image that deeply touches the religious experience of the Jewish people.

This is also why the Christian Chagga in Northern Tanzania practicing the Kikuyu Religion identify Christ with the Holy Mountain, Kilimanjaro, in a hymn. The mountain is a symbol that witnesses to the presence and power of the high God. Carl F. Hallencreutz develops the continuity and discontinuity in the use of this symbolic identification which in no way weakens the validity of this religious symbol: "Without in any way denying the validity of what the traditional symbol signifies and communicates, it states in terms of a witness to Christ:

It is Jesus, your son,
Who makes visible
what is prepared for our salvation.
He is the Mountain
full of eternal brightness . . . " (1979:100).

It is in this sense that Christ is the Pipe. He is the Mediator among Christians as the Pipe is the Mediator among the Lakota. Yet this is not an analytical statement but a symbolic identification which touches the deep levels of the Lakota psyche. Neither does a discussion on the similarities and differences of this symbolic identification invalidate the power of this symbol.

However, my praying with the Pipe is not accepted by some Lakota, including not only American Indian Movement members but also some in the Ecumenist I group who believe the two religious traditions should remain separate. One Lakota objected, since the filled

Pipe traditionally is not taken apart in ceremony. But he missed the symbolism. Taking a Pipe apart outside of a ceremony has no symbolic value. But in ceremony it symbolizes death precisely because it is contrary to the natural ritual condition of the Pipe. He also was unaware of his own tradition. In every Lakota war party there was a Pipe man who carried no weapons and did no fighting. His purpose was to pray. Before going out on the warpath, he took a filled Pipe apart, leaving the filled bowl in the camp and taking the stem with him. If they returned victoriously, he put the pieces together and prayed in celebration. If they were killed, the separated pieces were a symbol of death (Wissler, 1912:15).

This began a period during which Lakota people requested my prayers with the Pipe. In the late 1960s, Enos Poor Bear requested this for his inauguration as Tribal President. In recognition of this prayer he gave me a beautiful star quilt at the powwow celebration. I have prayed with the Pipe for the sick in hospitals, for the blessing of homes, for the prayers of petition during Mass, and on many other occasions.

But without doubt the most significant celebration of the bringing together of the Lakota and Christian religious traditions was the funeral of Benjamin Black Elk, son of the famous Black Elk and interpreter for both Neihardt's *Black Elk Speaks* and Brown's *The Sacred Pipe.*[7] I was the main celebrant in the Mass that took place in the Manderson school gym before about a thousand people. The Sacred Pipe was carried in procession to the altar by an Episcopal lay reader. I was wearing a red chief's blanket made into a chasuble decorated with beadwork, since red is the sacred color of power which had been manifested through Black Elk's Lakota and Christian traditions. In the sermon I shared with the people what Ben told me. Although the visions of his father as a Lakota holy man were known through the world, the last and most important chapter of his father's life as a Catholic catechist was still to be written. And through most of his life he had doubts of conscience. When he lectured on the Sacred Pipe, was he betraying himself as a Christian? But now that he saw the Sacred Pipe and Christ were really one (again, a common religious form on the phenomenological level), the doubts of many years had vanished. And a deep peace came upon the log cabin in Manderson. At the grave, Fools Crow and I both prayed with the Pipe. Ben Black Elk's daughter, Ester DeSersa, has continued this tradition by asking me to pray with the Pipe at the funeral of her son, Byron, and her aunt, Lucy Looks Twice.

CONTEMPORARY TRADITIONAL LAKOTA BELIEFS

In this section we will examine the Lakota's belief in God, the spirits, healing, life after death and the Buffalo Calf Woman bringing the Sacred Pipe.

Belief in God

Today the characteristic Lakota belief in Wakantanka, the Great Spirit, is that of a personal transcendent God. He is Creator and Provider. He rewards the good and punishes the evil. Most believe in the Christian doctrine of the Trinity, that is, three Persons in one God, and in Jesus Christ as the Son of the Great Spirit. Many Lakota claim that they always believed in the same God as the Christians, even before the white man came. Nevertheless, the Name of Christ is not prominent in Lakota ceremonial prayers. Some AIM members no longer publicly profess a belief in Christ and say they are going back to the "original Lakota beliefs in the Great Spirit," at least as considered by them.

But to determine what this past belief was presents many problems. One of these problems has been the debate on primitive monotheism which has been going on since the last century. Edward Tylor (1871) produced the evolutionary theory of gradual development from animism to polytheism to monotheism, while Fr. Wilhelm Schmidt resorted to an evolutionary theory in reverse, claiming an original monotheism for all people and evidence of a negative sort to support a theory of degeneration (1933, 1935). Raffaele Pettazzoni denies both of these positions:

Although monotheism presupposes polytheism, it is not derived from polytheism by a gradual and inevitable development, as the evolutionist theory would have it. It derives from it, if at all, by revolution, by a radical religious upheaval, the work of some great personality. . . . [On the other hand] the theory of primitive monotheism is founded upon an equivocation . . . The Supreme Being of [primal] peoples is but an approximation to the ideal monotheism. There is a divergence, a difference of less and more, between what is postulated and what the data furnish and all the efforts of the anthropological arguments to explain this difference as the result of secondary degeneration . . . presupposes the existence from the beginning for what does not take shape till later times and under particular historical circumstances (1956:2, 3).

Most of the anthropologists and missionaries who actually lived with the Siouan tribes confirmed this position by stating that *Wakantanka*, or Great Spirit, did not originally refer to a personal Supreme Being (Fletcher 1897:193; Lynd 1862:150–52; McGee 1897:182–83; Pond 1867:33; Riggs 1880:266) Walker states that in "old Lakota, *Wakan Tanka* is two words and designates a class of Gods, and through them all the Gods. It is never used to designate a single God; but the interpreters invariably interpret the term *Wakan Tanka* as the Great Spirit" (1917:57). Raymond DeMallie, who with Elaine Jahner is the leading authority on the Walker papers, is in agreement with this position: "Rather than a single being, *Wakan Tanka* embodied the totality of existence; not until Christian influences began to affect Lakota belief did *Wakan Tanka* become personified" (DeMallie 1987: 28). Powers also agrees with this position: "Both the notion of a Supreme God and Son of God are foreign to original Lakota belief" (1986: 118).

Fire Thunder brings out another difficulty in understanding *Wakan Tanka* as a Supreme Being. He states that "Walker is confusing the *ka[n]* of *waka[n]*, holy, mysterious, etc., with *ka[n]* to be ancient, full of years" (Deloria 1937:38). The Lakota word *kan*(ancient) is a poor one for the eternity associated with a monotheistic God, since it means "aged, worn out with age in opposition to former youthful strength" (Buechel 1970:283).

Although James Dorsey is unwilling to commit himself to a general denial of monotheism among the Siouan tribes, "he has been forced to conclude the concept needs considerable modification" (1894: 365). Kroeber agrees with Pettazzoni in stating that many religions of primal people recognize a supreme deity but it lacks some of the features of the exclusive monotheistic pattern of the Hebrew, Christian and Mohammedan religions, so that it shows "merely analogical similarity" (1948:314). Despite all this, the missionaries did choose *Wakantanka* as the most suitable word to use for the translation of "God."

However, another important insight into this investigation is that different categories of thought are involved. Dorsey, at the end of the last century, recognized the analogical nature of such comparisons, stating that the Indian divided phenomena into the human and superhuman rather than the natural and supernatural (1894:365). Benson Saler has a detailed discussion on the supernatural as a western category of thought (1977:31–53).

I would like to suggest another approach: namely, the difference between implicit and explicit monotheism. Explicit monotheism is a conceptual knowledge and cannot be present on a merely symbolic level. It is achieved only by reducing symbols to concepts through a process of philosophical reflection. Monotheism may be implicit in the religious experience of primal people, but the philosophical distinctions necessary to formulate an explicit monotheism are simply not present. I suggest that, like the natural and the supernatural, monotheism and polytheism are western categories of thought and these cannot be projected onto the thought patterns of primal people. The Lakota were neither explicit monotheists nor explicit polytheists: they had not arrived at the necessary level of abstract reflection. Moreover, symbols are vague and ambivalent. This is why Hultkrantz in his exhaustive study of ethnographic and historical resources (1953: 193–99) came to the conclusion that Wakantanka covers "both the conception of a vaguely personified supreme divinity that the natives believe they recognized in the different phenomena, e.g., the sun and the thunder, on the one hand, and the conception of independent divinities behind these phenomena on the other hand" (199).

But we need to examine Radin's ecstatic discovery of monotheism in Sword's formulation of God: "Wakan Tanka is like sixteen persons; but each person is kan (aged). Therefore they are only the same as one" (Walker 1917:153). Radin comments: "Clearly this is an explicit monotheism avowedly mystical. The Deities as intermediaries have disappeared: they are merely aspects of the Great Mystery. . . . Such is the creed of the priests. No pretense is made that this holds for the people. Among them the sixteen aspects of godhead are sixteen deities. . . . The significant fact remains that such a mystical Supreme Essence was postulated and actually became the official creed of all shamans" (1924:47–48).

I believe that Sword's understanding of Wakan Tanka developed, under the influence of his being ordained as an Episcopal deacon (Walker 1917:159), into a Lakota Christian monotheism, but it is not the Lakota monotheism that Radin had in mind.

Nonetheless, we can learn from the Lakota religious experience of God. In attempting to express the meaning of the word *wakan*, several old Indians, after consultation, made the following statement to Densmore:

An ordinary man has natural ways of doing things. Occasionally there is a man who has a gift for doing extraordinary things, and he is called *wakan*. Although this is a supernatural gift, he can use it only by effort and study. A man may be able to do things in a mysterious way, but none has ever been found who could command the sun and the moon or change the seasons. The most wonderful things man can do are different from the works of nature. When the season changes, we regard it as a gift from the sun, which is the strongest of all mysterious *wakan* powers (Densmore 1918:85).

And Sword makes this claim:

When I believed the Oglala *Wakan Tanka* was right, I served him with all my powers. I became a *Wiscasa Wakan* (shaman) and conducted all the ceremonies of the Lakota. In war with the white people I found their *Wakan Tanka* the Superior. I then took the name of Sword and have served *Wakan Tanka* according to the white people's manner with all my power. . . . I joined the church and am a deacon in it and shall be until I die. I have done all I was able to do to persuade my people to live according to the teaching of the Christian ministers (Walker 1917:159).

In Densmore's material, if one admires a man of extraordinary ability, how much more should one admire the powers working in nature. In fact, according to her informants, a thing is wakan insofar as it does have power. And what converted Sword was not speculation about God but an experience of power: "In war with the white people I found their Wakantanka the Superior." In the minds of these Lakota, *wakan* meant power, despite Power's claim to the contrary (1986:119–20). Power's treatment of *wakan* is an example of linguistic analysis becoming too narrow. Equally important as the etymological meaning of a word are its psychological associations. Most Lakota are more aware of a word's associations than of its etymological sources. I think that linguistic analysis and symbolic amplification are complementary methods.

The concept of Wakantanka entered a new era when the missionaries used the word to translate the Christian term *God*, since, as Densmore noted, translation begins a whole process of association: "A majority of English words expressing religious ideas are associated with the teaching of Christianity. In many instances, therefore, the native idea must be gained largely from the connection in which a word is used" (1918:88). Consequently, on a linguistic level there was a mutual influence between Lakota and Christian religious traditions.

The Lakota Wakantanka was susceptible to Christian influence both because of the vagueness of the Lakota concept and also because of the Lakota religious experience. The vagueness made the Christian God attractive. The Christian God is clearly personal and has a personal knowledge of each one of us. The fact of God becoming man and entering human history has an intimacy which was wanting in the Lakota religion. Secondly, the ordinary Lakota's religious experience of power was appropriate for accepting the Christian God as an experience of power. On the other hand, Lakota religious experience affected his knowledge of Christianity. When Sword said, "In war with the white people I found their Wakantanka the Superior," he was obviously understanding the Christian God according to his Lakota understanding of power.

BELIEF IN SPIRITS

Belief in spirits is an important dynamic in the practice of traditional Lakota religion today, showing a remarkable continuity with the past. The Lakota reverence towards nature is the result of their belief that animals, plants, and rocks all have their own spirits. They are commonly referred to as people.[8]

John Makes Shines told the following story. "There was a man named Dried Meat. He killed a deer for a hungry family. He told them he was in a bad mood for having done it. They laughed at him and said he was going crazy and that he was living too much by himself and that he should come into town. He called all his friends—ants, spiders, frogs, deer—and they all surrounded him. A buffalo appeared on a north bank kicking up the dust. The next day the entire family was found dead."

A Lakota man comments: "If we care enough for an animal, its spirit will continue to live. If we don't, its spirit won't continue. Because of this, the Indians took feathers from a dead eagle. If you see an eagle flying clockwise over you, it is something good to happen, if counterclockwise something bad. Ranchers in the midwest are poisoning eagles, claiming that they are killing their lambs. They haven't proved it. Now they are having a drought and they have to sell their animals anyway. There are special spirits for certain things. The spirit of a deer can bring back a marriage partner or it can cause two married people to separate. The spirit of a spider can destroy records in an office. It happened in the Pine Ridge courthouse. The spirit of a bear is good for healing."

In the 1965 Sun Dance, Fools Crow made what sounded like a strange remark: "I do not want the children to say the animals are feeling bad. I do not want the children to say the horses are feeling bad. I do not want the children to say our dogs are feeling bad." In the Lakota world view there is no sharp distinction between man and animal.

The ordinary Lakota man can have his own guardian spirit, a subject which Ruth F. Benedict treats (1923). The old man Good Lance gave Hunter the spirit of the eagle: "Spirit eagle always circles our place. You can hear his whistle and good luck comes to us. The spirit helped us by touching the mind of the person in charge of housing so that we got into a new house."

A Lakota woman told of the guardian spirit that her husband obtained on a Pipe Fast. "The stone he had on the hill is in the drawer. The spirit of the stone guards the trailer. We have owl feathers [for a peyote fan] in the trailer and we can still notice the smell. One night there was a spirit owl inside. We could hear his wings flutter. So my husband cedared the feathers and the owl is no longer there." So the presence of some spirits is desirable, while others must be appeased.

But yuwipi practice has shaped the Lakota belief in spirits more than any other influence. There has developed a set of beliefs that can be considered a "yuwipi theology." Hunter states that "the medicine man fasted four days and four nights. They asked the Great Spirit for help. So the Great Spirit took pity on his people and gave them helpers. They called them *inyan wicasa*, "stone men," or lightning formations that come out of the west, the land of the thunder people. They come in the form of various animals. If a man dreamt about a bear and meditated, he belonged to the bear clan [i.e., cult]. Some have ghost spirits, spirits of old medicine men who had done good deeds many years ago and passed away, or even medicine women. There are various kinds of spirits that enter the Pipe ceremony. Each person has his own. Any spirit can become yuwipi through a ceremony."

Iron Rope further explains, "They are called stone men from the stones used in the sweat lodge. The stones in the sweat lodge talk and they are spirits used in perfoming yuwipi. There are five stones and when they are heated up, they line up on their own accord. They put some kind of medicine on these stones and a blue flame appears. The rest of the stones are piled up around these five. In the meantime the men are singing and praying after they put water on them. Then all of a sudden you hear these stone men's voices and they answer questions. It is difficult to engage oneself in this. It is very good but also dangerous. All the offerings have to be done in the right way with no faults. And one of the participants, if he disbelieves, the stone men know and tell him. Then the spirits also know and they will fix him for disbelieving. When the spirits say that, it is very dangerous. That is why each one asks himself if it is I. If so, I want you to have mercy on me. I promise I will give you so many tobacco pouches as an offering. And so they will leave him alone. The one disbelieving promises that he will not be thinking like that anymore. The spiritual beings are good people but their minds are quick towards jealousy [a characteristic of the Indian people]. This attitude of disbelief is a violation of the sacred place. And that is why they call them stone men because they talk through these stones."

This is the same basic belief that Densmore describes in her section on sacred stones (1918:204–18).

A Lakota man tells of his experiences. "My wife had a stroke on one side of her face. I took her to Robert Stead to be cured. He conducted four nights of yuwipi meetings. On the fourth night during the meeting a spirit put a stone in her hand. She closed her hand around the stone until the end of the meeting. The name of the spirit is White Hair. Stead told us to wrap it in red cloth and put a blue and yellow ribbon on it. My wife was cured. We carry the medicine pouch in our pickup all the time. The spirit gave us a song that we sing on long trips. The blue ribbon stands for the night, the yellow for the day. The song is the following:

Le yuha cewaki yelo.	I pray with this.
Le yuha cewaki yelo.	I pray with this
Cannunpa kin le yuha ceweaki yelo	I pray with this Pipe.
Tunkasila hoya we yelo eye ye.	I send my voice to Grandfather.

"When I attended another meeting of Robert Stead, he told me that a spirit wanted to make friends with me. His Indian name is Roper. He will help you accomplish what you have to do. When I go to the Bureau of Indian Affairs office, where it is difficult to get things done, I ask my spirit helper, *Kola* ["friend"] Roper, to come and help me and he does. I know what to say and I get my business done. I had a cousin near the Buffalo Gap road by Cuny Table in the 1940s. Even a helicopter was looking for him. I went to a medicine man. He told me to take *wasna* [dried meat and cherries pounded together], tobacco pouch offerings and four flags of the sacred colors and go to the hill and pray. He would conduct a meeting and ask the animal helpers to find out. They would make themselves known. If a coyote appeared at my house, the cousin was dead. While I was praying, my wife and daughter saw a coyote near the house and when I came down, they told me. So we knew that he was dead. Later on they found his body."

An important conclusion can be drawn. In the minds of these Lakota, the spirits of any animal or deceased person can be present in stones and become stone men. In fact, as Buechel's definition suggests, this presence seems to be what makes a spirit a yuwipi spirit.

Hultkrantz explains the belief in the owner of the animals, that is, in the existence of a spirit animal to whom all animals of the same species in the world belong. Whether the Lakota had this belief is uncertain. One medicine man told me that he did not know if the eagle spirit he uses in his ceremony is the spirit of a particular eagle or a Spirit Eagle that manifests itself in all the eagles. However, the transmutation of spirits is a belief of theirs. A Lakota medicine man said that the yuwipi man, Eagle Elk, has the spirit of an old white eagle of great power, which is a deceased woman turned into an eagle. We will also see how the Woman bringing the Sacred Pipe turned into a buffalo calf. There is also a distinction between *yuwipi* and *lowanpi*, or "sing." The full yuwipi is when the yuwipi man is bound up and he calls the spirits in to untie him. But even when he is not bound, it is considered yuwipi since he uses the same spirits. One medicine man told me he used to be yuwipi but he is afraid of it. He is simply lowanpi now. The difference between the two is the spirits, the yuwipi ones being more serious and strict.

In practice, praying through the spirits holds the same place in traditional Lakota religion that praying through Christ and the saints does in the Christian religion. Although these two forms of prayer are normally compartmentalized, Charles Ree did pray through Christ once during a yuwipi meeting. Most yuwipi men see no conflict between the practice of yuwipi and their Christian Faith, as Iron Rope and Plenty Wolf told me. Dawson No Horse received his bishop's permission to be an active Episcopal lay reader and a yuwipi man at the same time. Certain psychological needs seem to be fulfilled at some times by the spirits and at other times by Christ. In this particular practice the Lakota moves back and forth between his traditional Lakota religion and the Christian one, which, as we will see, is a characteristic of the Ecumenist I group.

BELIEF IN HEALING

Healing is one of the main means through which people are led to a belief in the Pipe. Dawson No Horse was led to the Pipe through a personal healing. In 1963 he had a gallstone. Fools Crow prayed with the Pipe and gave him a quart of medicine. That night he felt good. He went to the hospital on Monday. Two X-rays showed no stones. The doctor asked him what happened over the weekend. Dawson asked Fools Crow if he should tell. He said yes. The doctor wanted to know the kind of medicine, but Fools Crow didn't tell, since it wasn't the proper time or place. This was Dawson's first experience with the Pipe. He had seen people praying with it before, but he hadn't paid any attention. Fools Crow went to Dawson and told him that from now on he was to pray with the Pipe and cure people. He put Dawson on the hill for one night. Fools Crow said that a man would come to him early in the morning. Dawson saw the man, who had a black side and a red side, braids on the black side and loose hair on the red. The braids were wrapped around a red cloth, the sign of danger. This meant that prayers would control any danger. The loose hair was there for sorrow so that those he prayed for could wipe their tears as those who lament in the Sun Dance. The man wore buckskin leggins, quillwork, and three rows of eagle claws around his neck. He had the most beautiful outfit Dawson had ever seen. The man said, "When you conduct meetings to heal, I will be there." The spirit told him not to go around from house to house asking people to come: Let people come to ask for help.

Shirley Little Eagle adds some important details: "I attended a yuwipi meeting of Dawson No Horse of Wakpamni Lake. He uses the ghosts of deceased people. He had a vision of an old man with long thick braids who used to Sun Dance. He saw him with his Pipe. During the meeting Dawson saw this man come into the room carrying his Pipe. He told the people to say prayers for their needs and they would be answered. Before he came into the room (the meeting was being conducted in the basement of one of the new houses there), I heard a loud bang on the outside door. It was locked. The basement door was also locked. I could hear him come down the steps and come down the line of people along the walls. If a person had pain, this spirit knew it. I felt a hand pat me where I hurt from my arthritis, on my ankles and other places. I also felt the gourd. I also heard an owl, the sound coming from way up. My sister was sitting next to me. We were scared and were hanging onto each other. All of a sudden, her hands were lifted up as though they were pulled. They were singing a Sun Dance song, "Grandfather, have pity on us," and her arms were raised like the Sun Dancers do. She felt a man with long braids and a necklace of shells. When she came to his waist, there was no more. No Horse's vision was of an old man with the longest hair, one braided and one loose hanging down to his waist, shell necklace and Peace Pipe. It was as though my sister didn't believe that her arms were pulled up, like the Sun Dancers when they raise theirs. She felt big fat braids. Animal spirits are not as scary. Yuwipi is dangerous but can be used in the right way."

Little Eagle was healed through the prayers of Eagle Elk. "I was healed from arthritis so bad that I could not walk or use my limbs.

When the doctors gave up at the hospital, my relatives sent a loaded Pipe to Joe Eagle Elk. He conducted three meetings for me. During the sweat lodge I was sitting outside the entrance with a Pipe. The first night he was tied up and laying on the floor covered with a blanket. He used the spirits of a deer, eagle, and owl, and when he really needs help, the ghosts of medicine men. The purpose of the first meeting was to ask the spirits if they could cure me. I wasn't able to hold the Pipe in my hands — the arthritis was so bad. They just laid it over the palms of my hands. I was scared because there was lightning inside the room so that the people could see each other. The spirits told him that they could cure me and told him the roots that would be used as medicine. The next day he went looking for the root, and just when he was afraid that he would not be able to find it, he saw one. He offered up tobacco and prayed and was able to pull it out by the roots with his hands. The herb looked like a deer, the roots like the legs and the top part like horns. The spirits told him that I would be able to run up a hill just like a deer. At the time I wasn't even able to walk. The second night he gave me tea with this root to drink and to put over the place where I hurt. After this meeting I was able to sit up. The third night was a meeting of thanksgiving. He gave me the medicine only twice after that within a few weeks and in a year's time I had the use of all my muscles and limbs. I am convinced that there are real spirits involved and that they healed me. I talked into a tape recorder for the Medicine Men Association at Rosebud, South Dakota, and they have it documented."

These examples show that belief in healing is still an important part of the traditional Lakota religion.[9] In fact, a number of Lakota told me that praying with the Pipe was for good health and a long life and the Christian churches for the next life. This fairly characteristic attitude leads us to our next subject.

BELIEF IN LIFE AFTER DEATH

Today the Lakota Christians believe in a life after death, a place of eternal happiness where God rewards their good life. That the Lakota believed in life after death in pre-Christian times can be easily seen from their Keeping of the Soul ceremony (Densmore 1918: 77–84; Fletcher, 1884:296–307). But the descriptions of this beautiful

ceremony give us very little understanding of the soul's final destiny.
The absence of any clear statement of belief among the examples in
the ethnographic literature may not be significant. The Lakota had
no dogma but only beliefs related to the ceremonies. But the absence
of any traditional Lakota belief that acts as an influence today, as was
the case with the spirits, is significant. This absence is the reason
that the Lakota readily accepted the religious symbol of Christ's Resurrection, a clear promise of eternal life which their own Lakota tradition lacked.

However, the Christian attitude towards the dead has many Lakota
associations. There is the desire to see and touch the body and to
bury the dead with their most cherished possessions so that their
spirits don't return to bother the relatives. There is also the belief
that the spirits of the deceased remain close by. Leona Bull Bear told
me that "one priest said in a sermon that if he dropped dead right
then and there, his spirit would immediately go up away from the
earth. But we believe that the spirits of the deceased are still around
the earth. The yuwipi men use them, and they are present in the experiences of ordinary people." This belief is verified by the frequency
with which Lakota people see visions of the deceased. Another Lakota practice is the all-night wake, ending with feeding the people
at midnight. The close relatives mourn for a whole year, after which
time they put on a dinner and give-away to end the period of mourning and to publicly honor the deceased. These are inspiring events.

The most striking Lakota contribution to the Christian belief about
the deceased is the ceremony of presenting spiritual food. Hunter has
this to say: "Before an Indian takes a drink of water and passes it on
to his people, he pours some on Mother Earth. It is an offering of
thanksgiving for the ones that Mother Earth took back to her bosom
so that these spirit people can partake of the water. In spiritual food
the four foods offered are water, meat, corn, and fruit because they
are the only ones that the Indians had. One gives a piece of food, not
a big one nor too small but just so. The right amount goes a long way."

Bernard Ice also shares his experience with us. "In a Peyote meeting
they take spiritual food either to the cemetery or place it in the fireplace. If the roadman conducts the service in the right way, without
distractions, you can see the spirits of the deceased at this time. Just
like the Bible after Jesus was crucified, the apostles were praying in

a room at night and Jesus appeared in the midst of them in spirit. Or Jesus appeared to the disciples on the way to Emmaus. After He blessed and broke the bread, He disappeared. The same thing in the meeting when you present spiritual food, the spirits really come around. Spiritual food reminds me of the Lord feeding the people with the five loaves. But the person who handles the spiritual food has to be perfect. Nowadays a lot of people use liquor, divorce, commit adultery and all that. That type of person cannot offer spiritual food.

"One time before I was blind, I was helping the fireman. A lady was gathering the food in a little glass. There was a cake to be blessed too. We brought in fresh coals and put cedar on them. We were getting ready for prayers. We were sitting by the door and here someone knocked on the door. It was quiet; the drum had stopped. We heard the knocking and opened the door and looked outside and there was nobody there. The dogs started barking out towards the hills. In that way we knew the spirits were there. The Indians use a dog for Pipe ceremonies since the dog is the only animal that can know when the spirits are coming around. They are the only animal that can see the spirits. When you prepare spiritual food and you hear dogs barking, then you know the spirit is coming. When a person takes the food outside a Peyote meeting, he or she is supposed to be by him- or herself. No one else is supposed to go out but instead to sit and pray for the deceased. When a person is putting spiritual food in the ground, he can hear the voice and see them walking around."

A woman relates a lengthy story about her son, which shows how dangerous carrying spiritual food can be. It would be best to relate the entire story. The boy has a pseudo-name. "Thomas was sick when he was a little over a year old. He had been all right but my dad went fishing and came back and laid a great big catfish on the table. The little boy came in just at the time the fish flipped over and it scared him and he got sick. I thought that he would get over it, but the sickness kept on. I took him to the Pine Ridge hospital, but the doctors were unable to do anything. I told them what happened, but they didn't pay any attention.

"So I took him to a medicine man. It got so that my little boy ran a high fever and had convulsions. That morning he had convulsions and even swallowed his tongue. They put a spoon in his mouth, and

I ran over to the medicine man and I offered him a smoke and I told him that I wanted him to come and doctor my boy right away. I was crying and wanted him to hurry up, but he said: 'Calm down; he will be all right.' But he took the smoke. He came over with his medicine bag. He smoked his Pipe and put it down and started talking to my little boy. He said, 'You are going to grow up. You are not going to die. You are going to get well. Sonny, I want you to listen to me. When you grow up, I want you to be a good boy. I want you to use the Peace Pipe, and you are going to pray with it. You are going to help people with it, carry it and doctor people with it as I am doing.' After he finished smoking the Pipe, he blew four times on the top of his head. After the fourth time my little boy came out of it. A cousin of mine fixed him a little Pipe, and I carried the Pipe for him. The medicine man didn't have to conduct a *lowanpi* [singing] ceremony. My boy knew he was destined for that. I think that is where the evil came in. As young as he was, that evil was trying to get him away from what he was supposed to do. That's my understanding of it. He remembered what I told him about carrying the Pipe. My boy mentioned every now and then that he wanted to Sun Dance. My boy also went to Native American Church meetings.

"The only time they included him in a meeting [i.e., with a specific duty] is when an old-timer died. Thomas had gotten out of the Wounded Knee occupation. The roadman conducted the services for that man. Since my boy was an American Indian Movement member, he wanted him to take care of the spiritual food. They were supposed to put the spiritual food in the casket, but they forgot to. So they wanted my boy to put it in the fireplace. I told the roadman that he was too young to handle that. You know how young kids are. They get into everything which they are not supposed to be doing. Even older persons can't hardly take care of that spiritual food. They might falter along the way. When you carry spiritual food, you have to watch your every step. From the time they put spiritual food in the ground they have to take care of it in the right way, not only at the memorial meeting but for the rest of their life. That means that they can't be gossiping, doing things out of the way like drinking. And if a person takes spiritual food and lives a bad life somewhere they will hurt themselves and be in tears. So I told the roadman that my boy was too young to take spiritual food, and I told him I didn't want him to do it. The roadman said, 'Don't feel that way. This is good what he is going to do. I am doing my very best to pray for him. You will find out that he is going to be a good boy.'

"Now I feel that he took spiritual food and didn't take care of himself and so he hurt himself afterwards. I think that was too much responsibility for a young boy to take. He went out to pray for AIM, and you know what trouble they were in. And that was overpowering for him, the people he was praying for. Because my boy had been in the Wounded Knee occupation, the roadman had him carry the spiritual food. He probably could have done okay but AIM people carry on; they drink. You hear about them. It seems to me that just kind of fell on my boy. He was too young to take care of a powerful prayer like that. It was dangerous for him. It would be good if he had a strong mind that could overpower the wicked and stay in the good ways. And so my boy died. At that time the roadman was praying with the Peace Pipe too. He was supposed to conduct a memorial meeting for my boy but he also died before he was able to do that."

BELIEF IN THE BUFFALO CALF WOMAN
BRINGING THE SACRED PIPE

The main sources for Lakota mythology and legends are Beckwith (1930), Deloria (1932, 1937b), McLaughlin (1916), Melody (1978), One Feather (1974), Wake (1905–1906), Walker (1917, 1983), and Wissler (1905, 1907). It should be noted that, according to Elaine Jahner, "Sword's narratives [contained in Walker] point toward terms permitting adaptation to changed cultural circumstances as his tales mediate between Lakota and Biblical beliefs, showing possible grounds for syncretisms. Sword's stories are close enough to both sets of beliefs to show how one can be interpreted in relation to the other and how philosophical thought stimulated by the Lakota world view could be carried on within the Christian one" (1987:50). Of all the Lakota mythology the most important is that which centers around the Sacred Pipe.

Although the Sacred Pipe has a widespread use among the North American Indians (Steinmetz 1984:27–80), it received a special religious meaning among the Lakota from the legend of the Buffalo Calf Woman bringing the Sacred Pipe. Among the traditions that were recorded (Brown 1953:3–9; Deloria 1938:21–23; DeMallie 1984:283–85; Densmore 1918:63–67; George Dorsey 1906; Fletcher 1883b:304; Hassrick 1964:257–60; Mallery 1893:290; Mekeel n.d.; Mooney 1892–93, pt. 2: 1062–63; Smith 1967: 1–3; Walker 1980:109–12, 148–49), Black Elk's account is the best known.[The basic legend is that when two hunters went out to seek game in time of a famine, they saw a mysterious woman coming over the horizon. One hunter had evil desires and was reduced to a skeleton. The woman sent the other one back to prepare the people for her coming. The next day she brought the sacred bundle with the Calf Pipe and presented it to the people with instructions. As she left, she turned into a buffalo calf, from which the original Pipe received its name.]

This is the basic myth. However, eleven versions are the source of widely different meanings of the Calf Pipe. In the Black Elk version, as recorded by Joseph Brown in 1948, the Pipe would become the center of seven religious ceremonies: (1) Sweat Lodge; (2) Vision Quest; (3) Girl's Puberty Rite; (4) Keeping the Soul; (5) Making Relatives; (6) The Sun Dance; and (7) Throwing the Ball. A red stone with seven circles symbolized these rites (Brown 1953: 3–9). Black Elk gave a much briefer account to Neihardt in 1932, mentioning only one ceremony, the Keeping of the Soul, but instead giving an incident not found in Brown. "Some hunters went out and got a buffalo and it was in the spring of the year when the calves are in the womb yet. They got the insides out and found a calf in it and cut the womb open and to their surprise it was a human in there. It looked like an old woman. The hair was pure white. All the men gathered there and saw it. This actually happened 80 years ago" (DeMallie 1984:285).

There is room here to summarize only the significant differences in other versions of the basic myth. According to the version the informant Finger told Walker, the woman was without clothing of any kind except that her hair was very long and fell over her body like a robe: "The woman told the good hunter that when she entered the village, '. . . the men must all sit with their heads bowed and look at the ground until she was in their midst.' One man failed to do this and a puff of black smoke blew into his eyes so that from then on he had very sore eyes as if biting smoke was in them. The woman entered the circle and served food first to the little children and then to the women and then she bade the men to look up and served them" (Walker 1980: 109–11). Thomas Tyon confirms that the woman was very beautiful and

completely naked with long hair (Walker 1980:149). A contemporary
medicine man told me she was completely naked as a temptation to
the hunters.

In the Sword version the woman feigned to give the Pipe three
times and gave it the fourth time, a ceremonial practice still in use
today. She stayed four days and taught them everything possible. She
told them that buffalo and other animals were to be eaten but that
certain foods were forbidden: snake, lizards, toads, crabs, buzzard,
eagle, owl, crow, hawk, magpie, cat, moles, weasels, and squirrels. She
also said that those who fought within the tribe must be friends. But
those who were enemies (outside the tribe) were not to be friends;
and as enemy outsiders will remain. She said that everything done
in warfare was to be accounted as good deeds. The chiefs were to use
the Pipe to resolve a feud that would develop from avenging a murder
within the tribe. (Deloria 1938:21–23). Percy Phillips states that "from
the first enemy that shall be killed through the power of the pipe an
ear shall be cut off and tied to the pipe-stem. The first scalp to be
taken shall be treated in the same way. . . . A few days after the pipe
had been brought, there was a quarrel within the camp in which two
people were killed. In accordance with the woman's command they
cut the ear from one and tied it to the pipe stem, together with the
scalp, and that ear and scalp are on the pipe to this day" (Dorsey
1906:327–28).

Ernest Two Runs said that "after the woman left, they went buffalo
hunting and found the woman among the buffalo; so they killed the
woman and cut off her ears and tied them to the Calf Pipe, now meaning 'Whatever I hear with my ears is the meaning of my generation'"
(Mekeel, n.d.: 3). This version is unusual in claiming that the woman
was killed. John Smith reports: From the quiver on her back she took
six bows and arrows. These she gave to six young men known for
their bravery and truthfulness. She told these men to go to the top
of a certain hill where there grazed six hundred buffalo. In the middle
of this herd would be found six men. These men were to be killed
and their ears cut off and attached to the stem of the Sacred Calf Pipe
(Smith 1967:3).

In the Lone Man version, speeches are prominent. The chief makes a
speech welcoming the maiden, and she in turn gives lengthy speeches
concerning daily living to the whole tribe and individually to the

women, children, and men and finally to the chief. She said that "the time will come when you shall cease hostilities against other nations. Whenever peace is agreed upon between two tribes or parties this pipe shall be a binding instrument" (Densmore 1918:65–66). In the Iron Shell version, the woman represents the Buffalo People and is proud to be a sister to the Lakota. She talked four days with the women, children, men, and the leader on how to take care of the pipe. Before leaving, she lit the pipe and offered it to the Sky, the Earth, and the Four Directions (Hassrick 1964:257–60). In an account of Captain J. M. Lee, one hunter was about to kill the woman because she was not of their own tribe. She said that the purpose of the Pipe was to establish peace within the tribe, and no one who kills a member of his own tribe must be allowed to smoke it (Mooney 1896, pt. 2: 1062–63). Finally, Garrick Mallery gives another version in his explanation of the Baptiste Good winter count:[10] "with the pipe she gave them a small package, in which they found four grains of maize, one white, one black, one yellow and one variegated. The pipe is above the buffalo. She said 'I am a buffalo, the White-Buffalo Cow. I will spill my milk over the earth, that the people may live.' She meant by her milk maize, which is seen in the picture dropping from her udders" (Mallery 1893:290).

What shoud be noted is that the heart of Black Elk's entire account is the seven religious rites of the Lakota. His tradition reflects not only an intense interest in Lakota ceremonial life which was missing in the others but also perhaps his "final attempt to bridge the two religious traditions that his life had so intimately embodied" (DeMallie 1984:71). Certainly, by developing a close relation between the seven rites and the Buffalo Calf Woman, he gives these ceremonies a more deeply spiritual meaning within his own Lakota tradition.

This association does not necessarily mean that all seven ceremonies originated with the Buffalo Calf Woman. Black Elk himself told Brown that the sweat lodge and vision quest ceremonies existed before the bringing of the Calf Pipe. Plenty Wolf told me that the Lakota received the Sun Dance from the Arapaho. Leslie Spier has a scholarly confirmation of this position based on a comparative study (1921: 494). Walker indicates the possible diffusion of the Lakota Making of Relatives ceremony from the Pawnee because the Lakota "hunka" appears to be a foreign word related to the Pawnee term, "hako" (1917:

122n). The value of the Black Elk tradition is not in historical reconstruction but in the theological development of the major traditional Lakota religious ceremonies. Even in recent years the Calf Pipe tradition has been changing. Eagle Feather of Rosebud has substituted for Black Elk's Throwing of the Ball ceremony the offering of the Pipe in the four directions (Mails 1978:88). And a young medicine man reflects the twentieth-century environment in saying that the Buffalo Calf Woman was almost naked as a temptation to the two hunters. But this can be expected since even in the last century James Dorsey already noticed "material change in the transmission of myths" among the Winnebago (1894:369).

CONTEMPORARY TRADITIONAL LAKOTA CEREMONIES

The traditional Lakota ceremonies practiced today include the offering of the Pipe to the four directions, heaven and earth, the sweat lodge, the Pipe Fast, and the Sun Dance. Minor ceremonies include a semiprivate Making of Relatives, naming ceremonies, and the piercing of ears. The administration of Indian herbs is a religious act accompanied by prayer.

Offering the Sacred Pipe to the Four Directions

Praying with the Sacred Pipe after offering it to the four directions, heaven, and earth, is done by a considerable number of Lakota people. This common use of the Pipe is not reserved to the specialist, that is, the medicine or yuwipi man. It is in this way that I, too, pray with the Pipe. The Pipe is always filled with tobacco, since the offering of tobacco is part of the ceremony, a practice of all the tribes in North America (Steinmetz 1984:45). It is permitted to have the Pipe permanently loaded with tobacco and sealed with sage. In a simple prayer the Pipe is not usually smoked. Individual Lakota pray privately in this manner out of personal devotion and on public occasions as a prayer of thanksgiving or petition. I was deeply moved when the Red Cloud community gathered for a Pipe ceremony with me at the death of my father. However, the offering of the Pipe is not only a ceremony in itself but also a part of every Lakota ceremony.

The Sweat Lodge Ceremony

Brown (1967:31–43) and Powers (1977:89–91) give descriptions of this ceremony. The sweat lodge is a ceremony in itself as well as a preparation and conclusion of other ceremonies. In Lakota the ceremony is called *inikagapi* (from *i* "by means of," *ni*, "life" or "breath," *kagapi*, "they make" or "cause"). Sweat lodge structures of bent willows can be seen all over the reservation. When a ceremony is to take place, blankets or canvases are thrown over the framework and rocks are heated in an open pit. Cold water poured over the hot rocks in a confined place results in a humid ceremony of considerable suffering, sometimes becoming almost unbearable. Purification is not the only purpose. The sweat lodge ceremony is also a means of petitioning for any need and of offering thanksgiving. The sweat lodge ceremony can even become identified with a yuwipi ceremony when yuwipi songs are sung and the sparks start flying from the heated stones in total darkness. A middle-aged Lakota told me that spirits communicate with him in the sweat lodge. The two spirits are Spotted Eagle and Grey Eagle. He had been praying for a certain woman, and the spirits told him that there was no darkness in her and that his prayers were carrying her. That is all they said. We can recall Hunter's and Iron Rope's comments on the presence of spirits called stone men in the stones used in the sweat lodge. During another sweat lodge ceremony, a Sun Dance song was sung as a prayer for those marching in the Longest Walk from San Francisco to Washington, D.C., associating the suffering of the sweat lodge with that of the Sun Dance. These examples also illustrate that there is no sharp demarcation between ceremonies but that they merge together at times. Benedict noticed this merging when she observed that during a Pipe fast the Lakota "insert skewers through the flesh and tie these to a pole from which the suppliant attempted to tear himself free" (1923:27).

The sweat lodge ceremony is also conducted in connection with the Pipe Fast, the Sun Dance, and yuwipi. It is not always done with yuwipi, and when it is, only before the yuwipi ceremony and not after. The sweat lodge before a ceremony is one of preparation and purification. The purpose of the one after is not quite as clear. Richard Moves Camp has an enlightening explanation: "It allows one to drink water and pray with the Pipe to complete the [Pipe Fast] ceremony.

The main purpose is to untie the knot that connects the person with the sacred ceremony so that he can go from the sacred world to the profane again. He also has to live with the responsibility of his vision and the concluding sweat lodge allows him to purify himself for carrying that out." Here a young medicine man has the intuition of the sacred and the profane which is characteristic of Durkheim's and Eliade's treatment. He discovers in the ceremonial world the ambiguity of the sacred/profane dichotomy. A person entering the sacred place and sacred time of the Pipe Fast must separate himself from that state by untying the knot before going back into ordinary life. The implication is that the sacred is a dangerous power that must be controlled. On the other hand, the person purifies himself to carry out the vision in the same ordinary life. The sacred thus appears to be a positive, creative "power.[11]"

The sweat lodge ceremony has always been important in Lakota tradition. Sword stated that the purpose of the sweat lodge is to revitalize the person through the steam called "the spirit like of the water" (Walker 1917:67). Today's explanation results from a more sophisticated level of reflection, but the continuity is there all the same.

The Pipe Fast

This ceremony has been more commonly known as the vision quest, a rendition of *hanbleceya* (from *hanble*, "dream, vision," and *ceya*, "to cry" or "crying for a vision"). According to Buechel, the verb *hanble* means "to fast and dream or attain visions; [and as a noun the meaning shifts somewhat] a religious prayer ceremonial" and *hanbleceya* as "to cry in the prayer of vision seeking" (1970:165). *Hanble* can be more literally translated as "to go and stand upright" (from *han*, "to stand upright" and *bla*, "I go," "*e*" being a euphonic change), which is what a person does when he goes on the hill. From this examination of the Lakota, it seems that the notion of prayer and fasting is more an essential element of the ceremony than the crying for a vision, elements which have been lost in the term *vision quest*. And so one medicine man claims that a better name for the ceremony is the Pipe Fast (*cannunpa hanble*), since a person going on the hill to fast with the Pipe is not always seeking a vision. He may be praying for many different intentions or offering a thanksgiving. The term *Pipe Fast*, then, has the advantage of turning one's attention to what is more essential in the ceremony—namely, prayer and fasting—since one can successfully complete this ceremony without attaining a vision. Although crying for a vision is undoubtedly the highest form of this ceremony, prayer and fasting are more fundamental. This is brought out by Plenty Wolf's testimony: "The reason why I went up on the hill was that I had a daughter who was very sick and about to die. I wanted to say a prayer in an Indian way to help her get well. I also prayed for my boy who returned from the Sioux sanitarium [an Indian hospital for tuberculosis patients]. After all those prayers, I lost both of them. But I still went on my Pipe Fasts. One day I went to Manderson up on a hill and prayed for four days and four nights. On the last day it seems as though I lost my memory and I went down into the bottom of the bank. I prayed down there, and then I returned back on the top of the hill again. There was a big pine tree when I came to, and there were some graves, and I was standing right above them. I wanted to come back down but these graves were in my way so I prayed to God again. Then I returned back down after my prayer, and there I was standing at the place where I was standing before. Over towards the East I saw a man coming with a flute, and he was playing some different tunes on the flute. He came and passed by me. The man with the flute that went by was a coyote. The coyote had a ground squirrel in his mouth, and he went on by me. That is what I saw in my vision for four nights and days.

"The last Pipe Fast I had was for three days and nights. Early in the morning just before the sun came up, I started praying and I heard something. It seemed like someone was coming. I looked toward the South and it was the Great Spirit that was coming in the form of a skeleton. He came up to me, so I hit him with my Peace Pipe. Then I went into a coma, and when I came to, I was standing where I was originally with my different-color clothes and all my instruments. 'Did you hear what your great-grandfather told you?' I answered back and said no. 'Everything he told you, you will not know now, but he will appear and you will hear everything he said to you when you go back to the sweat lodge.' I wondered who it was that said those words. And I looked around and I found a bunch of pigeons that were sitting on a limb, and they were the ones that were talking to me. That was all said by those pigeons. I was sitting there, and towards daybreak

I heard a lot of women that were talking and laughing, and I looked towards the East and I saw a bunch of women running around and going down the hill [a temptation]. I prayed to God immediately. After I saw this, I stayed there. Early in the morning after the sun came up, the people from down below, who put me upon the hill, got me down. Then I entered the sweat lodge. After the sweat lodge the elders [the spirits] told me that I would have one gourd and the Pipe. If anyone comes to me for curing or anything else, I will do my best to help them in their needs. Now my elder told me that where I have seen the coyotes and the ground squirrel and heard the beautiful sounds of the flute should be remembered. But where I had seen the women should be forgotten since I had not spoken to them. Instead of speaking to the women, I prayed. So my elders told me that two years from now I would have to repeat my Pipe Fast."

The vision gave George Plenty Wolf the animal spirits which he used in his yuwipi meetings. He continues: "Out in the badlands there are a lot of ground squirrels. They are a little smaller than a regular ground squirrel, and these are the ones that I used in my yuwipi meetings. Yuwipi men have to use all the birds and animals. In my yuwipi I use what looks like a grey lizard (which comes around and kills mice), wolf, eagle, owl, robin, and hawk. I can talk with the spirits of these animals in my yuwipi meetings. The man with the flute who turned into a coyote said that the coyote is very poor and if I doctor poor people, they would get well. The coyote gave medicine roots which I got and used. Right now they are hard to find. I got them from Slim Butte. The skeleton told me to do the yuwipi. I never talked with the skeleton, but the dove asked me if I understood what Grandfather said. I said no. The dove said that Grandfather told me to take the yuwipi to doctor people. I should take my Pipe and pray to the south and the skeleton would help me with his powers to doctor people."

Another medicine man told me that his Indian name, the Man Who Carries Coals, comes from this vision: "I was making a Pipe Fast. On the third day it was very hot. The Indian way is to depend upon the elements, whatever the Great Spirit sends. It was in the afternoon and I was standing with my Pipe. I was woozy, hardly able to stand up, and the Pipe was getting heavier and heavier. I had to keep pushing up the Pipe. And then I had a vision. I saw a man walk very slowly to a fire and take up the coals into his hands and walk around the fire very slowly. And I recognized that man to be myself. A year later there was a very old man who was sick and I went to doctor him. I had a helper. But this man was skeptical and did not believe that I could heal him. I saw this in his face when I smoked the Pipe. I told my helper to cedar him. There was a wood fire in the stove and I went over and got hot coals out of the stove and held them in both my hands and told my helper to put cedar on the coals and I cedared the sick man. When he saw this, he believed that I had the power to heal him. I prayed for him and he was healed. I also carried hot coals in several Peyote meetings. And my hands were never burnt, no signs of hot coals. I believe that I got this power from my visions."

John Iron Rope related one of his visions. "The spirits will be coming towards you singing. Then all of a sudden I saw this man who was a skeleton. He was jumping up and down and turning himself around. He told me to recognize him good. Then he comes as close as he possibly can. 'Recognize me good. I am all skin and bones, full of skeletons. When a man is sick and is skin and bones, if you treat him, you can restore him to health.' Then I saw four skeletons, in the four directions and each one of the four colors. The spirits told me: 'when you go to a sick person, you will say it is impossible to restore him back to health. But always remember what we told you.' When the singing starts, this man that is a skeleton will be the one that will give the treatment. He will be using those rattles. When a person is very sick, some will not believe he can be restored back to life. People who visit the sick person will be amazed. Gradually he will be restored back to life and put on weight. Some yuwipi men have the power of healing through the vision of a bear. But my power is from the skeleton."

A Lakota medicine man recounts: "John Fast Wolf, my grandfather, was a medicine man. He made a four day and night vision quest because his mother was very sick. And she recovered. He saw a snake wrapped around him at night. The next day it disappeared. Also a man, almost skin and bones, told him to look over in a certain direction and he saw men during the night. The next day he saw that the men were plants which he used for medicine." All three of these examples of skeleton visions should be compared with the one in Dens-

more's treatment of the sick (1918:251). Plenty Wolf's visions show a
remarkable continuity with those of Siyaka (1918:185, 187).

But not all Pipe Fasts lead to visions. One medicine man recalls
one of his experiences. "In the early morning there was a deep frost.
I was standing with my Pipe and the ground was white and my buffalo robe was white. I felt the chill. I dropped the buffalo robe and
stood in my breech cloth feeling the chill over my whole body. My
Pipe was getting heavier and heavier. My hands dropped down and
I had to pull them up over and over. Then the sun started to come
up. The first rays were on my back. Then I turned to the north and
the sun warmed my right side and to the east and the rays were right
in my face and to the south and the rays were on my left side. And
I thanked the Great Spirit after feeling the chill of the frost that He
warmed me with the rays of the sun. It was an experience I will never
forget."

Renewal is a prominent element of a Pipe Fast. Catches insisted
when he conducted mine, that everything should be new: the knife
to clear the sacred place, the string of tobacco pouches, the wooden
bowl, and the Pipe itself. The wooden bowl is used if a person needs
medicine during the fast. Otherwise it is a symbol of emptiness and
should be held up when one petitions the Great Spirit for one's needs.

The Pipe Fast may become a means of seeking Lakota identity,
sometimes discovered relatively late in life, or an initiation into man-
hood. A growing number of Lakota make a Pipe Fast to understand
themselves and to seek a purpose to life. It is the yuwipi man who
is the normal one to conduct the preparatory sweat lodge, put a person on the hill, conduct a yuwipi or lowanpi meeting while he is there
and the concluding sweat lodge. Understanding this entire process re-
quires a discussion of the next ceremony.

The Yuwipi Ceremony

As we noted in the historical section, yuwipi became a
major ceremony during the reservation period. Feraca (1961), Fugle
(1966), Hultkrantz (1967) Hurt and Howard (1960), and Powers (1962) all
describe yuwipi meetings. I will add additional information. First I
will let Iron Rope briefly describe a meeting. "Everyone sits on the
floor along the walls. The four directional flags have to be set up [in

cans filled with dirt]. Then the string of tobacco pouches will go around in the form of a ring. The altar will be made of dirt in a circle with a string of tobacco around it. Then he [the yuwipi man] places the Pipe before the altar and fills it with tobacco. When all these things have been prepared, he prays with the Pipe. Then he sings. I will be sitting on the floor. We have some rattles which will be used when the stone men come. They will pick up the rattles. And they do all the dancing and maybe voices will be heard. This is a thanksgiving that a woman is making for recovering from sickness. Before the stone men come, I call for them and I ask everyone around if they have any request you wanted granted to talk freely of it. When they come, you might have some questions you will have to ask them. So I advise you to keep them in mind because if you ask questions, they will be able to answer. The stone men will be present because when you have prepared, they will come. . . . [Why do you have to be in complete darkness?] Ministers and white men think that when they are in complete darkness, it is evil. That isn't so. The stone men are very much afraid of light. That is why we have it in complete darkness. Because they are spirits, they see their way around and they don't knock things down. They even see. That is why there has to be complete darkness. If there is light, they will never come. This is not evil doings. No evil is going to come, but these spirits are good and kind. [Do you see the sparks?] Yes, flying around. There is a certain song I will sing, and that is when they will come in. You see sparks when they bounce. They are not here to do any evil things, and you shouldn't be alarmed. I pray to God and then to these stone men, begging them to fly down because God made these things possible way back from traditional times. The stone men are mediators, souls of relatives at one time. I pray with the Pipe in the four directions. I pray to the west first because that is where the thunders come from mostly. I pray first to God, then to the animals, and then to the thunder. God told me to say these prayers mentioning these animals and the thunder."

Hunter confirms the need for darkness. "The electrical stone men are called this because they come from the storms. So they will never come in when there is a little light showing. They will tell you. I don't know why, but their power fades towards the light. The light drains their power. That's why they don't have strength in the light. But when everything is dark, that is when they have power. Their power is connected with the darkness, but they don't do anything bad or wrong. That's how they work. At night when meetings take place, everything is asleep; all the animals are asleep. But in the daytime there is quite a turmoil. That's why they don't work in the daytime. At night everything is quiet, and they can work at night and travel great distances."

Yuwipi men are making changes in the ceremony, showing that it is a living tradition. Dawson No Horse has the regular four cans with flags, white, red, yellow, and dark blue, on each corner of the sacred place. He has two cans with feathers, plumes, and thin strips of colored cloth on each side of the altar and two more on each side of the Pipe rack on his left. At one meeting I attended, about six people presented him with their Pipes to be blessed. After presenting each one to the four directions, No Horse placed them on the Pipe rack to be prayed over during the meeting. These Pipes are smoked after his at the end of the meeting.

Instead of a dirt altar, which is the common practice of the older yuwipi men, he has one of cloth. The first layer is a red square; the second a pink one turned so that its corners touch the middle of the red sides; the third a white square placed directly on top of the red one; the fourth, a red circle and finally two strips of cloth, a yellow one up and down and a red one crossing it. He uses this type of altar because of a vision. Instead of using tobacco pouches or ties, his helper poured a thin trail of tobacco from a sack in an oval shape around the sacred place. After the meeting, No Horse stated that the older yuwipi men served dog but he did not believe in it. Hunter told me that the purpose of strangling the dog before the meeting was that the spirit of the dog would see a vision and return to the meeting to tell the yuwipi man. These changes are significant considering the conservative nature of traditional Lakota ceremonies.

Songs are essential to all Lakota ceremonies since they do not take place without the proper songs. Densmore elaborates on the relation between song and the world of the spirits (1916; 1953). I attended a yuwipi meeting delayed a considerable time because the singers had not arrived. Songs are related to the Pipe Fast. Iron Rope told me that "in a Pipe Fast the spirits will be coming towards you singing. The voice on the Pipe Fast will teach you certain songs. When I sing the songs I was taught, the spirits or stone men will come back." During

No Horse's meeting they sing a Sun Dance song, "Great Spirit, have pity on me," which brings in the spirit of the Sun Dancer which appeared to him during his vision. We can recall the song the spirits gave Two Bulls, which he sings on a long trip for protection. Sometimes songs are sung before a simple Pipe prayer. When Hunter and I prayed in the presence of the Calf Pipe for his recovery from sickness, both he and Looking Horse sang a Pipe song before we each offered our prayers with the Pipe.

Kemnitzer (1976:269–70) and Powers (1982:68–80; 1986:179–95) have excellent analyses of yuwipi songs. Hunter sang a series of seven yuwipi songs for Stanley Looking Horse and Mark Big Road which are included here.

Yuwipi Songs Sung by Lawrence Hunter

1. Kola lecel econ wo
   Kola lecel econ wo
   Kola lecel econ wo
   Hecannon ki taku yake iyecetu
   kte lo eye ye.

   Friend, do it like this.
   Friend, do it like this
   Friend, do it like this
   When you do this, whatever you ask,
   it shall be done.

   Hocaka wanji ogna ilotake ki
   Cannunpa ki opagi yo eye ye
   Hecannon ki taku yacin ki
   iyecetu kte lo eye ye.

   When you sit inside one sacred place,
   Offer tobacco with the Pipe.
   When you do this, whatever you ask, it shall be done.

2. Nitunkasila ahitonwan yankele ye.
   Cekiye yo, cekiye yo
   Ahitonwan yankelo eye ye.

   Your Grandfather is sitting looking down.
   Pray to him, pray to him.
   He sits there looking down.

   Repeat stanza

3. Tunkasila wamayank uye yo eye
   Tunkasila wamayank uye yo eye
   Mitakuye ob wani kte lo eya ya,
   hoyewayelo eye ye

   Grandfather, come to see me.
   Grandfather, come to see me.
   So that my relatives and I will live, I am sending my voice.

   Repeat stanza

4. Wakentahanyan wau welo eye ye   From above I come.
   Wakentahanyan wau welo eye ye   From above I come.
   Nitunkaŝila umasi ca wau welo   My Grandfather told me to come,
      eye ye   therefore I come.

   Wankatahanyan wua welo eye ye   From above I come.
   Oyatewan nihiceyapi ca wau   A people are crying, therefore I
      welo yelo   come from above.

5. Wakinyan ki kimemeya   The Thunders come to stop in a
      kinajinpelo   circle.
   Wakinyan ki kimemeya   The Thunders come to stop in a
      kinajinpelo   circle.
   Kola wanji nihiceya ki wanyanki   Friend, look upon one person who
      yo yo he ho   might be crying.
   Wakinyan ki kimemeya   The Thunders come to stop in a
      kinajinpelo   circle.
   Kola wanji nihiceya ki wanyanki   Friend, look upon one person who
      ye yo he ho   might be crying.

6. Leciya ŝunka wan yutapelo eye ye   Over there they eat dog.
   Leciya ŝunka wan yutapelo eye ye   Over there they eat dog.
   Wakinyan oyate ki sunka wan   The Thunder People eat a dog in a
      yutape, wakan yutepelo eye   holy way.
      ye

7. Kola kinapi you ye, kinapa yo   Friend go out, go out.
   Wananyan kinapaya yo kinpi yo   In a holy way go out, go out.
      eya yo ho   From above looking down I sit; go
   Wankatanhan ahaitonwan make   out.
      lo kinapi yo   From above looking down I sit; go
   Wankantanhan ahitonwan make   out.
      lo kinapi yo

   The first song is one of preparation. The second one calls the spirits in. The third, fourth, and fifth are sung during the presence of the spirits asking for help and healing. In between these songs the sponsors and others mention their needs and ask for prayers. The sixth song is a kettle song, and the last one asks the spirits to leave in a good way.

Plenty Wolf's Yuwipi During a Pipe Fast

The transcript of this meeting, obtained on a tape recorder, is included here because of the direct experience which it
may give the reader. The meeting was on the occasion when Plenty
Wolf put a young boy on the hill after a sweat lodge. He prayed for
him in a yuwipi meeting and brought him down from the hill, concluding with a sweat lodge.

The Pipe Fast began with the customary sweat lodge. Plenty Wolf,
the young man, and his father crowded through the small opening
into the dark, dome-shaped structure. Hot rocks were passed in and
a bucket of water. Plenty Wolf closed the flap, putting them in total
darkness. One could hear the sound of cold water hitting the hot
rocks generating steam.

The following prayer was said. "First of all Grandfather, if we commit any sins (wahtani), forgive us, Great Spirit. In these dark days one
of our common boys, upon this earth he lives and his body is from
this earth. We know that his body comes from You, Great Spirit. And
he wants to take up the Pipe and give thanks to You. And this common boy has a father ill, and therefore he will do some suffering for
the benefit of his relatives, and he promised to take up the Pipe and
live with it hereafter. And to this day, Great Spirit, we want to thank
You for everything. And hear him and bless him, we ask in this way
[i.e., with the Pipe]. Therefore, Grandfather, he likes to take up the
Pipe that he and his relatives will live. And drive from them all temptation, distress, and troubles to come. And tonight this boy is going
to praise You in this way. And help him plan for his future and lead
him not into temptation. There shall be no discouragement, and may
he have good thoughts towards You and patience. But, make his plans
so that he will understand the good things that are to come. And then
he will come back safely from this starting point. And another thing
too. A lot of men fail, but may this boy succeed. And all the relatives
and friends here, if there are any bad thoughts, take these thoughts
away from them. So that this boy here may understand and know all
these things and the right way, while he stays on the hill and make
him a good plan. For this I offer You in this way. This boy here, he
put one foot farther among our common people, so bless him. And
we ask, Great Spirit, to give him a good plan for his life so that he

may carry on. If it be possible, if You want to use him as a servant, may it be done through Your will. And all these things, he will thank You for helping him. We pray in this way with the Pipe. Great Spirit, You let the thunders work for You and also the four winds here. And all these things, they watch this earth here. Therefore, that is why I offer You this Pipe in this way."

The boy's father started singing. After the singing, Plenty Wolf continues his prayer. "Great Spirit, I am praying to You first of all. All my friends and relatives, we want to live and pray to You. [Repeated.] That is why I am praying to You. Up towards heaven I am praying to You for my friends and relatives. We want to live, and I am holding this Pipe and praying to You. [Repeated.] God, all these animals are my friends. That is why I am walking with this Pipe. But, I live the life of suffering and hardship walking with the Pipe. It is not going to be an easy life. And all the steps that I take, I must at all times watch myself. So I carry this Pipe with me, and I sit here praying with You now. And all those things that he wished for are granted to him [the boy]. And tonight he is going to stand there alone, and we want him to come back safely when it is over. I ask You praying in this way [a period of silence].

"In that silence Grandfather said that He sees us all gathering here for this occasion, that tonight the boy is going to stand alone but he will be protected. Grandfather will be praying for you. That is it, and this is one of the thanksgivings that you will do. Grandfather said this is the way to do it. If there is any sickness or what you ask for in a Pipe prayer, He will always give him an answer and help. This occasion that you are going to go through, Grandfather is well pleased. Now in the easterly direction, in the red tipi there are some red men, and they are slapping their knee and saying, 'We never realized that anyone would come approaching in this way.' In the midst of these men, I came to realize this Pipe. 'No one ever dared before to enter this house but you came to us inside. [This undoubtedly refers to a vision Plenty Wolf had.] But you have come, and you have known us as being good friends to you.' Whatever you do, don't stumble and stagger and fall. Or you might turn back with this Pipe and bad things might happen. No matter what takes place, I must carry on faithfully and hereafter we will go on in a righteous way. Open up and pass in the Pipe and matches. We will be going shortly."

This sweat lodge had only one opening of the flaps for smoking the Pipe. After the Pipe was smoked in silence, Plenty Wolf, the boy, and his father came out and got dressed. The three of them along with a few other people, including me, went by car to the location of the Pipe Fast. We formed a procession and walked up a steep hill. On top of the hill, the string of tobacco pouches was stretched out on three sides and the fourth side left open. The boy went inside the sacred place and Plenty Wolf followed with his Pipe, offering the following prayer:

"Great Spirit, before I pray, forgive us our sins if we have any. I offer this Pipe to You. Grandfather, Great Spirit, here is a common boy who has a father who is ill and one day he was in misery. Another day he regained his health. He wants to have a healthy life. He called upon You. With a healthy body he came up this hill now. He is happy, and he wants to thank You in this way since help came in every way. I offer You the Pipe in this way. Great Spirit, we thank You for this day, for preparing him [the boy] for this day. All his relatives and friends, may they have a peaceful life. Nothing bad will happen to his family. I pray to You in this way. And this boy here, his wishes are that he likes to leave some bad habits and lead a good life. And, therefore, Great Spirit, he wants You to put a good plan on him and take away all the snares. And all the things that can hurt the physical body [such as excessive drinking], may You help him to do away with them. Hereafter, he will depend upon You and that You give him his wishes. I offer the Pipe to You. And this boy here will have a good education. And he said that he would offer the Pipe to You in this way, and now here he is. And give him all the things he will need to get an education so his family can live as white men. That is why I offer this Pipe. There are some among people who are sick in the hospitals, and may they get well during the summer months and be happy. That is why I offer this Pipe to You.

"Therefore, Great Spirit, I won't say it way up high above You, but there are some animals between heaven and earth that are working for us. And all these four winds here and all the animals are going to be my friends, and that is why You give me this Pipe to use in this way. And, my boy, you are going to take this Pipe, but the life you lead will not be easy. That is what they told me and that is very true. But, nevertheless, I carry this Pipe with me amongst my people. But

I fell many times. Today, therefore, this boy is going to take up this Pipe. And help me, all the animals. We come to make an offering of the tobacco pouches. But there is a boy who wants to take up this Pipe. Hereafter, all animals help me. Tonight You are going to watch this boy; help him. All the bad things and evils may you [the animals] take them away from him, all the bad temptations, that he will not hear any unkind words, or that he might not see any bad things. But all he will hear, we ask, is for good things and to see a good vision. And when this is over, while he pulls through safely, where he comes from he will go back cheerfully. That is why I offer You this Pipe. Grandfather, we pray that all the animals watch over him. And this sacred hill is made holy because all You see here now are these pouches and these offerings. And there is one in the midst of us, he is going to be left alone here. Watch him until the end of his time. That is why I offer You this Pipe."

After the prayer was finished, Plenty Wolf instructed the boy in the following words. "When you feel sleepy, just lay down. If there is anything approaching you, you will know. And whatever might bother you tonight, pray to the Great Spirit alone. You will know that there is a Great Spirit. This Pipe here is just like a firearm. There is nothing to be afraid of. These are the things I want to tell you. If you feel sleepy, lay on the other side, but if it is towards morning, face the morning. When the morning star comes up, be sure and pray to him."

After these instructions the fourth side was closed with the string of tobacco pouches. It was already night, and the group descended in the darkness and in silence. We returned back to the house where the sweat lodge had taken place to prepare for the yuwipi meeting. Its purpose was to pray for and with the person on the hill. After Plenty Wolf had prepared the altar and the sacred place, the lights were turned out and he offered the following prayer.

"Friend, I am doing this; Friend, I am doing this. Thy will be done; Thy will be done. And in this midst there is a Lakota praying. I am doing this and it will be done. Whatever he wishes, it will be done; whatever he wishes, it will be done. While in the midst gathered here, is a man on the hill praying with the Pipe and therefore we are going to pray with the Pipe also. He is out there because his father is sick. He is only a boy, but he wants to go through with this. We are here to know the outcome of the man on the hill. While he is standing out there, there is a lot of risk and there will be some temptations and he needs help and that is why I'm going to pray for him. He likes to go to higher advanced school, and that is why he is praying at this time also, and we will pray for him. And he goes to some high school now. That is what he is thinking about and that is why he is standing on the hill and we will pray for him.

"Grandfather, Almighty, during these dark days first of all forgive us our sins. And we offer You this prayer with the Pipe. Therefore, Great Spirit, today this boy has a father who is ailing and he is praying to You today. All his bodily needs, he left them here. And the life that You gave is from You. Tonight he is going to pray to You using the Pipe. He doesn't want anything bad to happen but only good. And everything he wishes You grant him and we will make this offering to You. And Grandfather, tonight you protect him and let nothing tempt him, and that is why I pray with this offering.

"Hereafter, Almighty, Great Spirit, let no bad things befall, such as sickness, that they may live years to come, and that is why he is standing on this hill making this offering for his friends and relatives. Maybe there are some relatives of his who may have sickness of some kind. You take it away. Some of them are in the hospital. I want You to help all of them and heal them that they may live a healthy life. I offer this Pipe to You. And all of us gathered here, maybe they have something in their minds for offering: financial, working conditions, family planning, and business transactions. Almighty, Great Spirit, whatever their thoughts are, grant them. Whatever they want in their daily needs, grant them, and we offer this Pipe. And the children are all scattered seeking an education, places where they are, the white man is teaching them how to accomplish themselves. Therefore, You help them to gain their education and to live among the white man, helping themselves. I offer this Pipe. And there are lots of boys in foreign lands fighting wars, protect them and guard them and help them in their needs and with Your power that some day they will come home without any bodily injury.

"Therefore I offer this Pipe. Almighty, Great Spirit, between this earth and heaven there are some animal helpers. All these four winds, these animals take charge, and on this earth there are some animals. All these which watch the earth, Almighty Great Spirit, may they help me with these prayers for the things which I ask of You. These few short hours with the animals, help me as I offer prayer in this way."

At the end of this prayer the singing and drumming started. "Hear me, hear me." This was repeated many times. The singer called one of the animals by its name: "Hear me, hear me." The singer called the second, the third, a spotted eagle, and the fourth by name (the missed names were not clear on the recording). The drum stopped, and after a pause a new song was begun. It was an offering to Grandfather, and the rattles were being used. The song included the words "all my friends and relatives in need of You and that is why I am praying to You, Grandfather." The Pipe was mentioned in this song. When the song ended, Plenty Wolf said: "Oh, this is it. This occasion was coming up, and he knew about it, and that is why the Grandfather is present here among us." There was a silence in which Plenty Wolf talked with the spirits. He then repeated what the spirits told him: "This doing is very good, he said. Grandfather is very pleased, and all of you here are helping. Therefore, that boy standing on the hill is most welcome and thankful. Grandfather will watch him and guard him and He will help him." Then, Mrs. Plenty Wolf made the comment, "Well, Grandfather, we are all here together as a common people. Grandfather, this boy made a great sacrifice, and he walked on it fulfilled. And this was done in a humble way. Then it is a thanksgiving. Therefore, Grandfather, give this boy all he wishes for. And while he is up there, I want him to come back safe and sound. That is what my prayer is. Grandfather, I ask You, at least two of you, go up there and check upon this boy and have a report made. He did it in good faith, and I want a good report of him. I pray in this way. And, Grandfather, have two of you go up there and see him and to have a good report on him. Grandfather, that is it."

Then the boy's father said, "Grandfather, I thank You myself and all my relatives. They take this occasion and carry on this work in this way. And I am the only relative that is living. A long time ago my father told me this. I wasn't interested in it. But now at this time I am thankful that my boy is standing on the hill, that at least one of my sons is inspired so that he is doing this. And I am also thankful that he did it with the common people. I am really thankful, Grandfather, for all this. And hereafter I wish my boy to think a lot of You and depend upon You hereafter. And whatever good is done out of it,

I am thankful. There are lots of things I am well pleased of. Several days I have been suffering. One of my generations became known to You. Therefore, I know that You make this possible for him. My body is getting better, and my mind is good. While before this, I wasn't like this. Sometimes I felt awful bad, but today I am very well. All that I have to say is thank You for all of this. And, hereafter, if there are some occasions like this, we will be glad to attend.

"There is something I would like to tell truthfully. My grandfather used to do these things. When I was small, I was sick and suffering. He wanted me to grow up so he took one of these stone men and he suspended it around my neck. And he told my mother not to get after me. But one time my mother was harsh, and this stone was gone, and just the leather was hanging around my neck. I felt as though the stone was inside my backbone. [A part of the tape recording is unintelligible.] All these things I know and I should be the one doing this. I practically grew up on this. I forgot about all these things, but I now come back to it. One of my boys loved Grandfather and did this for Him and it is a great thing for him [the boy]. Therefore, I say thank you to Grandfather."

Mrs. Owen Brings, Plenty Wolf's daughter, said: "This boy is standing. I want nothing to happen to him. Tomorrow I will offer tobacco. I pray that if the boy wishes anything, You, Grandfather, will grant it to him. And I want You to help his father. And tomorrow I will get some things for this occasion."

Mrs. Plenty Wolf said: "They all got through talking now. Grandfather, You heard all of us."

The singing started again and ended followed by a pause. After the pause Plenty Wolf said: "Grandfather reported back that the boy is standing up there praying and he has good courage. There are some among him, with him, so they can hear him praying. There is nothing to be afraid of. We are all here so he will get out with nothing happening. That is it." He then continued: "During all this occasion here, Grandfather is here. He is also watching and praying." There is a pause during which Plenty Wolf talked with the spirits. He then said: "There is nothing to be afraid of. He is in that sacred place there. Nothing bad will enter. He is happy. What all of us common men have asked for him, Grandfather will grant it. All these prayers that have been put forth for yourselves, Grandfather will answer. We all wish that he will pull through this. In the future Grandfather will depend upon this boy. But, hereafter, try to live faithfully and all things that you ask for will be answered." There was a pause and then the words: "That is it." Mrs. Plenty Wolf asked, "Are you going to say something else?" Her husband said: "Well, Grandfather went up there and He came back, and this is what was reported. And when we get through here tonight and tomorrow, they will be there with him so that he will get out in good faith. That is it. For all the good things You said we will make prayers through the Pipe."

There was more singing, and then Plenty Wolf said: "Grandfather, You told me to do it in this way. I am doing this as You told me to do it. I am doing now accordingly. So hear me; have pity on me. That is it. Everything in prayer and in song we praise the Grandfather. So He will hear your prayer. He prays in those sacred hills, and that is where he prays for us. The spirits will go up on those hills and pray for you." The singing continued again. The rattles started, and the drum began faster beats. Plenty Wolf prayed: "God have mercy upon me. I want to live and that is why I am doing this." [Repeated several times and a part was missed.] During the singing Plenty Wolf said: "Grandfather heard you, and He is very much pleased with the singing and praying." Another song contained the general idea that they were singing for the boy standing on the hill: "See Me, recognize Me. I am standing here." Then Plenty Wolf said: "Grandfather is going to put all his attention to him now, but remember that you say your prayers also because we will now be praying for him. Tomorrow you might notice some good things happening. That is it." The lights were now turned on. The bowl of water was passed around, and everyone took a sip from it and said "mistak oyasin" or "for the sake of my relatives." The Pipe was passed to everyone to smoke or kiss with the same words.

During the morning of the next day, Plenty Wolf led a group to the hill to take the boy down. He offered a very brief prayer there: "Grandfather, Almighty Great Spirit, on this day, the boy, all his relatives and friends here, we all thank You and offer You this Pipe. Grandfather, this boy has now fulfilled his promise. And all his relatives may they live a long life. And in this world may they live happily, and that is why I offer You this Pipe."

During the concluding sweat lodge, the following prayer was said.

"Great Spirit, this boy has made his promise and has fulfilled his promise. From the sweat lodge he went and now he has come back again. Therefore, Great Spirit, grant him a good life and his family. And if there is any sickness in the family, I want you to heal them. And in that way the family will walk happily. That is why I offer You this Pipe. And this boy here, Great Spirit, I want You to hear him hereafter and answer his prayers, and by doing that he will give You thanks in years to come. I offer this Pipe in this way.

"And here with us, I want You to give Your blessing to all of us and help those who are in need, especially those who are sick somewhere and this sickness will be cured and give us a healthy life. These are the things we ask, especially during the summer. I offer You the Pipe in this way. Great Spirit, those who are relatives seeking jobs and money and business transactions that we can't accomplish, these are some of our daily needs, and now I want You to help us and give us our daily needs so that we can thank You in our prayers. And that is why I offer You this Pipe in this way.

"Grandfather said that what you ask for in prayer, may he [the boy] be heard hereafter and he will walk joyously. Your Grandfather and the other spirits pray upon these hills; they will be praying for you. And beware at all times and always pray to Grandfather. And in all our prayers, Grandfather, hear us and remember us. And the common people, everywhere they are sick, Grandfather will protect them and give them back their health. So this is it, and hereafter this is the way you will be praying in the future. In the easterly direction there is a red tipi, and inside there are three red men clapping their hands on their knees [gesture of surprise], and they shook their heads and said: 'We never thought his boy would make it through, but through Grandfather he made it through.' Recognize these men. They are friends of yours. And take this common Pipe. Go forth with it. This is that common Pipe that you are going to walk your life with. Boy, walk always in alertness. You might walk and stumble or stub your toe, or you might even fall down, or you might even turn your back with your Pipe. Do not do this or something bad will happen. Therefore, always walk with alertness hereafter and for all your friends, whatever they ask for will be granted. I offer this Pipe in this way. And after this we go on. May we have a healthy life and give us our daily needs and protection. In this way we offer You the Pipe."

The flap was opened and the Pipe was passed in and smoked. After this the people came out of the sweat lodge and the ceremony was completed.

Many observations could be made of these sweat lodge and yuwipi ceremonies. They form a tight-knit unity. Plenty Wolf asking for the forgiveness of sins, doing the will of the Great Spirit, and the use of the term "almighty" all clearly the result of his Catholic influence. But, the ceremony was very Lakota: his familiarity with the animals, which are his friends and spirit helpers, the red men in the red tipi from his vision, the serious responsibility of taking up the Pipe, the frequent prayer for good health, the stone men (i.e., the spirit in the stone around the father's neck), the importance of the sacred place, the assurance that if one lives a life worthy of the Pipe, his prayers are always answered. An interesting mingling of the two worlds is the prayer for a good education in the white man's world.

It should be noted that the frequent expression, "standing on the hill" brings out the root meaning of *"han"* "to stand upright" in *hanbleceya.* Nor is a vision in the strict sense sought in this Pipe Fast. Rather, the power of prayer with the Pipe is emphasized.

THE SUN DANCE

In Lakota, the Sun Dance is called *Wi wanyang wacipi* (from *wi,* "sun," *wanyang,* "to gaze," and *wacipi,* "they dance"; hence, "sun-gazing dance"). The Sun Dance has become the high point of Lakota religion today, with several hundred people attending the 1979 tribal one held at Porcupine from July 30 to August 2. A description follows.

On the evening before the first day, the center tree arrived late, 10:00 p.m., on a truck which brought it about six miles. The tree was about fifty feet long and was carried a short distance by the dancers from the truck to the Sun Dance grounds. With the help of automobile headlights, the dancers tied their own colored cloth offering and the ropes used for the piercing onto the tree. Fools Crow tied the rawhide effigies of a buffalo and a man on it. There was a short period of very busy activity, after which Fools Crow prayed briefly, the dancers raised the tree and dropped it into the ground, and the dirt was filled in.

On Monday morning at 4:30, an announcement blared out over the public address system that all the dancers should get up. During all four nights they slept with relatives in the tents scattered throughout the camping area. The dancers drifted towards the sweat lodges on the west side of the dancing area where one other person tended the fire which was heating the rocks to be used in the ceremony. The dancers filled their own Pipes and placed them on a rack near one of the sweat lodges. There was a separate sweat lodge for the men and women; No Horse conducted the one for the men. The group sang Sun Dance and Pipe songs, and everyone was given the opportunity to speak and pray inside the lodge.

At 6:45 A.M., a procession of 47 men, including 11 boys, and 28 women, but no small girls, formed. Fools Crow with Yellow Boy carrying a large buffalo skull and No Horse carrying a chief stick with eagle feathers led the procession, the youngest male dancers being the first in line and the women dancers last. In addition to No Horse and Yellow Boy, there were two helpers in jeans and three in skirts. Fools Crow made the four customary stops, the last one at the east entrance. The Sun Dance singers were in the procession and sang the first song without the drum. Any prayers offered were said too low to be heard at a distance. The dancers circled the tree and gave their Pipes to two helpers, who put them on two racks on the west side of the circle. Most dancers offered their Pipes to the four directions and turned clockwise before presenting them.

The dancers formed two straight lines and faced east as the songs continued, now with the drum. The dancers were led to the west and made a complete circle facing west, north, east, and south. The singing and dancing always stopped in the south position throughout the entire Sun Dance. Three or four helpers took Pipes from the rack, circled the tree, touching the Pipes to it, and passed along the rows of dancers so that the one whose Pipe it was could claim it and present it to the people appointed to accept the Pipes. The Pipes were accepted only after the three feints, after which the music stopped. These people, both men and women, took the Pipes clockwise to the group of singers, one group being on the north and the other on the east. The singers smoked the Pipes, at times asking help from people close by.

Dancers had their own style of dancing: some on one foot, some on both; some with a great deal of bodily movement, some with very little. Individuality was also expressed by difference in the color of skirts and dresses, in the designs of body paint, in the carrying of wands, sacred hoops, coup sticks, etc.[12] On the very first morning after just a few dances, the piercing began and continued throughout the four days so there was never a large group of dancers pierced at any one time. During the piercing the dancers formed a large circle around the tree; the ones being pierced were part of the circle. They were pierced in a standing position instead of lying down. Those dragging buffalo skulls did so right behind the circle of dancers. About twelve dancers were pierced the first morning, one to three at a time. There were four to seven men, some with their Pipes, always facing the sun and following its course throughout the day. These dancers never went into the shade during the rest periods but were allowed to sit or lie down. When returning from the shade to dance again, many embraced the tree.

On the second day Kermat Bear Shield was pierced and tied to the tree for six hours. Another man was pierced in the back in two places and danced all day with a buffalo skull hanging from his back about waist high. These two men joined those facing the sun. On the third day Bear Shield dragged buffalo skulls. A teenage boy was pierced with the intention of staying pierced all day and night. When he got sick from the sun, another one took his place to fulfill the pledge. However, the second one was also overcome with heat, and no one took his place. A dancer by the name of DuBray tried to drag eleven buffalo skulls. He had a rope around his body, and three dancers tried to pull him free of the skulls. But he was still unable to budge the skulls, so the dancers dragged them around. Finally No Horse was pierced and tied to a rope around DuBray to help him, since DuBray was undergoing the torture partly as a thanksgiving for No Horse's recovery from a sickness. With the help of dancers, both of them tore free. Later, No Horse pierced a woman on the right shoulder as she stood in the circle of dancers, and she broke free from the tree. On the fourth day Cordelia Attacks Him danced most of the day with eagle feathers attached to skewers in her shoulders. In the afternoon she was pierced and tied to the tree. Her daughter was also pierced in the right shoulder and tied to the tree. Since the mother broke free first, she encouraged her daughter, who was having some difficulty.

Matthew King, the announcer throughout the Sun Dance, made

comments from time to time, the following one being typical. "We will not have the same power until we have the faith of our grandfathers, but we are going that way. No one will tell you how to pray, how to live. You must go to the sacred hoop, to the tree. You must prepare yourselves; you have to find yourselves. The power you are going to talk to, you have to do that yourselves. Come into the sacred hoop. Go into the arena. Wisdom is free. You have to seek and find yourselves. I said many times before that there is no other way. Find God the hard way. No other religion is so severe and trying as the Sun Dance religion as exercised by our traditional people. We must understand what they were doing. We received many blessings from the Great Spirit. Everything we receive, even life, we return in thanksgiving. We pray to understand the law of nature, which is God. We must obey all the natural law regarding the ceremony.

"An Indian who had been in the white man's jail never prayed so hard. He thought of the Sun Dance, and today he is taking care of the sweat lodge, heating the rocks. Indians are harassed and suffer prejudice from the white man who think they have a superior power but they are destroying themselves. This is Indian tradition. It might be millions of years old. This is Indian torture, which is different from any other race. We believe in piercing, with the law of nature. When anyone committed something unusual from natural life, it was the duty of everyone to hold the man responsible. Everyone was under the law of God. They don't depend on the policeman in the white man's way. The Indian is peaceful. The Indian is not greedy but generous. There were many societies among Indian people which upheld the natural law. Members of the White Horse, Lance Bearers, and Fox societies memorized their regulations. There were no written laws but only those stamped in the brain. At the spur of the moment he doesn't go to the chief of police or head man for advice. Each one knows what to do. They prepared according to what we know. The warrior went fasting and prayed four days and nights without the necessities of life, food, water. He stood on a high hill with the wind blowing, with darkness, with the spirits of the deceased surrounding him. It was scary. And he made a commitment. The Indians must have a good life. They must comply with nature."

The number of dancers fluctuated from day to day. On the first day there were 47 men and 28 women, on the second 47 men and 37

George Plenty Wolf praying with the Sacred Pipe before the raising of the cottonwood tree.

The cottonwood tree at the center of the Sun Dance grounds.

Frank Fools Crow helping in the sweat lodge ceremony.

Frank Fools Crow instructing the Sun Dancers before the procession.

Frank Fools Crow leading the dancers into the Sun Dance grounds.

One of the women Sun Dancers.

Sun Dancers facing one of the directions.

Fools Crow with three dancers during the ceremony.

A singer giving back the Sacred Pipe to a dancer so that the ceremony can begin again.

Two Sun Dancers.

women, and on the third day 37 men and 37 women. I saw two teen-age boys, who had been pierced the day before, in jeans at the concession stand buying soda. I failed to count the dancers on the last day.

During the first three days the dancing stopped at 5:00 P.M. On the fourth day at 4:00 P.M., the last Sun Dance song was sung while the dancers were in a line facing east and the spectators passed by, shaking hands and embracing them.

And so ended a ceremony in which six symbols—the drum, the eagle whistle, the Pipe, the tree, the buffalo skull, and the sun—caught the Lakota imagination. The almost constant beat of the drum, the eagle whistle blown in unison with it, the offering of the Sacred Pipe, the tree which was embraced as a source of strength, and from which they tore themselves free, the buffalo skull placed in a position of honor on the altar and dragged in torture around the sacred circle and the sun, bright and hot and unmerciful, all engulfed the consciousness of dancers and spectators alike.

Since the Sun Dance songs have such a great importance in the ceremony, I am including the seven songs which Edgar Red Cloud sang. He was a singer for 50 years and the leader for 25 of those years. However, only the first, second, and fourth songs were used in the 1979 Porcupine Sun Dance.

The Seven Sun Dance Songs of Edgar Red Cloud

1. Melody without words.

2. Wakantanka onśimala ye
     wani kta
   Ca Lecomon we eya he

   Great Spirit, have pity on me;
     I want to live.
   Therefore, I do this.

3. Kangi Gleśka k'un,
   Kangi Gleśka k'un,
   Okicize ohiwayin kte lo,
     cannunpa ki yuha cekiya
     yo.

   You Spotted Crow,
   You Spotted Crow,
   Pray with the Pipe, so you will
     win a war.

4. Anpo ki kolawaye,
   Anpo ki kolawaye,
   Anpo ki hinajin ye yo.

   My friend, the Dawn.
   My friend, the Dawn.
   The Dawn, come and stand

[Repeat the previous stanza
  once]

5. Melody without words.

6. Wicaśala wan tewahile k'un,   A man I love
   Wanweglake śni.   I didn't get to see him.

7. Kangi Gleśka k'un, mni   Spotted Crow, do you want
     wacin so?   water?
   Mni yacin so? Mni yacin   Do you want water? Do you
     so?   want water?
   Ehayakeya.   You say it.

   Kangi Gleśka k'un loyacin?   Spotted Crow, are you hungry?
   Loyacin? Loyacin?   Are you hungry? Are you
   Ehayakeya.   hungry?
                                   You say it.

MINOR CEREMONIES

      I shall offer a few comments on the minor ceremonies. Although only a trace of the heyoka tradition remains, in the "clown dancing" at powwows, this used to be a serious obligation (Wissler 1912:82–85). Here I can offer only an indication of the literature available on this important subject. In summarizing a study based upon Murdock's Cross Cultural Survey, which includes reports from 56 cultures, Lucille H. Charles comes to the conclusion that the function of the clown is to bring a "renegade element" of the unconscious into the consciousness for the sake of "self integration" (1945:32). Verne Ray has a distributional study containing excellent ethnographic source material (1947). Julian Steward has a good general treatment (1931). James Howard has a brief discussion of the Dakota Heyoka Cult (1954,) and Thomas Lewis gives a description of contemporary heyoka dancers on the Pine Ridge Reservation (1970).

      There is also an informal adoption ceremony before a small group of people which consists of praying with and smoking the Pipe. Piercing the ears is usually done during the Sun Dance. Naming ceremonies usually take place at powwow celebrations. A medicine man will pray with the Pipe for the child, sing an honoring song, and give the name. After that there is a give-away. The increase in these ceremonies is a sign that Oglala Lakota religion is beginning to affect more and more areas of their lives.

RITUAL VIOLATION, DISHARMONY, AND SIN

Although there is some freedom in the performance of Lakota ceremonies due to the individualism characteristic of Plains culture, there are certain requirements which must be fulfilled. Now ritual violation involves the concept of taboo. Although taboo can be social, Frederick J. Streng points out that in its religious context it "became equated with the sacred perceived ambivalently as both holy and dangerous, pure or impure, as opposed to the profane which was as the ordinary or neutral. The ambivalence of taboo was used to establish a map of man's relationship to the sacred. On the one hand, there is the conception of the sacred as power, as a positive, expansive, inclusive force that is accessible to man and brings him blessing and holiness as he comes into contact with it. On the other hand, there is the sacred as a negative, separate, exclusive power prohibited to man, which causes death or pollution if man comes in contact with it" (Streng 1980:123).

In the Lakota tradition the Sun Dancers could embrace the tree because they were in a state of ritual holiness until they had performed their vow (Deloria 1929:410). But there was a taboo forbidding those in a profane state to do so. In the minds of the Lakota, a woman was punished by death for stepping over the Sun Dance tree after it was cut down (Densmore 1918:114). This taboo manifests the sacred as dangerous, while the Sun Dancers embracing the tree manifests it as a positive power.

But ritual taboo still exists today among the Lakota. One young man had this comment: "A medicine man prepared a sweat lodge for me. The pipe was loaded, and then he got scared. He was also praying for my separated wife, and he was afraid people might think he was a double-crosser. However, last night he cut six pieces of my flesh, which I put in a cloth and offered to the four directions, the heavens and Mother Earth. I asked that no harm would come to me since the Pipe was loaded and the ceremony not finished. I prayed and smoked the Pipe." A medicine man gives another example of ritual taboo in saying that a woman in her menstrual period must respect the Pipe and not be in its presence during a ceremony. In his mind this taboo does not involve impurity but rather a feminine power, due to her special relationship to nature at this time, which neutralizes the power of the medicine man. He claimed that a woman failed to do this one time and her bleeding never stopped and she died. Plenty Wolf relates two instances: "In the days when only horses were used for transportation, there was a man who used the Pipe in the sweat lodge. One time this man lost his temper and he kicked the Pipe. The following day when he got on his horse, it bucked him off and he broke his leg. He was taken to the hospital in Omaha, Nebraska, and there he died. In Sheridan, Wyoming, there was a Pipe ceremony, and at that time there was harassment by the police. The police broke up the Pipe ceremony, and after that there was a big flood which did a lot of damage. By these two examples it shows that the Pipe cannot be misused since it is dangerous."

After the 1978 Sun Dance at Green Grass, Stanley Looking Horse told Hunter that he was concerned with a large number of children in the dance. They were too young to understand what they were do- ing and if they made mistakes, harm could come to the parents or relatives.

The concept of taboo is influenced by both their Christian and La- kota traditions. In their Christian tradition sin is a moral taboo, that is, an offense against a personal God. In their Lakota tradition, by vir- tue of the very personal relationship which they have to the entire world of nature, addressing even the spirits of trees and stones as Grandfather, they also believe that the violation of taboo is disobedi- ence to the spirits. This Lakota belief comes closer to the Christian belief in sin than anything else in their tradition.

Richard Moves Camp attempts to bring the two traditions together, making this comparison: "The equivalent of Christian sin in the In- dian tradition is breaking one's commitment to the Pipe. When one prays with the Pipe, he is obliged to do it in a good way, not for evil purposes. The Pipe brings harmony between men when they smoke it. You can't lie through the Pipe. To go against these things is a sin."

The claim has been made "that among the Canadian Dakota an- cestral sin is a cause of sickness. Sickness came to them only from the wrongdoing of a great-grandfather and much still derives from that cause. . . . Sins that cause illness in dependents are of at least three types: ritual transgressions, torture or mockery of animals, crimes against a person or against the group . . . the medicine man names the sin . . . and the patient feels better at once because we know the cause" (Wallis and Wallis 1953:432). This belief is similar to the Christian one of original sin. Either there has been a Christian influence here or else at least one tribe arrived at the notion that what our ancestors did can affect our present-day lives. However, the precise nature of sin still differs very considerably between different cultures.[13]

2

THE NATIVE AMERICAN
CHURCH

*This chapter is divided into a history of Peyote and the
Native American Church on the Pine Ridge Reservation;
my presentation of a papal Blessing to the Native American Church; their beliefs in God, Peyote, the sacred ceremonial objects, the water woman, the last days; visions;
healing and the transcription of two Peyote meetings.*

HISTORY OF PEYOTE AND
THE NATIVE AMERICAN CHURCH

For the ritual use of Peyote in Mexico and its diffusion
to Oklahoma and throughout the United States one should consult
LaBarre (1975). One can find the legal development of the Native American Church in Slotkin (1956). Vittorio Lanternari has a very concise
history (1963:63–100).

Various dates connected with the introduction of Peyote on the
Pine Ridge Reservation have been given. Wissler (1926; 90) accepted
Shonle's date of 1909 from the Omaha (1925:55, and map, facing 58).
LaBarre put a questionable diffusion from the Omaha in 1906 or 1907.
(1975:122) Driver and Massey put a secondary influence, without any
primary one, from the Omaha in 1909 or 1910 (1957:272). But Densmore quotes a Winnebago informant, John Bearskin, as saying: "In
1903 or 1904 John Rave and others came to South Dakota, Minnesota
and Wisconsin and instructed the people in the peyote religion (1931
MS., Part II, p. 14). Jim Blue Bird, one of the original organizers in Allen, confirmed the 1904 date in writing to Dr. Omer Stewart (n.d.).

Emerson Spider told me that the first time the Winnebago came they did not have the Bible but brought a Half Moon without smoking. Then, shortly after, perhaps only one year later, they brought the Cross Fire with the Bible. According to Bernard Red Cloud, Silas Yellow Boy always talked about a Half Moon fireplace without smoking coming from the Winnebago. Radin states that he knows "that practically all the overt Christian dogmas were introduced between 1905 and 1910 by an Indian named Albert Hensley" (1933:202). Spider mentions Hensley as one of the first bringing Peyote to Allen, but he does not know the exact date. Putting all this information together makes Blue Bird's 1904 date highly probable.

A number of other dates are given which indicate the existence of Peyote on the reservation for a number of years previous. According to Nancy Oestreich Lurie (1961:44–45), the Winnebago Mountain Wolf Woman reported eating Peyote with the Sioux in Martin, South Dakota, near Allen in 1908. The Pine Ridge Superintendent, John R. Brennan, wrote in 1918 that Peyote had come to his attention seven or eight years before (Stewart, n.d.).

However, there seems to have been Oklahoma influences also, the first of which was apparently even before the 1904 diffusion from the Winnebego. Bernard Red Cloud relates the following incident from Silas Yellow Boy's early life. "Silas was a jockey, and he was thrown off his horse at Allen and knocked unconscious. He was taken to a doctor, probably in Martin, South Dakota. Since the doctor was unable to do anything, he was taken back to Allen. There were four Indian men from Oklahoma who were visiting and attending a powwow fair. With Charles Yellow Boy's [Silas's stepfather] permission they gave Silas some Peyote tea. They did not have an altar but put cedar on a fire and sang songs and gave Silas medicine. The old man Red Bear [Silas's real grandfather] had not yet heard of Peyote and stayed outside the house, and only Charles Yellow Boy and his wife went in. After Silas came out of his unconsciousness and recovered, the four men left. This was before there were any meetings on the reservation. Silas wanted to know where the Peyote that cured him came from. So Jim Blue Bird and Silas rode saddle horse to the railroad in Nebraska and took the train to Oklahoma.[1] Silas heard the same songs and saw the same four men in Oklahoma that doctored him in Allen. Silas claimed the the old man Red Bear, who used the traditional Pipe in the meetings, was open to accepting Peyote from the Winnebago because Silas had been cured."

There may have been another Oklahoma influence. Blue Bird wrote Stewart that a Southern Cheyenne, Red Bird, taught the old man Red Bear at Allen in 1906 (n.d.). Although the date has no verification, Bernard Ice confirms the substance of the statement in saying that Red Bear had relatives in Oklahoma and learned the Peyote ways from the Southern Cheyenne Tribe. However, instead of using the ceremonial cigarette, which he would have learned from Red Bird, he used the Lakota Pipe, at a time when the Half Moon fireplace derived from the Winnebago had no smoking.

The Half Moon fireplace with smoking of the cigarette began on the Pine Ridge Reservation at Wounded Knee during the second decade of this century, very possibly from Silas Yellow Boy's experience in Oklahoma. Yellow Boy, one of the original members, told Red Cloud that Levi Sitting Hawk, Dick Running Bear, and he conducted meetings there with the cigarette before the 1916 Deadwood trial (to be treated below). Yellow Boy recalled how he had to leave the meetings before sunrise and travel back by horse to Manderson where he lived. During that time there was no ceremonial breakfast so that the meeting could break up more quickly, since there was always the fear that the police would raid the meeting. The Wounded Knee meetings were started because of both the convenience of location and a desire to get away from the Cross Fire influence at Allen.

Important conclusions can be drawn from the above evidence. There is a double diffusion of Peyote practices among the Oglala Lakota on the Pine Ridge Reservation. The Half Moon without smoking, which was later absorbed by the Cross Fire in Allen, and the Cross Fire both came from the Winnebago, probably in 1904 and 1905, respectively. The present Half Moon fireplace with the cigarette is a result of a diffusion from Oklahoma either through Red Bird's or Yellow Boy's Oklahoma experience and was established at Wounded Knee early in the next decade.[2]

1916 was an important year for the Peyote movement because of the Federal trial in Deadwood, South Dakota, of the U.S.A. v. Harry Black Bear (U.S. Government 1916). On May 19, 1916, Harry Black Bear was indicted for giving Peyote buttons to Jacob Black Bear, Paul Black Bear, Jr., John Black Cat, and James Real Bull. In the September trial the above men, along with John Brennan, Dr. Cross, Philip Fast Wolf, John Hand Soldier, and Grant High White Man, were all witnesses for the prosecution. The prosecution wanted Peyote interpreted as an intoxicant and the accused convicted under the act of 1897 "prohibiting the sale of intoxicating drinks to Indians." However, the judge accepted the defense attorney's position that the law under which the case was being tried did not apply to Peyote. Thomas Sloan, a member of the Omaha tribe and an attorney, was the main defense witness. This trial not only clarified the legal status of Peyote but also allowed meetings on the Pine Ridge Reservation to be brought out of the cellars and into the open.

The 1920s were dominated by the registering of charters. Although no mention was made of the Half Moon and Cross Fire fireplaces in the charters, each group got its own independent of each other. Articles of Incorporation of the Native American Church of Allen were filed October 5, 1922, followed by those of South Dakota, of Washabaugh County, of Porcupine County. On the Rosebud and other reservations in South Dakota, Articles of Incorporation were filed by the counties of St. Charles, St. Francis, Norris, Sisseton, Buffalo, Rosebud, and Charles Mix. This flurry of activity resulted both from a misunderstanding of the nature of charters and from each group's desire for the prestige of having its own charter.

In this same period the Half Moon members obtained one charter for the state of South Dakota on February 3, 1927, with Richard Running Bear, Levi Sitting Hawk, Jessie Sun Bear, and Albert Running Bear filing the declaration. The incorporate title was the Ancient Native American Church. They obtained a national charter from Oklahoma in the 1930s. This charter was renewed in the 1940s and twice in the 1950s.

In 1923 the state of South Dakota passed a law prohibiting the transportation of Peyote across state lines. Thus, unknowingly, since Peyote was not mentioned in any of the State Charters, South Dakota was caught in the contradiction of granting a charter to the Native American Church and at the same time making its sacrament illegal. This law was not repealed until 1962.

Diffusion of the two fireplaces on the Pine Ridge Reservation can now be traced. There was a quick diffusion of the Cross Fire to Porcupine and Potato Creek. Charles Red Bear, Frank White, and William Black Bear brought it to Porcupine. (We have already treated the beginning of the half Moon with smoking at Wounded Knee.) According to a Rev. A. F. Johnson, in 1919 "the west end of the reservation had no peyote, or at least very little (Stewart, n.d.). If Wounded Knee is considered part of the "very little," this statement seems to be true, since all the evidence I could gather indicates the 1920s and 1930s as the period of diffusion to the other western parts of the reservation.

According to Phyllis Mesteth, Sam Lone Bear was conducting meetings, and her father, Joe Sierra, was the fireman in the town of Pine Ridge before 1930. Silas Yellow Boy married Susie Big Crow in 1924 and moved to Wolf Creek and conducted meetings there. When Susie died, Silas married Nellie Kills Enemy in 1936 and moved to Loafer Camp west of Pine Ridge. In 1958 he moved to the town of Pine Ridge, where he conducted meetings. These meetings survive today, with Bernard Red Cloud conducting them. However, the Wolf Creek meetings did not survive Silas' departure. Today Wolf Creek is the center of the Body of Christ Independent Church.

In the 1930s, Lawrence Hunter said that he was a member of the group that started right across from Holy Rosary Mission at Ben Marrow Bone's place. Ben had been a Catholic catechist. Some of the group were Philip Broken Leg, Vincent Catches, Noah Wounded, Charles Wounded, Joseph Running Hawk, and his brother, Bill. Hunter claims that Ben Marrow Bone, Joe Martin, and Philip White Bear filed the declaration for the national Charter from Oklahoma in the 1930s. These meetings lasted until 1945 or 1946. During the 1930s, Joe Martin took Peyote to Slim Butte, and Joe Catches, a brother to Pete, took it to the Pine Creek area. Beatrice Weasel Bear continues meetings in Slim Butte and other Weasel Bears at Pine Creek to the present day.

And so by the end of the 1930s, the permanent sites of the Native American Church were established: the eastern part of the reservation for the Cross Fire and the western part for the Half Moon. Attempts at diffusion were made in other areas but failed. Sam Lone Bear conducted meetings for primarily mixed-bloods at Rockyford in the 1920s, but these meetings did not survive him. Steve Red Elk told me that people tried to conduct Peyote meetings in Manderson during the 1930s but the strong Catholic community there had the police run them out.

Although 1934 is important as the year of John Collier's policy demanding freedom of religion to the Indian people, there was strong opposition to the Native American Church in the Oglala Sioux Tribal Council. According to a letter of James Blue Bird to the Hon. Theo B. Werner, the Oglala Sioux Tribal Council adopted a resolution to prevent the use of the Peyote sacrament in the Native American Church. Blue Bird also asked his congressman to get next to John Collier so that something could be done about the South Dakota law passed in 1923 prohibiting the transportation of Peyote across state lines. BIA Superintendent James McGregor was very much opposed to the use of Peyote. W. O. Roberts, who was at least tolerant, contended that "if the organization has merit, it ought to grow; if it does not, it will be strangled out like all other useless growths" (U.S. Government 1936). Fr. J. B. Tennelly, Director of the Catholic Indian Missions Bureau in Washington, D.C., defended the principle of religious freedom for the Indian people. In a letter to Adelbert Thunder Hawk, who was an ex-member and now a vigorous opponent, Fr. Tennelly stated: "The United States Government is pledged to respect freedom of worship in this country. It may not lawfully hinder the spread of any form of religion. The Catholic Church also maintains that every person is responsible, not to the Government, but to God, for his religious beliefs, and has no desire that the Government should interfere with the exercise of religion" (Tennelly 1936).

Another development of great importance is the amount of Peyote available. Dr. George Morgan, who attended Peyote meetings for many years and did extensive field research in southern Texas, has gathered this information. Solomon Red Bear, Jr., told him that in the 1920s and 1930s it was normal for fifty buttons per person to be consumed at the beginning of the meeting. And more were available. Multiplying fifty by the twenty to thirty people attending a meeting, one can appreciate the quantities available. Morgan himself can verify that in the 1960s it was not uncommon for a thousand buttons to be used at a meeting. However, in the late 1960s, Morgan observed three factors in his field work in Southern Texas: ranchers were closing off Peyote fields because of excessive trespassing; an association of Peyote with drugs was made due to the hippies; and the Navaho purchased large quantities. From the examination of official records, Morgan noted that the Indians from New Mexico and Arizona were responsible for about 80 percent of the total regular sales in 1974. In addition, getting Peyote by mail became difficult for several reasons: first of all, there is a need to dry Peyote before mailing, and the dealers have all the sales they can handle in person and on the spot; secondly, interstate laws are doubtful on purchase through the mails. The Lakota are saying that Peyote is getting too expensive. The expense not only includes the cost of the Peyote (which in 1980 was about $70 per thousand dry), but also the cost of automobile travel of about 3,000 miles; the inability to go into the Peyote fields and pick one's own makes one dependent upon a few Peyote dealers.

Because of these factors, during 1970 to 1975, 500 Peyote buttons were the normal amount used for a meeting. Since 1975 it has been getting as low as 200. Formerly, in the Half Moon if all the Peyote was not finished, the officials would finish off what was left over. Morgan makes the observation that it is getting to the point that Peyote is becoming more symbolic than being a real medicine. Recently, Renee Mills, Emerson Spider's son-in-law, told me that if Peyote is not available for a particular meeting, they could conduct a service by tying the drum, singing, and reading from the Bible for several hours.

The relationship between the Half Moon and Cross Fire fireplaces has a history of its own. In the early days Half Moon and Cross Fire members did not attend each other's meetings. Jim Iron Bear went from Allen to Wounded Knee to attend Half Moon meetings. Today, although members attend each other's meetings, Half Moon and Cross Fire meetings are not normally conducted outside their respective areas. There has nonetheless been a mutual influence between the two fireplaces. In the early days William Black Bear introduced spiritual food into the Cross Fire over the objections of Jim Blue Bird. In more recent times Emerson Spider brought in sixteen sets of songs instead of the twelve which the Cross Fire members had been using up to that time. He also introduced the practice of bringing in water at midnight to be blessed and drunk ceremonially.

But the Cross Fire has also influenced the Half Moon. Tom Bullman, a Cross Fire member, claims that in the early days the Name of Jesus was not used in the Half Moon meetings and that the explicit Christian identification of the Half Moon today thus involved an historical development. At times, the influence involves tension. When Spider baptized two Red Cloud children in a Half Moon ceremony in Pine Ridge, he showed great concern that he might be offending some of the members of that fireplace. Bernard and Christine Red Cloud said that it is through their family that baptism was introduced into the Half Moon. Christine said that "the Half Moon members were all baptized in one of the traditional Christian Churches and buried in their cemeteries. It seems as though we are ashamed of being members of the Native American Church. I was baptized in the Native American Church because I wanted to be buried in their cemetery at Denby." Christine's reason is a typical traditional Lakota view of the Church as a burial society. Bernard Red Cloud, in contrast, said he got baptized as a sign of total commitment to Christ.

However, friction between the two fireplaces still exists. Bernard Red Cloud comments on the fact that members of each fireplace make jokes about each other. Half Moon members say that Cross Fire people go to meetings just to read the Bible, while Cross Fire members say that Half Moon ones go just because they are out of smokes. Emerson Spider made a very significant statement at the South Dakota State Convention of the Native American Church in June of 1977. He said that there had been a grudge between the two fireplaces for the last five or six years. But he insisted that the Native American Church is one church with two fireplaces. If one doesn't live a good life, neither fireplace will do a person any good. But if a person lives for Christ, both fireplaces are good. Yet, he expressed the feeling that the Bible should be in the Half Moon. But, as a sign of unity, he asked the ministers or roadmen there what their intentions were: "Do you want to conduct your meetings Cross Fire, Half Moon, or both? Declare yourself so that I know where you stand." Emerson himself is conducting both ways, and a few others indicated their desire to do the same.

There is some important history concerning the use of the Pipe in Peyote meetings. As we have seen, the old man Red Bear used the Pipe in his meetings from the very beginning. Bernard Ice recalls one of Red Bear's meetings before he was blind: he was a boy of about eight, and Red Bear was in his nineties; this would make the meeting in the early 1930s.

"My family went to Allen for a visit since we had a grandfather over there. They had this meeting down the creek. My parents went to the meeting. I was with a playmate, Aloysius High Hawk, and we decided we wanted to go inside, mainly because we wanted to smoke the Peace Pipe. They didn't use the cigarette. The Peace Pipe was taken care of by the old lady Red Bear. Before the meeting they carried her in on a blanket since she had difficulty walking. Aloysius and I had been ice skating along the creek. The meeting was inside a log cabin. The altar was made out of a white sheet about two feet square. A blue half-moon was drawn out of war paint. The chief Peyote was on the moon. A bucket with live coals for the cedar was in front of the cloth. The chief Peyote was cedared first. Then the old lady handed the Pipe to the fireman, who cedared it and handed it to the old man. He took it and filled it with tobacco mixed with red willow bark, and he prayed with it in the four directions and set it down on the sage in back of the chief Peyote. After this they passed the Peyote around and the singing began. There were a lot of people, and by the time the staff completed one round it was midnight. Red Bear got the staff back and sang the four songs and laid the instruments down. Then they had the morning water. They cedared the water.

"Then Red Bear picked up the Pipe and lit it. Then he passed it around and everybody took four puffs. I tried that, since that was the reason my playmate and I went in. Even the women smoked it. It went clear around and back to the old man again. Then he cleaned the Pipe and put the ashes in the bucket. Then he put the empty Pipe down and the fireman prayed with the water and they passed it around. Next they passed the Peyote around and started singing again. There was no smoking of cigarettes during the meeting, just one smoking of the Pipe. That is the way the old man Red Bear conducted it. When the old man died, the Pipe was buried with him. Red Bear passed his way of running meetings, but not the Pipe, to Abraham Running Bear, who passed it on to Levi Sitting Hawk."

Emerson Spider and his mother also saw the old man Red Bear pray with the Pipe. Eva Gap, widow of George Gap, said her father, James Hawkins, used the Pipe during meetings. Six people always smoked the Pipe: the roadman, chief drummer, cedar man, fireman, sponsor, and water woman.[3] In his final sickness her father passed his way, along with the Pipe, to her former husband, George Gap. George was a Cross Fire at the time. In 1948, Hawkins told George: "Son-in-law, you will take my ways." Because of this, George turned to the Half Moon ways and at times used the Pipe. With both men, if other people wanted to smoke the Pipe, they could. Eva said that during her father's meetings some people put cedar on the fire and offered up prayers through the cedar smoke instead of smoking the Pipe. The Pipe was smoked four times, just like the cigarette. In confirmation George told Omer Stewart that he attended his first Peyote meeting in 1922 with the Omaha Indians in Nebraska and was cured of tuberculosis at that time. He began conducting Cross Fire meetings in 1928. But he did change affiliations, since Bernard Red Cloud saw George conducting a Half Moon meeting around 1950.

Beatrice Weasel Bear told me that the Pipe was used once several years ago in one of their meetings. The roadman, chief drummer, cedar man, and fireman were the only ones that used it. The Pipe is not normally used in meetings because there are people present who are unable to handle it. If they are drinking or leading a bad life, they could take Peyote to reform their life but they should not handle the Pipe. The cigarette (rolled with paper derived from the corn husk) is smoked during the meeting instead of the Pipe but symbolically stands for it.

Emerson Spider made a Pipe for use in Peyote meetings around 1956 or 1957. But, when he presented this to the State Convention, the Cross fire members disapproved.

I prayed with the Pipe during two Peyote meetings. Both meetings were sponsored by John and Beatrice Weasel Bear, and the roadman was Phillip Eagle Bear. The first meeting was conducted on May 17, 1974, asking for a safe trip to and from Scotland, where I was to study for a year. Several roadmen from the Pine Ridge Reservation turned down the invitation to conduct the meeting when they found out that the Pipe would be used. So Beatrice turned to Phillip Eagle Bear from the Rosebud Reservation. It was decided that I would smoke the Pipe with three other men, none of them officials. This was done in the early morning and in addition to the four regular smokes with the corn husk cigarette. Each of us was sitting in one of the four directions in the tipi. On my return, a thanksgiving meeting was put up in a tipi on April 3, 1976, and the same procedures were used as in the first meeting. Thus the prayers started at the first meeting were completed. Beatrice felt very much relieved. (A transcript of the second meeting is given below.)

THE AUTHOR'S PRESENTATION
OF THE PAPAL BLESSING

My bringing back from Rome a Papal Blessing from Pope Paul VI for the Native American Church on the Pine Ridge Reservation, certified by a beautiful document, is also part of their history. I presented this Blessing to the members at a memorial meeting held in the fall of 1975 for one of Beatrice's sons, who had died a year before. During the midnight water call I made the following comments.

"I was in Rome as a pilgrim this summer during the Holy Year, and while there I thought of the Native American Church. And I asked the Holy Father to grant a special Papal Blessing to the Native American Church on the Pine Ridge Reservation. Pope Paul is the highest representative of Christ on earth. And he stands in a very special position between man and Almighty God. And his blessings are very powerful. They really bring down God's protection and peace and grace when he gives a blessing. So there is a picture of Pope Paul [on the document]. And there are pictures of four churches. There are four Basilicas in Rome. Basilicas are churches that have a special position. They are considered a little more sacred than the ordinary churches. This is why they are pointed out to be Basilicas. They are churches of special grace. We know very much of St. Peter's Basilica. We all heard of that. There is also St. Paul's Basilica, St. John Lateran's Basilica, and St. Mary Major's Basilica. I was able to make a pilgrimage to all four of these Basilicas and pray for the Native American Church in these special places. The thought struck me that even in Rome a person cannot get away from the four directions. One prays in the four directions even in the center of Christianity. And so the certificate says: 'Most Holy Father, Rev. Paul Steinmetz humbly begs for the Native American Church on the Pine Ridge Reservation a special Apostolic Blessing.' Then there is in Latin: 'In the year of Our Lord the Pope has granted this Apostolic Blessing in the City of Rome on June 16, 1975.' That was the day the Apostolic Blessing was given.

"So I think that it was a very important day for the Native American Church on Pine Ridge. So now you have Pope Paul's special blessing. And it has special meaning this year because it is a Holy Year. There won't be another Holy Year until another twenty-five years. We have to wait twenty-five years. The next one will be the year 2000. And so the Apostolic Blessing has an even greater meaning this year because it is the Holy Year. I suggest that a keeper of this document in some way be elected or be chosen, someone to take care of and guard this document of the Apostolic Blessing, because it is very sacred. I think that the keeper should be a man or woman who is living a good life, who is above reproach, who would guard it personally or be sure someone else is guarding it, who would perhaps bring it to meetings. And after all of us are gone, after everyone in this tipi is departed into the next world, we certainly hope that there still will be a keeper of this Papal Blessing, that it would be preserved in this Church even beyond our own time. And so I present, then, this great Blessing from Christ through His visible head, Paul VI, as my little gratitude for everything the Native American Church has done for me."

This blessing was also presented during my thanksgiving meeting, which will be treated below.

BELIEF IN GOD

The nature of the Peyote rite as it originally came into the United States from Mexico will be discussed below. However, there is no doubt that today the Oglala Lakota in the Native American Church have explicitly Christian beliefs. From my observations I have always heard the concept of God expressed in Christian terms with a clear monotheistic tendency, as was noted among the Navaho by David F. Aberle (1966:178). Yet, it should be noted that Half Moon members also address God by the traditional Lakota, *tunkasila*, "grandfather," indicating important psychological associations with their traditional Lakota understanding of God, associations which Cross Fire members do not make. The significance of this distinction was brought out by the fact that when I used the word *tunkasila* during a prayer in a Half Moon meeting in the Cross Fire Church at Potato Creek, a prominent Cross Fire member told me that the term was not used there. All the members believe in the Blessed Virgin Mary, the angels and saints. The Half Moon members respect the world of nature primarily because of their belief in the presence of spirits, while the Cross Fire members have the same respect primarily because of their belief in the immanent presence of God. So there are differences.

BELIEF IN PEYOTE

There is no Lakota word for Peyote. When speaking in their own language, the Lakota use *pejuta* or "medicine"; the word *Peyote* is employed only when they are speaking English. According to Buechel, the literal meaning of *pejuta* is "grass roots." The word for pills, or white man's medicine, is *pejuta gmigmela* or "round medicine" (1970:440). As *pejuta* refers to natural plants that can be used for medicinal purposes, it is an appropriate word for Peyote.

Peyote as a constant source of visions can easily be exaggerated. At least today, most members consume rather small amounts, as was noted before. In the meetings I have attended, I have been unable to observe any significant change in outward behavior other than an added fervor in praying and singing. James Howard states: "likewise my own experiences in eating peyote have tended to confirm my belief that the auditory and visual hallucinations supposedly so important in the diffusion and perpetuation of the religion (cf. LaBarre 1906:45) are actually rare phenomena. In fact, I suspect that many of the 'visions' attributed to the consumption of peyote by American Indian peyotists are as much a result of a lack of sleep, the hypnotic eighth-note drumbeat, and the habit of staring into the sacred fire, as to the hallucinogenic properties of the plant" (1967:2). This is not to say that Peyote does not facilitate visions but rather that it is only one influence in a total religious setting. We will see the importance of visions below, noting that most visions seem to have taken place in the past.

According to some members of the Native American Church, Peyote does help them arrive at an understanding of things. Bernard Red Cloud has this to say about understanding the sudden death of his teenage daughter. "We were living a good life and we had a bad experience in Deloris' death. And I almost got away that time. Different people talked to us. 'You have the instruments and you belong to the Native American Church. Now the Almighty wants to know if you mean business. So he took one of your children to see how you are. Are you going to believe Him or not? It's up to you. The Almighty took one of yours and put a seed in heaven, one of your own blood. Are you going there to see her, or are you going to lead a bad life. The Almighty will touch your heart; you will get blessings. He took that nice-looking girl and put her up there so that your whole family could think about that and get up there. That girl made a road for you. It's all made for you. She prepared the way.'

"I was tempted to think that I always lived a good life. Maybe there is no God, or maybe He doesn't listen to me. I'm just wasting my time. I could go out and have a good time where the bright lights are. Just before that happened there was music and joy in the Native American Church. But, when Deloris died, I didn't enjoy the music at the funeral meeting; there was nothing there. It was there, but it was my mind saying that. It took a year for it to come back. I couldn't get away from the Native American Church because I didn't know how to go into other churches. They have different rules. And I can't read the Bible very well. This is the only place I can go. But it took a year. [Do you feel the Almighty has blessed you through Deloris' death?] I think so. Now it is up to me and my family. If we want to see her, we have to take the right path. That's what the Peyote done to me. It showed me that and got me this far."

Bernard Ice states that Peyote is not like a narcotic: "when you eat it, your mind turns to the Great Spirit and to Jesus Christ. In one song I can learn what it might take twenty or twenty-five years in school." Francis Mesteth remarks that the purpose of Peyote is to clear the mind: "The mind is functioning in all kinds of manners, thinking of many things. When you take the medicine, God's spirit power is in the medicine. It clears the mind. Everything you hear is clear. You can see good and you can talk to God. We don't have an education and we don't understand big words, so we use the medicine. If you take Peyote in a meeting and think about things, it will come to you. If you eat a lot of Peyote, it will show you a lot of things." Joe American Horse states that "when you take Peyote, you have an inner eye that clears up, that tells you what is right and wrong. My father, Charles, told me that if you take a lot of Peyote, your eye is cleared up and you can see." Beatrice Weasel Bear says that she is glad that she turned to the Native American Church and used the medicine, since it really made her think about the Almighty and how far away she had gotten from Him. Peyote can serve as the Last Sacraments, Eva Gap relates: "My grandmother wanted her Last Sacraments. They were going to call a minister, but she said she wanted them in the Peyote way. William Black Bear gave her four Peyote balls, and my father sang four songs. They said the Lord's Prayer, and she said Amen and breathed her last breath."

BELIEF IN CEREMONIAL OBJECTS

The ceremonial objects considered here are the altar, drum, staff, cedar and gourd rattle.

The altar is a rich source of symbolism in the religious imagination of Native American Church members. Hunter had these comments. "The various tribes of Oklahoma formed the Half Moon fireplace as the symbol of the Native American Church. Many people have gone on the path of this life and beyond. The mound is Mother Earth, where you come from and you are going to go back in there. It is the same as the Bible passage, 'from dust to dust.' As you eat Peyote, the altar becomes a grave into which many a man has gone. The Half Moon altar is an open fireplace. In the Cross Fire they say you have to be perfect. The Half Moon way welcomes all, no matter who they are. In the Half Moon you can go in even if you are a drunk; you can go in and redeem yourself. The Half Moon is like a regular horse; the Cross Fire like a thoroughbred horse. People use different symbols in the ashes—like the eagle, which is the symbol of courage and good health. Because the water bird is timid, innocent and pure, they use it as a symbol to cure a person who is really sick. They use sand instead of earth because the sand is not a symbol of the grave like the earth is. They use the sand because they want the person to get well and not die. I saw the sand altar place used only once up here by Philip Broken Leg."

Bernard Ice gives us an example of how many different symbols can cluster around the symbol of the altar. "I often wondered why the moon was there. It could be something else. In the beginning, Adam and Eve were in the garden of paradise. They disobeyed God's commandment and hid themselves. They thought that the sun was light so that they could hide themselves in the night. But the moon is there also. They can't hide from God, since night or day He has His light. [The Lakota word for "moon" is *hanhepi wi*, or "the night sun."] Then God said that the woman would have to go by the moon to count her periods. The Indians could also tell the weather by the moon. There is a wet and dry moon. Because it sets like the dipper, it is either wet or dry. If it sets up it holds water; if it tilts, it spills the water. The Indians used the moon in many ways as a calendar to count the year, the season, the weather. So they kept track of the moon. So they use the moon right on the altar.

"The moon shining even when Adam and Eve sinned is one of the reasons why the Half Moon is open to everybody, even sinners. The moon is just like life; new moon, quarter moon, and then full just as we grow up. Then as we grow old, the moon also diminishes. Then they put a mark on the moon altar which is the road of life. Sometimes the roadman makes four marks across the road of life. These stand for the four directions and the four corners of the world. The white man spent a lot of money going to the moon. Here we have it right here on our altar. There is no life in the moon but it controls life here on earth. Earth, moon, and sun keep perfect time; God controls that. We use the fire in the altar because we can't get along without it. It keeps us warm and cooks our food. They put cedar on the charcoal in the fireplace and then they make the offering to the Almighty in prayer through that fire. But you have to handle that fire just right so that you don't get burnt. If a person becomes careless and forgets God, he can hurt himself.

"There are all kinds of colors in the fire: blue, yellow, orange, red. That is where they get the designs and colors for their beadwork. In the Half Moon the main design in the ashes is the bird—either an eagle, dove, or water bird. The eagle is king of all birds. He flies higher than any other bird. The eagle represents the Great Spirit, since he is the highest, king of kings. When you see a marshal or FBI person, he is wearing a badge with the eagle. The person with the eagle on him is someone that you have to show respect towards. The American flag in the White House is hanging from a pole. On top of the pole is an eagle. The eagle is also on top of the dome of state capitols. It is the national bird. Somebody shot an eagle and it cost him $5,000. When Congress passes a law, they put the seal of an eagle on it. So in a meeting when all the prayers and singing have been completed, they put the eagle in the fireplace. God approves of the prayers since the seal is right there on the altar.

"Again the symbol is a dove. John baptized in the River Jordan, and a dove descended on Him. Through that, Jesus contacted the Spirit. The water bird is from the east—from Minnesota, the land of ten thousand lakes. That also represents the Holy Spirit. The water bird flies above the lakes, and when he sees something to eat, he can dive into the water. If he sees a sinner, that could be represented by a fish. Or it might be a human that is suffering and needs help. He can get him even out of the water. Or he could get the sickness out of the person and he could get well. When they have a doctoring meeting, they use the water bird in the fireplace.

"In the Cross Fire they use the star. Jesus Christ, the offspring of David, is the Morning Star. When Jesus was born, the three Magi followed the star. Maybe someone wants to be reborn again. There are also individual variations in the fireplace. Francis Mesteth uses a triangle. This stands for the three Persons in one God. If you look at a dollar bill, it has a triangle on it and an eye in the middle. That's the all-seeing eye of God. If you use different designs, then you should explain them by the Bible."

It should be noted that these remarks are coming from a Half Moon member. And the richness of his imagination should be admired. Beatrice Weasel Bear, another Half Moon member, has this to say: "Joe Sierra introduced new designs into the Half Moon fireplace, all connected with the servicemen. He knew this by eating the medicine and praying. He put the triangle there, which stands for the three Persons in the one God but also when a serviceman returns home dead, the flag is folded into a triangle and given to the relatives. At midnight he put the heart there, representing the Sacred Heart of Jesus as well as the purple heart given to servicemen for brave deeds. At the main smoke he put the star for Jesus, the Morning Star, and for the gold star that is given to Gold Star Mothers who lose a son in war. Finally, the eagle, which is the king of all the birds and closest to the Almighty and also the emblem that servicemen wear. The year that the submarine *Thresher* went down, Joe Sierra poked fire for George Gap, who was a Navy man. That year they had a memorial service at Denby over at Sitting Hawk's place. In the morning he prayed for those people who went down in the *Thresher*. That morning instead of the eagle he laid down an anchor. And that was real good, I thought. He was really wise, I think."

The drum also has many symbolic meanings. Hunter comments. "The drum has water in it like Mother Earth. The star on the bottom of the drum is the morning star. 'One day He will come from the east and He wants me to prepare to meet Him'—that's a morning star song. Jesus says, 'I am the bright Morning Star.' And so as we behold Him, we ask Jesus that we have life everlasting and peace. As you beat the drum, the sound goes south to the land of spirits and to those who are there. Some are drummers, some roadmen, firemen, cedar men, people who were in meetings, singers. The echo of this drum brings the spirits back so that from the outside they can partake of the meeting and listen because they will be remembered in the prayers. Through the spirits we can get a blessing."

Bernard Ice, who is blind, has this to say. (His remarks are so beautiful and rich that they require hours of meditation to appreciate.) "Sometimes I am sitting here at home all alone. But I am not alone. I have a drum, water, gourd. I sing the songs, and my worries are all gone. I feel good again and refreshed. The drum has seven stones, which stand for the seven Indian sacraments of life, the seven sacraments of the Catholic Church, and the seven nations of the Sioux. The seven Indian sacraments are the holy Peyote, the dirt Half Moon, the fire, water, corn, meat, and fruit. The thong on the top represents the crown of thorns that Jesus wore. On the bottom the rope forms a star. There is the speaking in tongues when the drum is used. The skin on the drum is the animal hide used for clothing. Jesus wore a robe in the Passion. The soldiers took it away and gambled for it. This is a sign of the evil forces which are about. Jesus' hands were tied with a rope when He was in custody. Everything is in the Bible. The drumsticks represent the rod of Moses in the desert.

"When the whistle blows at the morning star time, all the creatures on the earth wake up right away and they start for an area. The first animal that gets there shall live. One animal got there first, and then he drank the water and lived, and that was the deer. This deer is still here, and all the other animals are gone. The hide of that deer they put on the drum. There are a thousand tunes in the drum when you move your hand around and wet the hide. Having a thousand tunes is like having a thousand prayers and different voices in the drum where they are made one. There are different voices, singing, prayers, people—all praying to the same Man. Water in the drum is the water of life. You cannot be born without this water. After you come to this earth, you have to live by water—cooking and drinking it, everything. Charcoal is in the water. This represents the fire, the hereafter. After you die, you are going back into charcoal, back to ashes. Charcoal is in the water of life so that there is life after death."

The drum is tied right before a meeting and must not be untied until the meeting is completed. Emerson Spider has these remarks on a certain memorial meeting in which the drum was untied, a meeting at which I was present. "The drummer for this meeting was late and was unable to tie his own drum. He didn't like the way the drum was tied so he took it apart during the meeting to retie it, which is against the regulations. One person defended him when objections were raised. But just like the drum, both families were torn apart. The drummer began living with a woman married to his own brother and the one who defended him was separated from his wife for a while. I don't believe in superstitions, but that happened."

What Emerson failed to mention is that the drummer was in tears as he confessed his guilt in the morning.

Bernard Red Cloud states that "when you beat the drum, it brings out the sounds that represents the Thunders. It will go a long ways through the valleys and canyons. So, by using it, the sound goes up to the Almighty. Since it goes along the horizon, it must go up, too. Because the thunders are the source of rain, they put water in the drum. For the first man who tied the drum, there must have been a blessing on him because it has the crown on the top and the star on the bottom. The thunder beings bring the water and it brings the Son [Jesus]."

Hunter relates a vision he had of the drum. "I had a vision of being inside the drum that I was beating. Every time I beat it, it looked like the water was coming up. I wanted to get out but I couldn't. As I beat it slow, the water kept going down, but I couldn't get away from it. The last song I remembered was a chief song. As I sang it, God knew I was in this state. I kept muttering to myself: "Great Spirit, have pity of me." As I was drumming, I kept saying that all the time. As I looked at the chief Peyote, he was just a little old man—wrinkled up, stringy grey hair, barefooted. He was sitiing on the mound. I couldn't get past him. I couldn't get around him. He just sat there and looked at me. He was sitting there just like Father Time, sitting there watching me. And I couldn't hide anything that came to my mind because he knew it all. And I got singing and I came out of it. The only thing he told me: 'Try and do it right.' He said that if I didn't, I was going to hurt myself and somebody else, too."

The roadman's staff which is passed around to everyone and held by those who sing also has meaning. Hunter explains that "it is the staff of life, the cane. It is a prayer that the younger generation will grow to be old men and be wise with the staff of life as a cane and to teach it to their children and grandchildren. It is the support without which we can't go in." For Bernard Ice, "the staff is Jesus' staff." Francis Mesteth recalls that "Moses used a staff to part the waters of the Red Sea in leading the Israelites to the Promised Land." For Bernard Red Cloud, all the instruments—including the staff—represent the traditional history of the Indian people. Moses could do anything with his staff. He passed it on to somebody. Who has the staff now? Mr. Indian has it at a meeting. During a meeting the staff goes to each and everyone there. Each time a man gets hold of the staff, he puts his prayers on there and gives it to the next one. So the staff goes around and collects good thoughts and prayers and lays all of them at the altar. You don't go between the staff and the altar because the prayers are going up through the staff. I have the feeling that there are little strings attached to the staff. If you go between, you break that string for the man singing. That's how I feel. We use sage in there. Nowadays you can wash your hands. In the old days we used the sage. When you take the staff and the Peace Pipe, you hold them in sage. You purify your hands so that they are worthy to grasp the staff and the Peace Pipe."

Francis Richards also compares the staff to the one that Moses had. "His was a staff with power, the power to bring water out of rock and to turn into a serpent and cure people of their bites." Beatrice Weasel Bear shares her feelings: "When you are peyoted up and you hold the staff, it feels real powerful. During meetings it felt like it went way up, and when I was singing, I had the feeling that the songs were going way up." John Weasel Bear adds: "When I hold the staff, I feel nearer to God. The staff with the other instruments are cedared off with prayers, and they have God's blessings on them."

The fact that the staff did not remind anyone of the coup stick which the chief had signifies the non-militant and peaceful nature of the Native American Church.

Cedar is a means of offering prayer to God. It is part of the Peyote ceremony which can be taken out of the meeting and into the home. Hunter said that he had a chief Peyote and cedar at home. When he wanted to pray, he cedared the chief Peyote and thanked God. Red Cloud states that "at a meeting when you sing and pray and praise God, you have cedar in there all the time. I used cedar at home because it makes me feel that I am in the church, that I am pure, that I have some spirit with me. I feel the Almighty is close by. It's the smell that makes me feel that way. There is no fireplace in my home now. The quickest way to get to the praying is to burn cedar without putting up the tipi and making an altar. We have it all the time. My children saw the blizzard in Rapid City, South Dakota, over television, so they burned cedar and prayed that they wouldn't have it down here." Joe American Horse recalls that his father would put some cedar on a fire on Sunday and read the Bible. He had been a lay reader in the Episcopal Church, but they called him a cactus eater and excommunicated him.

The symbolism of the gourd rattle is illustrated by a vision Bernard Ice had: "One time I had a gourd, but I didn't have any rocks in it. I was sitting at a meeting and thinking about it. Then in a vision I saw a gourd laying on its side with little rocks coming out of it, just the size I wanted. When I looked up, there was a road going up. As I walked, the rocks were getting better—like agates, then like marble, pearls, and finally silver and gold. They turned out to be diamonds way up in the sky. The instruments can help you have a vision of the good road to heaven. Even these little rocks can do this. A vision like that helps because it gets your mind on heaven, or on the road of life. It always leads to prayer. It made me feel real happy. I didn't think that those little rocks would make me see a vision like that. I was thankful that I needed some rocks for my gourd and it made me see that good road. Maybe someday I will have diamonds in my gourd when I get up to heaven."

BELIEF IN THE MORNING WATER WOMAN

The prayer of the Morning Water Woman, usually the wife of the roadman, is an emotional climax to the Peyote meeting. Hunter gives us a beautiful understanding. "The Morning Water Woman is like Mother Earth. She is mother of all. From her bosom came the water. She gave to all her children, the plants, the various species of animals, from the tiniest ant to the biggest elephant, the eagle. The woman that nurses a baby is just like Mother Earth, giving to it that it will go out into the world strong and sturdy. When the woman brings in the morning water, she asks God's blessing on all, that everyone drinks it, the good and the bad, that they drink it because they are her children. She prays for everyone who is going to drink the water, first in the meeting and then in the whole world. God gave her the privilege to pray for everyone, no matter where they are at, in conflict or in peace. Anyone who drinks the water will remember where it comes from. The woman is a symbol of Mother Earth. They call her the Morning Water Woman, and she is mother of all. If your mother is gone, she is just like your mother. Or if your mother is living, you have a second mother. You came from a mother and to a mother you shall return."

Here is an example of moving back and forth between cosmic and individual symbolism. The shifting associations give us a poetic insight into this beautiful woman. Bernard Ice also shares a poetic vision. "I had a vision of the morning water. I saw the big dipper. When the handle is up and the dipper part down, it is the morning water time when the woman brings in the water. At that time the dipper is tilted over and the water drips out and hits the clouds. It lightnings, and the water comes through in a shower and hits the mountains and the hills. Streams start flowing down to the creek. The water woman comes up to the creek and gets the water in a bucket. She was facing east in my vision, with her hands up in prayer. She got the water that came from the dipper and took it into the tipi and blessed it. I saw it come from the big dipper."

BELIEF IN THE LAST DAYS

Some of the religious symbols of the Oglala Lakota are apocalyptic. Hunter claims that "both the Pipe and Peyote meeting has to go on and on until you find the perfect meeting. And that will be the second coming of Christ. So a meeting is never complete until you have a perfect meeting, and that is the end. That is the reason why one should not be artistic in building the fire in a Peyote meeting. A fire should build itself until that day when it becomes perfect by itself. When that day comes, the Blessed Savior will say 'thank you' and call us."

Bernard Ice compares the roadman blowing the whistle in the four directions when he goes outside to pray to the angels blowing the trumpets at the end of the world. "There is a Peyote tone which comes from the drum, gourd, whistle, and voice all coming together in the right way. This Peyote tone can heal a person. The trumpets blown by the angels in the four directions at the end of the world will sound like this Peyote tone." John Weasel Bear had a vision of a hole in the Peyote fireplace containing fire. "The four angels in the four directions are waiting. They are going to blow their whistles, the ones that are used in the meetings. When they do, they will drop that one bomb and it is going down into the hole and the fire that is down there will ignite and crack open the earth." Beatrice has another apocalyptic image: "Just like the Peace Pipe brought Indian people together to pray, so does the Peyote. The Sioux used to have many enemies. But now they use Peyote to make friends and relations. When all the tribes use the Peyote, it will be the end of the world. Even the Mohawks in New York use the medicine. They want Johnny to conduct a meeting over there."

PEYOTE VISIONS

Peyote visions do not necessarily occur at every meeting, but they play an important part in the life of the members because they lead to deep psychological transformations. First five visions from Half Moon members will be given and then five from Cross Fire ones.

Hunter states that "Jim Kills First was conducting a tipi meeting. He cedared the whistle and as he blew it, the sound went up and never came back. The same thing happened the second and third time. The fourth time it kept on going, but as he trailed it down, it started to come back and something heavy set on top of the tipi and we heard the whistle again, although it wasn't blown. He raised his arms and said: 'ha ho, thank you, Grandfather, thank you.' The presence of the spirits is a sign that your prayers have been answered." An interesting observation is that this was a vision apparently shared by the group.[4]

Hunter relates a healing vision. "We had a tipi meeting in Scottsbluff, Nebraska, at Joe Sierra's place. A Navaho couple came with a sick girl who got so sick with double pneumonia that they put her in the hospital. It was a large tipi, capable of holding 96 people in double rows. The Pine Ridge group got in late, and we sat at the end of the Half Moon altar. The sick girl's father had asked for prayers. Towards the main smoke in the morning, the staff came to us. I said that we are going to sing some songs and try to help out in every way we can. I got children of my own. I told my father-in-law to follow me one skip behind with the drum.

"I started singing, but somehow the song was different. It made me wander around in some hills as I closed my eyes. I was up in those hills walking around. I was trying to find something. I had this long stick, and I was poking around for something I was trying to find but could not. So I cut the song off and started the second one. I kept going like that, and I couldn't find what I was looking for. I opened my eyes, and I saw that I was making the people restless the way I was singing the song. I knew the songs, but they seemed different to me now. I started the last song. That song came to me. It was high. I found the thing I was looking for. It was a root. I picked it up, and I put a piece in my mouth and started chewing it, and I stuck a piece in my pocket. About that time the drumbeat came out right and the roadman started blowing his whistle and started yelling 'heya, heya.' Everybody started flapping their feather fans, and I kept singing that song and I got through.

The girl's mother came over and grasped me and said, "Thank you. As you sang the last song, my little girl came to the door [in a vision] and she was well." After the meeting they went to the hospital to see their girl, and when they came back they had the little girl with them and she was well. Finding the root in the vision had the power to make her well."

Beatrice Weasel Bear tells a healing vision which Joe Sierra had. "Joe Sierra had tuberculosis real bad. The hospital said he was going to die. He went to Oklahoma, and they doctored and gave him a lot of medicine. Pretty soon he had a vision. He was wandering off in some desert. Somebody told him to pray to his grandfather. At first he thought of his natural grandfather. But the voice kept on repeating 'remember your grandfather.' Then he thought of his great-grandfathers and other grandfathers in an Indian way. But he kept on hearing the voice. Then all of a sudden it dawned on him what the voice was saying, and he prayed to Grandfather, the Great Spirit, and he came out of it and got well."

A middle-aged Lakota woman relates a typical Peyote vision containing images of good and evil which had a profound effect on her life. "The very first meeting I had for myself I saw a vision in the fireplace, a vision I will never forget. There was the Half Moon, then a space, the fire, the water bird ashes, and the tail further on down. When I looked at that, I saw the Half Moon and the Peyote sitting on top, way up there. It looked real smooth and nice up there. The Peyote was way on top like a crown. In between I saw dark abyss. The body of the water bird was shining and sparkling. That was a real shiny city sitting there. When I looked at the city, I saw a lot of evil things going on there. Further on down, where the tail part was, I saw human skulls and bones covered with snakes. I thought that if a person stays on top, he will be all right. But if he falls down into the abyss and the city, he will end up with the bones and the snakes. If a person doesn't follow the Peyote road and goes down into the wicked city, he will end up with the skeletons. That's real death, real death. That's where all the snakes were going in between the skeletons, crawling all over them."

Bernard Ice shared with me a healing vision, involving a Lakota woman. "She became sick during a meeting, and they gave her Peyote. She was unconscious. During the meeting she didn't even move but just lay there. The next morning she didn't change. After dinner, Emerson Spider's mother made a suggestion. A long time ago if a person didn't move like that, they put the altar back and started a meeting again. We had to help her like that. So Emerson put the altar back with the fire and instruments. The staff made one complete round, and then her brother came in and sang. She moved when he was singing. Emerson put cedar on the fire and fanned her with an eagle feather. Her hand went up over her head. She got up and tried to grab something like she was asleep and just got up.

"Later she told me her vision. She saw an eagle. She wanted help, but the eagle didn't look at her. He looked the other way. When her brother was singing, a boy about ten to twelve years old, the eagle looked at him and then at her, and she started moving at that time. When Emerson fanned her with the eagle feather, the eagle started flying towards her, and she tried to grab the eagle's legs. That is what she was grabbing for. If she could grab the eagle's legs, she could get up. The reason she got that way was that she was trying to pray for everybody at the beginning of the meeting, for everybody in the meeting. They were all sinful. She prayed that she would take all the sins on her even if she would have to die. When she prayed like that, it did happen. It was like a big sack, real heavy. So that weight was on her and she couldn't move. She tried to find a way out. She was in darkness too. She saw a small hole that she could go through, but she could not find her way towards it. When her brother was singing, there was a little feather floating for that little hole and showed her the way. Her brother was singing, and he was a little boy, and he was sinless. His voice represented that little feather that showed her the way out. So she was able to grab the eagle's legs, and he took her out through the hole. When Emerson put cedar on the fire, the big sack of sins was thrown into the fire and burned up. She took the sins of other people on her and got into that position where she could not move for twenty-two hours. She walked into the meeting and took Peyote, and that is what happened."

In all these visions the images are drawn from the traditional Lakota religion to a much greater extent than in the Cross Fire ones, showing that deep in the Half Moon psyche there is a blending of the two religious traditions. But, let us now look at the Cross Fire visions.

Emerson Spider relates the first one. "There was a vision seen by White Bull of Martin, South Dakota. He was in a meeting with his father, one of the old-timers. The father didn't believe in the holy baptism. The son wanted to be baptized, but his father didn't want him to, so he wasn't baptized. The son went into a meeting and took a lot of medicine. He was a very young man, and he didn't care about anything.

"All of a sudden he looked at the people hard and enjoyed himself just by looking at them. All of a sudden his vision was going blurry. Then the people disappeared and he could not see anybody at the meeting. So he thought to himself: 'That's all right. Even though I can't see those people, I can hear them. I don't care. I will just sit here and listen to them singing. I really like their singing.' He just listened to them. He took a lot of medicine, so the medicine was working through him to show him the vision of being baptized.

"All at once he could not hear. The medicine stopped his hearing.

He could not hear a thing. So he thought about himself. He said to himself: 'Since I can't see anybody or hear anything, I don't care. I am just going to sit here and think about what I am going to do tomorrow. I want to go see my girlfriend. I want to go powwow. I want to think about the things I will do in the future.' So he did this. But finally, that went away. He could think about nothing or nobody. The only thinking he could do was think about himself. 'Why is it that I am this way?'

"'So even though I can't see anybody or hear anything or think about anything but myself, I am just going to sit here on the floor. I know I am sitting on the floor and I am leaning against the wall. So I am just going to take it easy and go to sleep.' So he was trying to touch the back of the wall he was leaning on, but he could not do it. So finally, he almost fell backwards. He tried to feel it with his hands but he could not do so. So he had nothing to lean back on to sleep or take it easy. So again he thought to himself: 'So I don't have to be sleeping or taking it easy. Just so I am sitting on the floor and taking it easy on the floor.'

"He did this, and all of a sudden the floor was moving. So he looked down and he saw that the floor was just a layer of bricks, no cement in between. As he was sitting on top of that, there was just enough to sit on. He could see nothing since it was dark. And the bricks were moving just as though it was going to fall over. So he thought to himself: 'I am just going to fall from here. If I die, that's good.' Then again he thought to himself: 'Maybe this is not high enough to get killed, so I might just have broken bones, and if I live, I will have a hard life and I may not be able to enjoy my life. So I might as well not do that. I am just going to sit here, sit real still. I am going to die here so I am going to take a deep breath. After I die, I don't care how I fall. I am going to be dead anyway, so I won't know anything. So I am going to do that.'

"So he took a deep breath and sat there for a long time, for what seemed like two hours without breathing. All at once he heard voices back of him. So he listened to the voices. There was shouting and crying and hollering. Some were laughing and some were saying that we are going here and there. He looked back, and all of a sudden he found himself sitting on the prairie, on level ground. In back of the people there was a big fire coming. It caught up to several people who were crying and hollering for help. Some of them were running with these people, and they came to a town, a big town with a lot of buildings. When he got close, he noticed that the buildings were all churches, so he didn't know where to go. He wanted to go with some people, but he didn't belong there. So he went to a church in which all the people were, and he went to the door and knocked on it, but the minister looked at him, and when he saw him, he closed the door on him because he didn't belong to that church. So right away he thought to himself: 'As soon as I can, I am going to get baptized and belong to a church so that I won't get caught by this fire.' So that morning that man got baptized."

The next two visions are similar. Emerson Spider tells the first one. "Tom Bullman got seriously sick one time. He was in bed for many days, and finally they took him into a meeting, and he took medicine. They were singing and praying, and towards morning all at once he saw a vision. He saw a house, a log house, just about to fall over. So they braced it with other logs so that it wouldn't go over. So he went into this house, and it was all messed up inside. All kinds of trash was laying all over. So he started to clean up, and he noticed that there was someone there helping him clean it up. Pretty soon they pushed all the trash out of there. And here he came to, and the house he saw was himself. The sickness was about ready to get him down and make him fall over. The logs bracing the house were prayers that were said for him. The man that helped him sweep it out was the Peyote. It cleaned him out, and that morning he was well."

Joe American Horse tells the next one. "This is a vision my father, Charles American Horse, had. My mother was my father's third wife. Before, when his children grew up, his wife and children died. He married one woman, and she died. So he married her sister, and she also died. They all died from a sickness they called 'quick consumption.' So my father took sick. There was no cure either by an Indian doctor or a medical doctor. When the doctor told him he had only six months to live, Black Bear in Allen told him that Peyote could cure any kind of sickness. At that time Peyote was outlawed on the reservation. Anyone caught with one button could be thrown in jail. So they said that they do it among the Winnebago. So he went with Little Stallion from Rosebud. They took a train in Nebraska. They stayed down there two weeks. They had meetings. The whole idea is to take as much medicine as you can. My father saw a vision. There was a river that he wanted to get across, and he was looking for a place to cross it. Then he saw a man coming towards him wearing what looked like a dark suit. But as he came close he saw that it was his skin which was all black and shriveled up. He thought the man had been smiling. But close up his mouth was all peeled. He looked at himself and saw that he had good clothes and a home but it was his soul. His soul was going to determine whether he was going to live or die. His sickness was from his soul. He found out that evil works in many ways."

In these visions we see that sickness is attributed to a spiritual cause. Peyote, by leading a person to identify himself with the source of the sickness and recognize it, becomes a source of healing power.

The next vision is the conversion experience of a young Lakota man. "I was a young man and I was no good. At a meeting all at once I heard a noise I thought was a car. It was in winter, so I thought that someone had started his car and left it on. But it lasted a long time, so I asked the fireman, who told me there was no car outside. So I thought that in the early days I was told by the old-timers that sounds like that come out of the drum. So I thought that the man was making the sound come out of the drum. So I sat listening to it. When a man had finished singing, the next man wasn't quite ready. So the drum stopped, but I noticed the sound was still with me. So the sound wasn't from the drum. So right away I looked for the sound all over the place where they were having the meeting. It was getting closer as I looked towards the altar.

"All of a sudden I saw the chief Peyote that was sitting in the midst of the people and that is where the sound was coming from. When I saw it, the Peyote was spinning real fast, and it was making that sound. And it came out towards me and I saw it. It was a sort of plate that was spinning fast. And in there were classes of people sitting on the plate. The ones that were trying to live according to God's Word were sitting towards the middle. And all those who were not obeying the laws of God were sitting way on the edge of that plate. And I heard people hollering and crying, and I saw jails and all other places that did not belong to Christ on the outside of the plate. And I was on the rim of it, and I was hanging on and praying that I would live a Christian life. And I was praying real hard and hanging on. And all of a sudden I woke up like, and I was sitting on the floor and hanging onto my cushion. This is a vision given to me by Christ through the holy herb [Peyote]."

The last vision is told by a Lakota whose name I have omitted. "I was a young man with rheumatism and in pain and getting worse every day. Finally, I could not sleep at nights, and I stayed awake crying. There was no medicine to ease the pain. I used all kinds of medicine, including Indian roots. One day my father had eighty-two Peyote buttons. He said: 'My son, I am going to get some boys to pray and sing for you. So you start taking this medicine when I am away.' So he got on his horse and left. So I started eating the medicine, and it didn't take long to eat it, since I was in so much pain that I wanted something to ease the pain. That is what made me eat the medicine so quick like. I ate the eighty-two buttons.

"All at once a vision came to me. It was far beyond words. It was a mystery of God that came to me, that I never did experience before. All at once I was laying there crying. I had a sister who was just a little girl. She came into my room and started to feel my leg where I had that pain, and she started crying. In my mind this sister of mine didn't have any sin of any kind. She should not be crying like she was, it seemed to me. I was a big sinner. I don't cry for my sins. I was crying for my health. I was crying because my body was aching. I didn't care much about my sins until that time when my sister cried. So I started crying, and I cried and cried. I was sorrowful for the sins that I had committed in my life. While I was crying I could hear myself as a young child crying, just the way my sister was crying. My voice was changed, and I cried just like a little baby. I didn't recognize my voice. I thought that someone else was crying. Here it was me. So I stopped and thought about it, and that's where I saw the vision, the miracle of the movement of the devil.

"The devil came into the room where I was laying. He was saying that I needed to wake up. There were good times going on outside. He said that you will be healed and get well real quick. We are going to have a good time. He showed me a lot of things, good times, drinking, women, and all kinds of things that go about in the world that would wake me up and make me do it again, the same things I have been through. So the devil was trying to do this. 'No,' I said, 'I don't want to be that way because sins got me into this situation, so I don't

feel like doing that anymore.' Here he grabbed hold of my toe and the
feeling I had was that he put his knees on the knee where I had this
rheumatism. He was trying to get me so I would wake up, but I just
lay there. There was a Spirit above me that was helping me. It was
going around. And I know that was the Spirit of the Lord that was
helping me to fight this evil. So they were fighting over my body,
which the devil wanted me to get up. But I just lay there and hung
on.

"So all at once I could hear a clicking sound, which was coming
from inside there. So I was looking around, and I saw a clock that
was on the bureau. So I thought that was the one making the noise.
So I looked, and I noticed that the clicking was getting louder and
louder until it seemed that it filled the entire house. It was so loud
that I got up and looked underneath the bed, but there was nothing
there. And here it showed me that there is a time for every man and
his time will come in his daily life. The clicking showed that there
will be a time for me to go and I will not be able to stop myself. No
one will stop a man from going at that time. So it wasn't my time
to go. So it showed me again the way to live for Christ in which it
is far beyond words to explain what I had seen there. Then I became
aware of what was happening around me. A man brought me an orange,
a sack of Bull Durham, and fifteen cents and placed them on the table.
I could hear my mother and relatives trying to cheer me up.

"Then all at once I saw another vision from above. I saw a man,
a figure of a man that was shining. That man stood right close to me.
He said that you are man enough to what you have seen and gone
through. 'I will come after you and take you in disguise up there. I
am going to teach you the things you don't know. I am going to teach
you all that.' So I wanted to be with him, so I said, all right, 'I will
do my best.' Even though I was in pain. Then all at once, this is where
it is a miracle and it is hard to believe. It threw me back to the days
when I got sick. I reviewed that, what I had seen, what I had been
through. I had to go over that again. I never experienced anything like
it before. The things I had seen, it showed like a telecast. If you re-
wind that and play it over, it is going to show the way it was exactly,
not any differences, over and over, no matter how many times. That's
the way it happened to me there. I don't think it can be done to a human; you can't review your life exactly as it happened. There are

things you are bound to miss and leave out. But not this one. It surprised me that God should do things like that. While I was laying there, I saw all the things I had seen: the people that came to see me, the pain, my father telling me to take the medicine, all the things happened again. I had to review all that.

"So it came time for the man to come after me. 'Have this place cleaned up,' he said, 'Sweep it all up. I will come after you in the spirit.' I told my mother about this, so she cleaned it all up. When it came to the time that the man was coming after me, I could see him coming. And I told my mother not to come near. And I know that my breath was coming back again. I could feel the devil was working pretty strong trying to wake me up. He didn't want me to go with that man to be educated by him, so he was working pretty hard to wake me up from that vision.

"The man said that I had to die to be with him so that he could teach me all things that I didn't know. So my mother saw me and started hollering for help. She said that I was dying now. I had some uncles, and they came running into that place. I was already out of my body. I saw my body laying there with my eyes wide open and ready to pop out like. So I went over there and pressed my chin, and here I closed my mouth. It had a funny sound when I closed it. And my mother told them to bring a spoon, that I had lockjaw. So in opening my mouth they cracked one of my teeth. In my younger days I had a cracked tooth to show for it. While they were doing this, they didn't see me standing there. And that man was coming after me. He stood in the doorway. He didn't come in because these people were crying. Especially my mother was crying real loud, and other people were hollering. They told an uncle to tell the relatives that I was dead. So that man who came after me, he cried. I could see he was crying. He turned around and went back.

"So I was in the center of the room and I didn't know what to do. I had a chance of going with the man that came after me. But again in my mind I was thinking what would happen to my father when he comes and sees me dead. I always pitied my father because he favored me, being I was the oldest child. So I made up my mind to go back into my body and stay there. This is what I did. I went back into my body and got up. I started singing songs which we never used before in the meeting. I think it is the power that sings through me.

I didn't really sing them, since it seems that somebody was singing through me that made these sounds at that time. About a half-hour later my father was back, and he brought some boys with him. My father told them to have a meeting. They had just a little medicine with them. I ate all eighty-two buttons. So they tied the drum and had the service that night. The next morning I got up and walked, and all the pain was gone and ever since then.

"And there is one more thing I thought about, which I would like to explain. The departed ones, I think that is how they go. It showed me how a man, when he is departed from his body, is in spirit. He can see, but you can't see him. I could see myself laying over there, and I could see my mother, but they couldn't see me. They almost ran into me, and I was standing right there. So it's God's vision to let me know who a man is when he is departed from his body, when he is in spirit. Some people say when a man is dead, he is gone. There is no more thinking and no more seeing. But, what I saw through that vision is that man is still alive and he can see and hear.

"[What did the orange, Bull Durham and money stand for?] One time my father told me that if a man says that he prays to God, you will know by the fruit which is the generation. His would be good to show that the man is praying. The fruit shows the generation, that I will have children of my own. I didn't have any at that time. Bull Durham must have stood for the tobacco we use now to pray with in the Half Moon. God was showing me that in the future I would be using it to pray with [the person is a Cross Fire member]. And money represents what we have to live on."

Here we have an impressive vision. Hearing his little sister cry made him realize that he was sinful, and hearing himself cry in the voice of a little baby showed him how deep an experience this was. The devil tempted him to a life of sin, and he fought the devil by simply lying there. This passivity made him receptive to the coming experiences. He then experienced the devil and the Spirit of the Lord fighting over his own body, an expression of the universal theme of the struggle between good and evil. The clicking sound prepared him for the main part of the vision by showing him that it wasn't his time to go and he need not be afraid of what was to follow, for the shining man would lead him down to deeper levels. As a preparation he had to review his entire life to acquire self-knowledge. Then the man told him to have the place cleaned up, symbolizing the purity needed for the experience of his being in the spirit. When the man did come, he told his mother not to come near since this was a dangerous power. The devil made one last attempt to stop the vision, or the spirit journey, by bringing back his breath. The shining man told him he had to die to be with him—a worldwide symbol of renewal. When his spirit went with the man, he appeared dead to the people around him, and they cried and told relatives that he was dead. The shining man waited at the door and cried. He was afraid of how his appearing to be dead would affect his father, so he made up his mind to go back into his body and woke up. Although the devil did not keep him from following the man to new knowledge, the love of his father did. Perhaps this is the reason why the shining man cried, since he was not sufficiently detached from his father to follow him. And perhaps he failed to realize that this death was only symbolic. But he did learn new songs, had a conversion from a life of sin, and experienced what life after death was like. We see here in a most remarkable way the presence of many of man's deep religious themes.

Dreams can be as important as visions. Bernard Ice had a detailed dream concerning the misuse of the Pipe and Peyote. "One night I was thinking about the Peace Pipe. Every time I make a short prayer and go to sleep. In my dream I saw a whole bunch of nice-looking Indians—broad shoulders, small waists, muscular, braided hair, with a feather and a blanket. The Indian's mind was good in those days, no television or liquor. I saw four of them riding horseback. Someone told me to look down the valley. I saw pine trees and a creek. There were some Indians there, but they looked awful. Their hair was long but not braided. They were deformed. They had chicken wings instead of arms. Some had beaks instead of mouths. There was something wrong with every one of them. Their minds were not developed either. They told me to look farther down, and there was a medicine man holding the Pipe. At one time the Indian had the Pipe with the right kind of tobacco. Here they were putting marijuana in the Pipe that ruins their minds. There were hippies at the place also. The FBI officers could stop in there and the medicine man could smoke it right in front of them and they would not know it, since they thought it was the Peace Pipe. That ruined their minds to the point that the Indians started shooting each other. And that is why they were deformed. It is going to be hard to put the right kind of tobacco back like it should be, I thought.

"Then I looked the other way and I saw their only hope, the Peyote fireplace. I tried to help the Indians by making the fireplace. I tried to make it, but I couldn't do it. It always fell down. It just wouldn't hold up. I couldn't put the moon there. But finally, I did get the moon altar and put the Peyote there. I was going to try and pray for those people. Some voice told me to do that. But I had to eat one of the Peyote first before praying. Somebody handed me one, dry. I started to chew it. It didn't even taste like Peyote. It tasted like clay. It looked like Peyote, but it was something else. Something was wrong—no power to it, no medicine, just clay. I couldn't pray because the Peyote wasn't real. There must be another way.

"The voice told me to look east to a little hill. On it there was something shining. The voice told me to go over there and take a look at it on the other side of the hill. There were some good-looking Indians over there. On this side the creek was polluted, but on the other side it smelt good. There was a clean white tipi on the hill. I walked over to the shining object, and it was an open Bible. They got their medicine from there, and they turned into real Indians. Then I woke up. I am blind, but in my dreams I can see all these things."

Francis Mesteth related a very significant dream which a woman had. "Just before my wife and I left to conduct a meeting in Arizona, a lady came up to our car. I didn't know who she was. She told Phyllis that the lady sitting in the car behind us had a dream in which I was sitting before her with the Peace Pipe, and there were some little round balls sitting on my right. She didn't know what the balls were, but she was worried because when you dream of the Peace Pipe, there is a meaning to it. She didn't want anything to happen to her or her family. The woman said the girl was really worried about it and I should go over and talk to her. But before I could, they drove off. So we thought we better go and chase them down and see what it is all about. We went east of Pine Ridge and tried to catch them, but we missed them somehow. When we got to a certain place, they were coming back, so we turned around and followed them to the gas station. We called her over and asked her what the problem was. She told me that she never knew me before, but she dreamt that I was standing in front of her with the Peace Pipe and four balls that looked like medicine.

But she couldn't clarify that because it was a dream. 'Does it mean I have to pray with the Peace Pipe or something will go wrong?' she asked. 'I don't want anything to happen, so I want you to pray for me.' I told her that I was leaving for Arizona and I would pray with the Peace Pipe for some people over there, and that I would pray for her over there at the time for whatever the dream is or whatever is wrong with her. She said: 'I hope you do, because I don't know what it is all about.' So I prayed for her in Arizona, and when I got back, she saw me and said that everything was all right, that nothing happened to her."

PEYOTE HEALING

Although some of the visions just described are examples of healing through Peyote, a few additional examples will add to our understanding.

Lawrence Hunter recalls doctoring a traditional medicine man; he was sick and could hardly walk or talk. "I had four little Peyote buttons, real small, in my pocket. They had the star shape on them. I had some Bull Durham tobacco stubs in my pocket also, and some of the tobacco powder got into the creases in the Peyote. They asked me to make pills for him. The little ones are the strongest. So I gave them to the medicine man. I fanned him with spotted eagle feathers and said a short prayer for him. Towards morning I sang the morning water song: 'They say get on your fast horses because Grandfather is coming; I want to get everything completed before He comes up and starts a new day.' During the song the medicine man sat up. After I finished, I passed the staff to him, and he said in a whisper: 'Son-in-law, I want to sing, and I want you to drum. In the morning you and I are going out to greet the Grandfather, and we are going to yell in thanksgiving.' And he could hardly walk or talk. So I said: 'All right, thank you.' So I beat the drum, and he sang four songs, and his voice just came out clear. He could only talk in a whisper. I guess the Peyote worked on him.

"After he got through, I put a blanket on him, and we went outside. The medicine man told me: 'See those people over there? They are coming after me. They are my parents, my mother that I have never seen and my father that I had known only vaguely, and some of my other relatives. They are standing there looking at me.' I kind of got scared. He got through going to the toilet, and so we came back towards the fireplace. As we were about to enter, the morning star came up and went down again. It came up four times. Four times the medicine man raised his arms and yelled. I helped him by saying: 'ha ho, Grandfather, thank you; You heard us for what we said. You heard us. Thank You.' We went back in, and everybody looked at us. The paleness in the medicine man's eyes was all gone."

Bernard Ice claims that if you get the right Peyote tone from harmonizing the drum, gourd, whistle, and voice in the right way, you can heal a person. He claims that Matthew White Face was healed of a stroke at a doctoring meeting he attended. Phyllis Mesteth says that a little baby was healed in Arizona: "There was an eight-month-old baby who had been in the hospital. There was no kind of milk formula that this baby would hold in her. The mother brought the baby to me and said, 'You Sioux people say Peyote is good medicine. I give you my baby; she is yours. I give her to you to get her well.' My husband, Francis, brought in some Peyote tea, and he cedared her with feathers. And we made four real tiny Peyote balls and put them in her mouth. And the little girl got all right, and now she is thirteen years old. She called me mama too."

Emerson Spider attended a meeting with Red Bear, William Black Bear, Oscar Spotted Eagle, and others. The whole congregation had a vision of Oscar running around all the walls of the room and jumping on the side of the man that they were doctoring, on the place where he hurt. He started to vomit a lot of stuff out of his system, and when he had finished, he was cured. Mrs. Gap tells how her father would say that if one of the members falls away and goes to a different church, when they get sick the medicine will call them back. Beatrice Weasel Bear relates that when Charlie Black Horse doctored someone in a meeting, he cedared the Peyote ball, put it on an eagle feather, and blew it, and it would go all the way across the room into a person's mouth. This same story is told by others. Oscar Two Eagles had a reputation for doctoring people in Peyote meetings; both Beatrice Weasel Bear and Ira Elk Boy attended his doctoring meetings.

Ira Elk Boy tells of another doctoring meeting he attended. "The man who was conducting the meeting said: 'It takes a good healthy man to doctor a person, and anybody who is in here could help me—

anyone who takes this smoke. When it comes time to actually doctor the person, that is the time I need your help. I want you to eat this Peyote as much as you can. I will pass five Peyote. Take one and make four balls and pray with them and give them to me.' I looked at the sick man, and he was laying down, and I also prayed for the leader to bless him on what he was going to do. He gave me five Peyote, and I ate one and prayed with the other four and gave them to him as he directed. There were about six of us who did the same thing. He doctored this person about 1968. The cedar man got up in the morning and put cedar on the fire, and the sick man got up and cedared himself. He asked for a smoke and said: 'I feel good. The ache is gone. Each one of you gave me Peyote with a blessing. I have the blessing inside me. So tomorrow I will be walking around. I am going to say thank you. That is why I take this smoke.' And we all felt good."

Despite all the accounts of healing through Peyote, there is a widespread consensus that Peyote has lost its power to heal today. There are many reasons given. Bernard Ice said: "We seem to have lost the power of healing. I am a diabetic and blind. I tried, but I can't get healed. Twenty-five years ago and more they healed. But, when the Indian got liquor, they lost the power." Solomon Red Bear feels that there could be healing meetings again. Christine Red Cloud says that healing doesn't take place anymore: "Perhaps we don't eat enough Peyote. Or perhaps the people are not together enough, that is, they don't get along with each other." Joe American Horse attributes the lack of healing to too many distractions: "At a meeting, everybody is taking out their fans and trying to out do each other, and everybody has tape recorders and it distracts. There is a Peyote power which comes when everybody prays together. But this can be broken by too many distractions. Again, if a person turns off a tape recorder, he doesn't like that person's singing. There is a bad feeling there." Beatrice Weasel Bear has this to say: "The medicine is powerful. It can be used for sickness. But the medicine doesn't seem to cure anymore because of the arguments people have. That disturbs the power. Also, there is so much disturbance during meetings." However, Bernard Red Cloud attributes the lack of doctoring meetings to the hospital at Pine Lodge: "When the meetings first started, they had doctoring meetings. But they did not have this hospital. There was only one doctor on the Pine Ridge Reservation. So at that time they really depended on Peyote to get well. But now they get shots at the hospital. When I got pneumonia, I never thought of putting up a meeting for myself. I ran up to the hospital and got well there. When you put up a doctoring meeting, it takes time, money, and Peyote. Everything at the hospital is free. Maybe that is the reason."

THANKSGIVING MEETING FOR
THE AUTHOR'S RETURN FROM SCOTLAND

This meeting is included because of its significance in the history of the Native American Church on the Pine Ridge Reservation and, in particular, because of its relationship to the Catholic Church. I included the transcript with little editing to give the reader a feeling for the long speeches and prayers taking place in a long, all-night meeting. Many valuable insights can be obtained through reflection on the prayers. (The Lakota is indicated by parentheses. Italic within the parentheses indicates an English word or phrase. Otherwise, English was the original. Brackets indicate added comments, not in quotation.)

Beatrice Weasel Bear began. "First of all, I want to thank you, Uncle Phillip, for coming here and Aunt Julie for coming to complete this meeting for Fr. Steinmetz. I want to thank my brother-in-law, Emerson Spider [State High Priest] for being here too. I want to thank my brother-in-law, Neulon Deon [State Chairman] for helping us. And also my brother, Douglas Chief. I want to thank Johnny [her husband] for helping me complete this meeting for Fr. Steinmetz. I want to thank each and every one of you that is here to help complete this prayer service that we have been talking about for so long. I'm grateful Fr. Steinmetz came back just the way we wanted him to come back, safely and in good health. And I want to thank him for bringing the Papal Blessing from Pope Paul. I want to thank you, Fr. Steinmetz, for bringing that back to us for the Native American Church, for what you have done for us. I really appreciate that. Tonight when I pray, I am going to remember Pope Paul and the Roman Catholic religion. I will pray for all of them and all their ministers all over the world and the ministers of all denominations when I take the medicine. We are all praying to almighty God. I am going to pray for the people here. We all know what this prayer service is for. We have a cake for Fr. Steinmetz which we had made for him. I want Phillip to take care of that too. Also, during the meeting sometime Fr. Steinmetz would like to pray with the Peace Pipe. Phillip will take care of that. He will know best. I'm really thankful that you all came. I am happy to see all of you.

"We are all having a hard time. I will remember those people who are having a hard time at the funeral meeting over there at Rosebud. I have been through that. I want to sympathize with that family that lost a son. I will remember all of those people in my prayers. It seems as though everything is so hard. It makes me sad the things that are happening. I hope that everything could be good for us again. Through prayers I hope that we could all have good feelings towards each other, all the time. Not only the Native American Church but others, relatives all over having a hard time."

Johnny Weasel Bear said: "(Uncle Phillip, remember my mother. She had surgery. She left $20 for the meeting. And also my sister. Douglas gave $20 and Louis Pretty Boy $20." Beatrice continued: "Cynthia Spider is here to help cook breakfast. Also, Wilson Plenty Bulls is helping with breakfast. I just want to mention that. Also, Wilson brought some medicine. Joe American Horse said he would be here and he will talk to you in the morning.) Fr. Steinmetz, I also want these people that donated money to be remembered. I was asking Uncle Phillip to remember them in his prayers and also in yours. Also, Jessie Spider donated some dried meat and corn for the breakfast. Also, my niece, Charlotte Red Cloud, donated some meat, too. She is helping with some other food which she will bring tomorrow. Also, remember them. Uncle said that if you wanted to say something, go ahead."

I said the following. "I want to tell you, Beatrice, that I'm really moved by what you did for me. It really touches my heart. I will certainly be praying for you tonight. I know that it will have special meaning in my life and I will find that out as I pray. There is some very special purpose in my life in having this meeting. I'm really touched, Beatrice, by what you have done. And perhaps all of you can pray that I be the type of priest that will do good for the Indian people. Pray for the grace and strength and understanding, for all that I need to work with the Native American people here. It's really a great honor and a great privilege that is being given to me tonight. I want to thank everyone here for coming to help and pray. All those who helped in the meeting, gave money to help in the meeting, for everyone here, for Beatrice and Johnny, thank you."

The first smoke took place. Before this, Phillip had said: "There has been some death among some people and Reuben Snake, some of you don't know who he is. He has been around there [Rosebud] for quite awhile. He lives with his father. I stopped at his place, and he was really crying. He asked me to do some things for him. But I didn't. I came over to this meeting. But here I can at least pray for him at this time. I will take a smoke and I will pray for him. His father's name is Reuben, also."

Then everyone prayed in low tones while they smoked the Bull Durham cigarettes. Phillip said, "I believe that in the Western United States the Indians used the sage in just about everything, in all their ceremonies. In the sweat bath they used this sage to wipe themselves and when they caught cold. I thought that I would explain this for the benefit of Fr. Steinmetz so that he will be familiar with what is taking place here. And I want to make an announcement for midnight. I am going to have the Rev. Emerson Spider talk, and I understand in conversation that he wanted to be here tonight. Tomorrow night he will conduct a service. I want you, brothers and sisters, to pray for him. It takes a lot of strength to go two nights. Reverend just came through an operation or a sickness, and he is not fully strengthened, and yet he is going to take part in this and tomorrow night and then bury that cousin of mine. I will remember him. I hope that during the main smoke you remember him. He is going to talk at midnight. And Fr. Steinmetz is going to talk just before the Pipe ceremony. During breakfast my nephew will speak. You know during breakfast we developed habits of joking. So we are going to occupy our minds while we are eating. Some of this food came from people who are sick and are wearied and in sorrow. During breakfast while the food is going around, some of the old-timers—Silas Yellow Boy, Joe Sierra—they tell us the food that is going around at breakfast is holy. So during breakfast Deon will talk. He will observe what is going on during the night, and he will assimilate it and will elaborate on what he will talk about. I thought I would say that. We are going to sing now. Take your time. There will be some more coming in and they will take up the whole space here."

Phillip Eagle Bear blew the whistle four times, and the singing started and continued until the midnight water. At that time he said, "Thanks to each and every one of you. We praise the almighty God. And the drumming too, it is good and encouraging. So I want to thank you all for it. So there is a time for everything. There is a time to stop and hear the Word of God. After we drink water, Rev. Emerson will talk. And then we will have some more singing. And then, towards the time of the morning star, I asked my nephew, Bernard Red Cloud, to load that Pipe. He is familiar with that. Then he is going to take the rug out [on which the Pipe was lying, bowl and stem separated] and lean the Pipe against the scaffold. And then Fr. Steinmetz will talk. After that, we will ask the fireman to light it. Then you can carry on with four directions. And Johnny will tell you who will smoke the Pipe. Just like we did the first time [the meeting before the author's trip to Scotland]. And when you get the Pipe back [after smoking it with the three men] you can say a word of prayer. I thought I would give you the program. (I have been wanting to come to meetings all the time but I couldn't do it. Sometimes my legs hurt. Sometimes I get so sick I can't feel anything on my lips)."

Douglas, the cedar man, prayed in Lakota in the early morning. "(God the Father, I am praying to You. God the Father, I am here praying to You. God the Father, have pity on me and have pity on these people. As we eat this medicine, have pity on us. God the Father, You will make it possible that my brother, Phillip Eagle Bear, will be able to pray. God the Father, You will see that his wife has good health. And also, God the Father, You will have pity on the chief drummer [Neulon Deon]. God the Father, You will have pity on us now and in the future. God the Father, You are the only one with the power to do this. And You will have pity on Bernard Red Cloud. God the Father, You will bless us and we will be in good health. God the Father, You will always make it possible that there will be a tipi where we can always pray. [This meeting was the first tipi meeting of the year on the reservation.] God the Father, You will have pity on me. That is the way I pray. God the Father, You will have pity on my woman. God the Father, whatever is good for us, You can do. That is the way I pray to You. God the Father, You will have pity on each and every one of us. This is the Indian way; this is the way we pray. God the Father, have pity on my cousin, Emerson. God the Father, You will have pity on my sisters. God the Father, You will take us to another night. You will take us safely. God the Father, You are the only one I believe in. That is why I am telling You this. God the Father, You will see to it that all of us are well. And You will see to it that we stay this way. God the Father, whatever is good, You will make it possible. God the Father, You will make everything good. God the Father, all of us and all our relatives that are here on this earth, You will remember us. At this hour, at this time, I am telling You this, God the Father. God the Father, I am telling You at this time. God the Father, I am telling You this. God the Father, You will have pity on us.)"

Then Johnny Weasel Bear talked in Lakota. "(Before I say anything else, I just want to say thank you. I also want to say thank you to my brother-in-law. I want to say thank you to all of you. And the chief drummer, I want to say thank you. The one who lost one of his relatives, cousin, I want to say thank you, too. I say thank you to all of you who were here last night. And I want to say thank you to all who helped in this meeting. Those who made donations to help in this meeting, I say thank you to all of you.)

"I want to thank you. I will remember you. I want to thank you, Fr. Steinmetz. When we pray with this water, I need prayers myself. I want to thank you. You brought that Blessing back for our own Indian religion. (I want to thank you for helping to watch over this meeting, brother Phillip. And cousin, Wilson Plenty Bull, I want to say thank you. [A few sentences were missed.] When I pray, I want you to help me. I hope all of us will be here safe, and I hope all of us will be together again like this.)"

Johnny began praying. "(First, I want to say thank you. Perhaps someone here is not happy. Also, God the Father, I pray that there will be another time when there will be prayers like this in the Indian way. That is why I am telling You this. At this hour when I am sitting here and praying, there is Fr. Steinmetz. I don't feel that I am the man that can pray for him, but that is the way I am asking You, God. God the Father, I pray that he is without sin. God the Father, at this hour have pity on me. God, I hope that there will be a prayer man who will help us bring back this Peyote way, this Indian religion. That is the way

I pray. Or if there should be a woman here who will pray, I ask that You will remember her [the water woman]. God the Father, You will watch over her. We do this in a humble way. You will have pity on her, God. And as we are having hard times in the *Native American Church*, Fr. Steinmetz is here to pray with us. God the Father, it is my belief that You chose this man to be here to help me. The poor Indians, we pray to You. We are happy that he brought this *Blessing*. Also that he is eating my medicine. You will have pity on him. You will watch over all these brothers, God the Father. And overseas, wherever Pope Paul is at, God is at. God, You see this. Since he went over there and did a good deed for us, God the Father, at this time You will bless him too. The *Roman Catholic Church*, You will bless each and every one of them, God the Father.

"At this hour we are telling You all this and also the *Native American Church*, we also have ministers and, God, You will watch over them too. It is You that they are working for, God the Father. That way You will have pity on brother Emerson. You will let him live and do this. Wherever we pray like this, he is one of the first ones to be here. God the Father, You will have pity on my brother. You will bless him, God the Father. Tomorrow night he will have a prayer service [the funeral meeting] and so when he is there, You will watch over him. And whoever he is with there, my sisters or my aunts or my cousins or my nephews, You will make it possible for him to do this and that he will be able to live. And You will make it good for him and make these things possible for him. Also my nephew, whenever I go over there, he thinks a lot of me. So at this time You will watch over him, his wife, and his children. You will give them good health, and You will always watch over them. You will also have pity on my aunt and my uncle. At this hour have pity on them. At this time when we had this tobacco, he took this tobacco and he used this tobacco and he talked to You. He prayed to You. And he has some children. Have pity on all his children and give them good health. I have a brother here who watched over this drum all night last night. He watched over this holy drum.

"And my cousin, You will watch over her. She came in here and did whatever she could do. You will watch over her. And all these people who are gathered here tonight, You will give them a *blessing* and good health. And God grant them whatever they want. God, You will make all their wishes possible. You will watch over my cousin, Douglas. You will watch over him. Whenever they have a meeting, he is right there to help out. You will watch over him. He will have good health, he and my aunt. You will make it possible for them to do this at least two or three more times with no problems at all. Or if they want children in their home, You will make it possible. I pray to You in this way and at this hour. And I pray for my brother and this fireplace. I pray that You watch over us. If possible at this time I will pray again. I pray to You that we will live like this and be happy on this earth. In any way You see possible, God, that is the way You will do it. It isn't what I want on this earth, God, it is You. Have pity on me. God the Father, You have pity on us and also the men of this generation. In the future, if it is possible, we will get a *blessing*. I want my mother to live a long time. I want my mother to be healthy for a long time. And my niece and nephews. At this hour last night we thought about them. My nephew, I pray that he will always be here. At this hour I pray to You. I pray for all my brothers, and I pray to You at this time. I say thank you to you, brothers, that we all pray here together. That is all I will say, and thank You. And brother Emerson, God will have pity on him. And at this hour we will have a prayer here for the *Native American Church*. And also Joe and his wife, and even those who did not come inside here, those who belong to the *Native American Church*, I pray to You for them at this hour, God the Father. At this hour, all my relatives who are here on this earth, God the Father, if I made any mistakes I am telling You, and so You remember them at this time. You are the one that can help us. Douglas, You will have pity on him. At this time, at this hour, all those who are officers of the Half Moon, You will make it possible that they will be able to do this. If You want anyone else to come in here, you will make it possible. And my aunts and my uncles and my nephew and all those who have prayed here, God the Father, all those who have prayed here, You will bless them. And my niece will get a good education.

"And also, God the Father, here and at this time, You will give us a *blessing*. My relatives will drink of this water and they will have good health. And one of the officers who is here, Francis Mesteth, give him good health. He prays like this too; he prays like we do. You will give him good health. At this hour You will also help my nephews and also my niece. And I thank You in this way so that all these people be in good health. And I pray to You in this way. And Loretta [his stepdaughter], You will give her a child. Through this fireplace may it be possible that she has children. From the bottom of my heart I thank You. I want to see a grandchild in good health. I want to see a grandchild in here. God, You have pity on everyone. And my nephew, God, You will have pity on my nephew, John. You will see that he gets an education. You will make it possible that he gets an education in the future. You will watch him. And all these who are here and who are going to school. You will help them get an education among the Indian people. You will make it possible that we will have good health, and my nephew, You will also see that he has good health. And this tipi, my son's tipi, You will watch over that. Or even those tipi poles that Rose Ann brought for us. Or my brother, Billy Richards, You will watch over him. And my little nephews, You will watch over them. There are some grandchildren here amongst us who are orphans, watch over them. You will love each and every one of us just like those tipi poles. But You will love us as one. And also my brother, Charles Stoneman, You will help him and watch over him. And all my brothers, wherever they may be and also my in-laws who are here and helping out, You will have pity on them. And if I should forget anyone, You will remember them and You will watch over them. And my cousin, Chris, he helps out here. You will watch over him. And my nephews, You will watch over them, and that drum carrier, You will watch over him, and You will watch over his children. And You will watch over my sisters and brothers and their families. And You will watch over them and they will have good health. And this man that someone brought, he will have good health. Or if he should want a place to live or a job, just like Mike, You will help him do that. And my young brother there, if he has a woman with him, You watch over him and his woman. And You will give them good health.

"God the Father, have mercy on me. I told You about my pains. Or those of you in here who may have aches and pains, if you are happy to be here, let Him know. Whichever it may be on this earth, if I have to live with this pain, or if it is going to be happiness, I will accept either or both. God the Father, I always want to pray to You like this, but at the same time I am having a hard time. That is why I am telling You at this hour. I want You to bless my brother and my niece. I want them to be happy. [Pause, crying for a while.] Then, God the

Father, at this hour all of us who have prayed here and whatever our prayers were, You will answer them. God, at this hour have pity on me. You are the one that watches over this earth. You are the one who is happy, and You will watch over us. At this time I will thank You. Have pity on me. At this hour when we are praying to You and all my people who were here praying, have pity on us. And at this hour You will bless us with this fireplace and this medicine. And bless Fr. Steinmetz because he is a good man and he helps with the *blessing* for this Church. You will make that good for him. You make it possible for us to have what we have [the Papal Blessing]. And You will make it possible to have what we want.

"And I want to tell You one more thing. There will be a new Tribal President. This Tribal President will have pity on the Indians who need his help. And all the needs among the Indian people, whatever we lack and everything we lack, we tell You at this hour, and we are asking for Your help. And that President, whoever he works with, You will have pity on them. And he will help us only in a good way. He will help the Indians in the best way possible. And You will make it possible that he will be able to do a good job for us. And whatever claims we have, he will help us through our claims [for the Black Hills]. And our children, we want them to have good health. In the Name of Jesus, Your Son, I am talking to You in this way. And You will remember me.]"

While the water was being passed around, Rev. Emerson Spider gave the following talk. [Ellipses indicate sections edited out.] "First of all, I would like to greet each and every one of you. I am thankful towards almighty God. And that goes for each and every one of you. I am very thankful that I get to see you this morning in this holy place. I know that the dear Lord is with us. I know it right away. . . . So at this time as I was sitting here, I think it is one of the best prayer services that has taken place. And I thank the good Lord that this is the first tipi meeting of the year that took place around here in this area. I am very thankful that the good Lord was with us. And I have been thanking Fr. Steinmetz for the last few months, and still I think that I can't say enough. And that's the way it is with each and every one here. We are grateful that we have a man like him to come into our church and participate in our holy circle here. I think it is the meaning of God that we have a man like him. Once again, we are very thankful you are here. If it wasn't for you, we would never be gathered here at this time. In the early part of the evening, they were thanking me and my cousin over there. The State Chairman and the minister being here, I think that is real nice. There are some leaders here, Half Moon boys that came around. I thought that was real good. All the ones that come here, I think that is real nice.

"As I said, I think it is the best meeting. The reason I said that is that as I was sitting here and thinking and looking at the fireplace, at what has taken place and what is going to take place [the roadman blew his whistle], we got the chief Peyote here, the divine herb that is given by God, and we got the Sacred Pipe that is here and we got the Blessing that is written on a piece of paper there by the high man, Pope Paul. As I was sitting here looking at these, why this is great. One of the greatest things that has ever happened to the Native American Church. I am grateful and thankful for it. . . .

"And I kind of talked for this man here [the author] that uses this Pipe here. I guess other people in other churches don't like the way he does here, praying with the Sacred Pipe. They were talking, and I said that somehow I think that is God's will. Some young people, you know they have different ideas, like I kind of noticed it this way. They are afraid of Jesus Christ. And they want to be on their own. They said: 'Could that Sacred Pipe (they didn't even say sacred), could that be used in religious ways [i.e., in Christian churches]?' I happened to be there. And when they said that, it seemed that no one could answer that. There were college people and ministers there. When it came to my turn to talk, I said, 'I don't care where you use the Pipe, if you use it right, that is going to be good. And if you are not going to use it right, I don't care where you use it, in a ceremonial way or in a church way, it won't be good. So what this man [the author] is doing, I think that has been good. He is using it in a good way.' I think that is real nice. So there that question was answered.

"I have to lead a meeting tomorrow, a funeral, which is the hardest meeting there is. But, again I was thinking if I have that true love, I should show it. So that is the reason why I am here. And there is one thing that really bothers me. I always wish that I was a healthy man so that I could take in anything, like being a fireman, two, three nights. One time I was that way. In my younger days I could stay up four nights, run meetings, drum, be a cedar man and a fireman. But now as I get older, this sickness is getting me down. And there is no cure for it, so I thought it was okay the way my brother was praying. Why is it that I am suffering here? The more I pray, the more suffering I have. But here in Holy Scriptures, I brought my Bible with me, you have to go through suffering. You can't be taking a good sail [i.e., an easy way] through there. You have to be suffering with your body to go through there. That is the way we enter the kingdom of heaven. . . .

"Let's have that true love towards each other before it is too late. Let's have that peace. We have it here, that Peace Pipe; let's have that true peace in our hearts. There were two boys talking at that time [at the former meeting, mentioned above]. They pointed at me and asked: 'Do you believe in Christ?' I said: 'Yes, I believe in Jesus Christ.' 'You must be a white man,' they said. 'Once you believe in Jesus Christ, you are a white man.' 'No, you got me all wrong,' I said. 'I'm a hundred-percent Indian. Not one drop of blood in me that is white. I'm a hundred-percent. When one receives Christ, that doesn't change a person into another one,' I said. 'If a white man believes in Christ, that doesn't change him into an Indian. Or an Indian believes in Christ, that doesn't change him into a white man. You got it all wrong, as smart as you are.' There were college people there. In the Scriptures it says the last days are coming at hand and these things will come about. People will be smart. You can't tell them anything. They get mad right away. . . .

"I'm going to tell the Word of God. When I lay down, that is going to be it. While I am alive, while I am breathing, I am going to tell others. I am going to tell this man over here. If he has ears to hear with, he will be saved. Some of us have no ears. Like myself, I have big ears, but sometimes the words come in one and go out the other. That's the way I am. Like I always said, we should close one side. And this liquor is killing off our people. The meeting I am going to run tonight, the liquor done that. The boy got killed right there [he was stabbed to death]. It is the liquor that did that. And this boy [in the previous meeting] who was saying that I was a white man, I said: 'Do you drink?' 'Yes,' he said, 'I drink.' 'Do you smoke?' 'Yes, I smoke.' 'You must be a white man,' I said, 'because you are using the white man's things. Those are white man's things. The liquor doesn't belong to the Indians; the cigarette belongs to the white man. And then you tell me that I am a white man; I'm an Indian. If you don't like this Christ and you want me to say that I'm a white man, who would I be if I gave Christ back to the white man? Would you come and join me as a good Indian, representing the Indian, being a true Indian? In the early days this white man came and tricked the Indian through this liquor and now we are using it and we talk big. If we are going to be an Indian, let's do it the right way. We have been talking about this Pipe; let's have respect for it,' I said. 'Then we could say "I respect the Pipe." Let's do it that way. . . .'

"Once a truth has been told here, let's take it. Sometimes I felt like getting up and going out [of a meeting]. I didn't feel like coming in here. Sometimes I did go out when my dad gave a talk. I didn't want to listen to him. I kind of stayed away. It seemed like I didn't want to go in because I might hear him talk again. I got scared of him. And one time I listened to my dad, and here I am. That's what brought me here. If you listen to a minister, to a man of God, it's good. But as I said, we want to be on our own. We say, 'I'm old enough' and 'What I do is nobody's business.' We say those things. Then we say, 'I'm an Indian.' But, if we are going to be an Indian, let's be a true Indian, a real one, not an imitation like. We are right in between being an Indian and being a white man. We are just like a monkey. . . .

"I have a brother who talks and makes men laugh, and I really like that. And one day even he was moaning, crying, and it seemed he wasn't himself. And I noticed right away that there was a time to moan and a time to be jolly. And we are doing this right here. We are praising the almighty God. We are making joyful noises to the Lord. We are doing that here. My cousin is representing Greenwood, South Dakota; Phillip is representing Rosebud; I am representing the state of South Dakota; one man from Potato Creek and from Pine Ridge, Wounded Knee, Porcupine; even from Nebraska, too—Scottsbluff, Chadron. Like boys coming back from school, where he goes to school, he represents the place he comes from. So we are all here. Thank you for your kind attention. (This is all I have to say and I want to thank you.)"

Phillip then said. "(While we are drinking water, I want to say thank you. All of you who have prayed, I want to say thank you. And Reverend, I really thank you. Whenever there is a man who is speaking and he is worthy of his words, it is good to hear him. And all of you who have talked, I want to thank you. Some of you have made good talks in here, and I want to say thank you.) We ask almighty God for a perfect night, quiet stars, a nice day so that the people can have a nice meal, so the people here can have a nice meeting. I just want to be thankful for that. (I didn't feel able to do this but you [Beatrice Weasel Bear] asked me to do this.)"

The singing then continued until early morning. During this time I sang the following song:

Our Holy Father Paul, yo wana yo wana yo wana yo.
Our Holy Father Paul, yo wana yo wana yo wana yo.
Jesus bless him, yo wana heana he ne no way.

Cannunpa wakan [the Sacred Pipe] yo wana yo wana yo wana yo.
Cannunpa wakan, yo wana yo wana yo wana yo.
Jesus bless it, yo wana heana he ne no way.

Pejuta wakan [the holy medicine] yo wana yo wana yo wana yo.
Pejuta wakan, yo wana yo wana yo wana yo.
Jesus bless it, yo wana heana he ne no way.

I thank you, Jesus, yo wana yo wana yo wana yo.
I thank you, Jesus, yo wana yo wana yo wana yo.
I thank you, Jesus, yo wana heana he ne no way.

In the early morning Phillip stopped the staff to make the following introductory remarks to the Pipe ceremony. "I really want to thank the fireman the way he handles the fire. Joe Sierra taught most of us. He said to do it neat. That's why I want to comment on the display of the wood. And again Joe used to tell us when we are going to put up a meeting, everything that you use in that meeting, be sure that it is first class. If you are going to have a good fireplace, be sure your sticks of wood are straight so you make the people feel good. You want wood that is good when you are going to pray to almighty God. That's the way the Indian people are.

"When I get the staff, I will ask my nephew, Bernard, to load the Pipe and take the rug away and put the Pipe against the scaffold and then you [the author] can talk just like Rev. Spider. It will be your privilege. You can talk ten minutes, twenty minutes, whatever it is, so that you get it off your mind, about your trip, about Pope Paul. You will feel better. If you are in a hurry, you leave something out and later on you feel sorry about it, that you didn't put it in. That one word makes so much difference. When you are finished with your talk, the fireman and you will light the Pipe. He will tell you the ones you are going to smoke with. That's the Sioux culture. The Pipe and the tobacco are their culture. It's their way of life. Do not hold the Pipe if you are going to tell a lie. So we will be at the moment of truth. We are going to witness all of this. When you get through, put the ashes in the fireplace. We will put the rug back the way it is sitting now. Then we are going to give my niece, Beatrice, tobacco. That's the way we are going to do that."

Then Phillip sang four songs while Bernard Red Cloud filled the Pipe. After the singing Phillip said, "I want to thank each and every one of you for your kindness and generosity up to this point. The reason I put the Peyote out is that we don't have time to eat the medicine. This is the Half Moon way. Some roadmen wait until the last round of songs. But, I believe in eating Peyote up to the main smoke. If we eat medicine up to this point, the Peyote will help you. That is the way the teaching of the Half Moon is. I thought that I would tell you the best way the medicine works. From here on out there will be praying, talking, and we will eat, too. It's going to take up a lot of time. Fr. Steinmetz, you can talk now."

I gave the following talk. "I really don't know what to say. You have a meeting for me in my honor. You accept me into your fireplace. You say I am worthy to partake of the holy medicine with you. I don't know what to say. And, then, you say that I'm worthy to handle your Sacred Pipe. And that's the greatest honor, I feel, you can give me. You say you accept me as one worthy to handle your Sacred Pipe. You wouldn't be able to say anything more wonderful to me than that. So I'll try to do the best I can to speak from the heart.

"I sang the song, 'Our Holy Father Paul' and I think we can all sing that song, 'Our Holy Father Paul' because we have his Blessing and he is your father now. And I sang, 'may Jesus bless him.' And I thought that all throughout the world people are asking Jesus to bless the Holy Father and they are doing that in Africa in their own African languages and in African ways. They are doing that in Taiwan in the Chinese way. They are doing that in the Philipines and in the Pacific Islands. They are doing it in Europe in a European way. And tonight we are doing it in the Native American Church way. And I know that all the prayers of the Native American Church went through that song and that those prayers crossed the ocean. I brought the Papal

Blessing back to you across the ocean, and now our prayers tonight go the other way to our Holy Father Paul. So it really made me feel good that the prayers went through that song to the one that gave us his special Blessing.

"Another song that meant a lot to me was when I sang '*Cannunpa wakan kin;* may Jesus bless the Sacred Pipe.' I really believe that this is the prayer we all have to have on our lips and in our hearts frequently. We are at a time now when we must have Jesus bless the Sacred Pipe. As Emerson said, there are some now who are turning away from Christ, who are taking the Sacred Pipe and turning their back to Christ, in opposition to Christ. They are really turning the Sacred Pipe into an anti-Christ. And so it is really necessary that we pray for the Sacred Pipe so that it doesn't come back on the Indian people in tragedy. And so I'm happy, then, that the prayers of the Native American Church went up through that song that Jesus bless the Sacred Pipe, that it always be in good hands, hands worthy to accept it.

"When I look, just as Emerson did, at the altar, I see there the Papal Blessing, the holy medicine and the Sacred Pipe. Three powerful things are brought together in this sacred tipi. Why did God bring these three together? And I think it is a question to which we will get only a part of an answer, or a part of a vision, tonight. I think we are always going to have to seek out the answer to that. Why did the Almighty bring these powerful things together in this tipi? We are going to have to seek out what is the meaning to that. It has a meaning in my life, a very personal meaning. It has a meaning for Beatrice, a deep personal meaning for her. I prayed with the Sacred Pipe for the first time at her father's funeral at this spot. And when Norman died, she told me that he had the prayers of the Native American Church and he was buried in the Catholic cemetery. And I brought the Papal Blessing to the Church at the memorial for Norman. And she told me something that really touched my heart. She said that at that memorial meeting she lost a son but she received the Papal Blessing for the Native American Church. I was deeply moved by those words. I see one little meaning. We have three religious traditions brought together here in peace and harmony. I think that it is a little prophecy that this is what must happen on the reservation, people brought together in harmony, people finding everything brought together in

Christ. I really believe that this is a scared tipi. I really believe that the Almighty is going to continue to tell us something tonight. He had a purpose in bringing these three religious traditions together in this meeting. It wasn't chance. It was His will, His divine will. And in a way the Pine Ridge Reservation can never be quite the same since this took place. This is an event that can't be erased. You can't say it didn't happen. It did happen, and the Almighty has a meaning. In a very humble way, we have to more and more discover that meaning in our lives.

"Oh, I learned many things from the meeting tonight and other meetings. I was praying, and I came to realize that what the Native American Church taught me was not just to pray for people but to pray with people, to pray the whole night with people, to suffer and pray with them. I really have a feeling tonight of being a part of this earth. I feel I am part of the Indian land and of the Indian people because of the experience tonight. And I look forward now to praying with the Sacred Pipe. And really, up to this point I really wasn't completely home. I prayed with the Sacred Pipe in this tipi before I left for overseas, and I prayed for a safe journey, and the people prayed for me. I really don't feel completely back until this is completed. When it is completed, I will know that I am home again, completely home. So this moment has a great deal of meaning to me. And I learned from the Native American Church humility, to really ask the Almighty in a pitiful and humble way for the things I need. It has been a rich experience for me.

"And I kind of see a door, a vision of a door, and I felt that going through this meeting was like going through a door. But I can't see what is beyond the door. And so I feel God has called me through the door and I don't know where it is going to lead me. And this is true, I think, of all of us. This is why we must put ourselves in God's hands and we have to trust Him and we have to believe that He is a loving Father. It is difficult at times, and yet we do have a loving Father. And I like to simply mention something Emerson told me that really touched me. He told me that when his father was about to die, he told him that he was his father on earth and he did the best he could to provide for him, that some of the times he wasn't able to. But after he was gone, Emerson should always remember that he had a Father in heaven Who could provide him with everything he needed. I was really touched with that; it really moved me. What a beautiful thing for someone's father to say.

"I continue, I guess, to grow more and more roots here, little by little. It doesn't take place all of a sudden but just like a plant. It starts with a couple of roots, and it starts to grow up. The roots keep on going deeper and deeper and wider and wider. I kind of feel that is my experience now. I kind of feel those roots getting a little deeper and further out. I really feel good. And I really thank Jesus for being here. And I thank all of you for the love and the respect that you have given me. I think that these remarks relieve my heart."

Phillip responded: "Thank you for the wonderful talk. You talked about some good things you have experienced. Each and every one here has experienced lots of visions. We eat this medicine so that with the mind's eye you can explore the depths of God's mystery. That is how each one of us is saved. Through that they can see their own salvation. There is no other way. So I thank you for the wonderful talk you gave us."

Bernard Red Cloud then lit the Pipe and gave it to me. I smoked the Pipe and gave it to the three other men, who smoked it with me. There was still some tobacco remaining in the bowl. I offered the Pipe to the four directions, heaven, and earth and offered the following prayer.

"Let us pray. We gather up the entire universe through the Sacred Pipe, the mountains and the valleys, the rivers and the streams, the flowers and the trees, we gather up all of God's creation and offer it up through this Sacred Pipe, the birds, the four-leggeds and all our fellowmen. And tonight through this Sacred Pipe we offer up all the prayers offered in the four Basilicas in Rome. Almighty God, we praise and thank You for this meeting. We praise and thank You for my return back here. We praise and thank You for that acceptance that I have received. We praise and thank You for all your wonderful gifts. We praise and thank You for the Papal Blessing to the Native American Church. And may this Blessing always remain with this Church and always protect it from all harm. May it give it strength; may this Blessing give it hope and peace. And so may this Blessing always be over the Native American Church as a shield to protect it. And Almighty God, we thank You for this miracle of bringing the Papal Blessing, the holy medicine, and the Sacred Pipe together in this tipi for this meeting. And we ask You to give us the meaning of this in our lives and in the life of the reservation and in the life of the Sioux people.

"Almightly God, we pray for Beatrice and Johnny. Watch over them for all the sacrifices they made and especially their family and their children. O Lord, be with their children. O Lord, bring back their children, that they may come back home here and especially Roger, bring him back. And Almightly God, pour your healing power into the heart of Beatrice. Give her strength and comfort; give her peace and understanding and always be with her, guiding her, protecting her.

"Almightly God, pray for Emerson in the meeting he is going to conduct tonight that it may be a meeting in which great goodwill be done. Help him during this meeting that it may turn out good. Almighty God, we pray for the reservation. We pray for peace; we pray for hope in the hearts of the people. We pray that they may come together now in prayer and harmony and that all that divides the people be expelled. Almighty God, we pray for the new tribal officials. They have a difficult job to perform, that they really bring greater happiness and greater hope into the lives of the people. Be with them, Almighty God. In these difficult days, Almighty God, we ask that the Sacred Pipe and this holy medicine may always bring people to Christ.

"Almighty God, we ask You to come into this tipi tonight and bless everyone here, to pour your great gifts into the lives of all those who are here and to their families and their relatives and their dear ones. Almighty God, we pray especially for those who are sick, for Cleo Weasel Bear, for Johnny's mother, for all those who are sick, that they may get well. Almighty God, we ask You to send Your blessings and Your grace into this community here in the Native American Church. And we ask You all this through this Sacred Pipe in the Name of Our Lord Jesus Christ."

I then touched the Pipe bowl to the ground in silence and emptied the remaining tobacco into the fireplace.

Phillip responded. "While you were praying, I was thinking God will lead His own people by their own ways regardless of what kind of formality they use. God will be in the midst of them. So I thank you for the wonderful prayer. I thank the audience for their patience. You can't tell these Fathers if you don't want them to take it seriously. They are very serious people. They are humble people. To serve God you must be a humble man. Father went to that school. I presume he got his degree, and from there he went to Europe and his footsteps led to Rome. Father prayed in the four directions, and there were the four churches in Rome. When he was through, Father asked the Pope for a Blessing through the bishop or whoever is in charge. The State Chairman is sitting here and the State High Priest. We must ask ourselves in what way we are going to use that Blessing. How are we going to benefit by that Blessing? It is up to each and every one of us. We can't go out of here and live a sinful life. Father did his part. Now it is up to us to do our part, to take care of a Blessing from one of the world's best-known figures, the Pope. It is not an empty gesture. It is something constructive. God bless each and every one of you. I will give Beatrice the main smoke. When she gets through talking, she will light the cigarette. We are going to wait. Some roadmen go on singing. I mentioned that we would eat medicine up to the main smoke because there would be a lot of things taking place."

After Beatrice's talk, which was not recorded, and her prayer, said in a low tone, the singing continued until the four closing songs by Phillip. During the morning Neulon Deon made a number of personal reflections, and the meeting was concluded.

Several observations should be made. The introductory remarks and other talks throughout the meeting display the profuse remarks of thanks so characteristic of the Half Moon meetings. The cedar man's prayer, with its frequent petition that God should have pity on people, is typical of the traditional Lakota religion. Emerson Spider's talk is proof of his evangelical spirit, the importance of the Bible, and the place of Christ for all Lakota people. Emerson also insists that a Lakota does not lose his Indian identity in accepting Christ and as a Cross Fire member defends my use of the Pipe. The State Chairman, the State High Priest, and the three most influential Half Moon roadmen on the Pine Ridge Reservation all came to the tipi meeting to recognize the importance of the Papal Blessing. My talk established an ecumenical relation between traditional Christianity and both the Native American Church and the traditional Lakota Religion.

THE FOURTH MEMORIAL MEETING
FOR A YOUNG GIRL

Bernard Red Cloud conducted this Half Moon memorial meeting for his young daughter, who died a violent death involving homicide. The meeting is more typical than the preceding one and is included for the understanding and appreciation which it gives of a Peyote meeting. It was a moving experience. (Parentheses indicate Lakota was the original language. Italic indicates an English phrase used in the Lakota.)

The roadman had these opening remarks. "(Before I begin this meeting, I want to thank all of you who have just come in here. I want to thank all the people who brought food here, and I want to thank Margie. I want to thank Fr. Steinmetz. I want to thank those that came from Porcupine, even John. John came from Porcupine and those that came from Potato Creek. This will be a memorial meeting. I am going to run it. This meeting is for the benefit of my daughter. It is a memorial meeting, but each of you will take a smoke [*cannunpa*, "Pipe"] here. So whatever your thoughts are when you are taking the smoke, it is up to you. I don't intend to be the only one to get a benefit out of this meeting. I want you people to say your prayers, too, at this meeting. I want you to get something good out of this meeting, too. That is my feeling for you people. I called for this memorial meeting, and you people are here. I have a large family, my wife and I. And at the time when I lost my daughter, I didn't know what to do. And here at that time the people, members of Peyote Church [*pejuta okolakiciye*, or "Peyote fellowship"], have helped me, and they talked with me, and they prayed with me at that time. And when you people prayed with me, talked with me, and helped me at that time up to now, you have built up my support and made my heart feel good. That is the way I feel now.

"This is the fourth and last memorial meeting. That is why I want this man to sit here again [referring either to the main drummer or to the cedar man]. This is what we are thinking about now, this fourth memorial meeting. Since this is the fourth and last memorial meeting for my daughter, maybe next year at the memorial meeting [for someone else], we will do something for her in memory of her. *Maybe at Easter or Memorial Day* we will do something for her again. Again,

I want you [his son] to take care of the fire for me at this time. Also, we lost a mother-in-law, my brother-in-law's mother. I had thoughts of a meeting around about the same time when he lost his mother. So I postponed my meeting to go over there and help him at that time. I wanted to help him. And I am glad that he is here at this meeting. I hope that his attending meetings and his praying help him. My feelings are that they will also get something good from this meeting at this time. Those are my feelings.

"At midnight we will have a smoke. I will take care of that smoke, and I am the one that will use that smoke. There used to be an old man who did what I am about to do now. He is the one that used to do this. But now he is gone, so I will do what he did. There will be an old lady coming in here during this meeting later on. Her name is Julie. As we go into this meeting, you will pray too. As we go along, you will pray for your own needs as well. There are some things I want to say and some prayers I want to say, and I will do that at midnight when I take the smoke. At the time I take the smoke, I will pray that this Church will grow stronger. In the future that is the way I want it to be. I will pray so bear your thoughts with me)."

Then he begins to pray. "(God the most powerful, this day and this evening I pray to You that You will bless all common men. With this smoke I pray this way that You will help each and every one of them. This night our thoughts are of You and we are praying to You. Four years ago I lost a member of my family. I lost a daughter four years ago and that is why I am praying this way again this day and this night. You are the most holy. You gave us good blessings. At this hour I pray that my family will be at peace. And we will say good prayers. That is why at this hour we will pray beneath You. And also the people who are here, whatever is in their minds and their hearts, hear them. That is why we are praying this way, and we really mean our prayers. [A woman was praying in the background at this time.]

"Sometimes I am not strong, and that is why I am still talking to You like this. That is why I am offering this tobacco pouch [sack of Bull Durham] so that it will build us up and make us strong. You will also watch over me when I am beating the drum. *Jesus* is only one heart with God. In *Jesus* there is only one heart. That is why, *Jesus*, I pray to You to watch over my family. *Jesus*, You are the only One. *Jesus*, You will watch over all things. That is why, *Jesus*, all our thoughts of

You are good. Although we know that her spirit is outside, maybe sometime this will happen to someone else and You will be with him. I am thinking of the best for me, and I am the one that will be strong. All these men here, these young men who are gathered here, all these men I want You to take care of them. Whatever their needs are and whatever their prayers are, You will answer them. And we will partake of this holy communion [Peyote]. We will do this throughout the night, and You will make it good for us. All these prayers, which we will say tonight, will make the *Native American Church* stronger. I pray that we will grow stronger and stronger. All these people who are here praying tonight, have pity on them and help them. That is why I am praying and I am asking You to help them. I am asking You to watch them.)"

At the end of the prayer, he had a few comments. "(All of you here tonight, I want to thank each and every one of you. And these men who are helping me, those who take care of the fire and others who are helping me and devoting their time to do what they are doing, I want to say thank you to them also.)"

The singing started and continued without interruption until the midnight water call. At that time the roadman made these comments: "(Now, we will call for water and we will pray. The cedar man will put some cedar on the coals, and when he does that, you will cedar yourselves. *I will call on my congregation and we will say the Lord's Prayer.*)" The Lord's Prayer was said in English during the four morning water songs.

After this, the roadman talked to his son. "(You do good work. That is why I am going to give you the smoke. I am asking you to say a prayer. Those of you who came here after the meeting got started, we explained the purpose of this meeting before. We could have taken time to explain the purpose to each and every one who came in after the meeting started, but this is a memorial meeting for my daughter, and I want all of you to pray. I never saw you for a long time, my cousin, Richard. And you are here now. It is good to see you here. Silas and Billy, you have come a long ways for this meeting. We sure appreciate that. Next year we will remember her. We will donate something to the Church. We are going to do it that way. We finished four meetings for her. We are sure happy that I could do that. I am glad that I came this far. That is why I appreciate what You did for me. I have come this far. I look back, and some of these people I haven't seen before. I sure feel good at this time. This is the reason I didn't go to gatherings but stayed home. I stayed home for four years now. I did everything right. I have been in the *Native American Church* for a good time. People consider this as a church, the Native American Church. This is the reason why I am doing this. [Several sentences were lost on the recording.] I felt very bad about my daughter's death. I didn't want people to see me that way. But this is the last meeting for my daughter. Maybe next year we will remember her. I am sure happy I could do that. I have come this far. They were real difficult times. I have come this far.]"

The fireman made this talk before praying with the midnight smoke. "I was in the service, and I had to get emergency leave when my sister died. It has been four years now. Our family is real close, you know. We never quarrel, or leave each other or anything. We always stick together. We are a real close family. Then no one could talk to my dad. I tried, but my mom talked to him that time. Our dad wasn't able at that time, so if it came to running a meeting, it was up to us. It was too much for him. His mind couldn't take it. My sisters tried their best to talk to him. The Native American Church is the only way we know how. We were brought up this way. Ever since I was a little kid, it was the Native American Church. This is the way I was brought up. The only way I know. Praying at midnight is the only way I know how.

"We talked about it, that we are going to have a memorial meeting and all this. So my dad said okay. My dad said that it was hard for two years. Everything is back to normal. My dad is working. Everything is completed for us now. We have a good home, and everybody is happy now. It is like it used to be. We come a long way now to this meeting. It took money and travel. [A few sentences were missed.] Every year we had the memorial, I wanted to be here. I was here even though I thought I wasn't going to make it. But I always made it. Francis, thank you for coming. John, I haven't seen you for a long time. Fr. Steinmetz, thank you for coming over and taking this meeting in. My uncle and aunt, I am glad you could make it. Brother Louie, you came over and helped me out in putting up the tipi. You really helped out. I want to thank you. That's about all I have to say now."

The fireman then prayed in Lakota in a low voice while he smoked the ceremonial cigarette and then passed it to the main drummer, the cedar man, and the roadman, who finished it and laid the butt against the altar.

After the water was passed around, the roadman said: "We will sing now, and while you are singing, we will heat up the tea. You will take your drumsticks and your feathers and you will cedar them." The roadman's wife made this comment while someone was preparing to go outside: "Before you go outside, this young lady here would like to be allowed a little time. She has some cedar of her own. She wishes to place this on the fireplace to say a prayer. She wishes to make a silent prayer, so if you give her a little time, she wants to do this. She is from Topeka, Kansas." This was done.

During the course of the singing, a man stopped the staff and made these remarks. "(At one time I was a healthy and able man. Now I have heart trouble. At this time when things bother me, it seems to be a little worse. When I was about to leave for this meeting, I was leaving my little daughters. I have some small daughters and a small niece. And also my mother is in a wheelchair at home. A lot of my neighbors living around there have a lot of money. They get paid their lease payments and there is drinking going on around there. So I want you to remember my family and say prayers for them. Before I leave here, I want to mention to you that I do have heart trouble and I am worried. That is why I am leaving this meeting and I want you to remember me in your prayers. This is the only place that I am at peace. When I eat this medicine, my heart feels better. That is what I want to tell you.)"

The singing continued. Later it was interrupted by the roadman's wife. "(I am going to take this food outside. I am taking this food outside for an offering. I am offering it to the red man in the Lakota way. We are putting this food out there for gratitude because we are thanking God for all that He has given us. When we put this food out there, we will receive food again and more food. When we do this we remember *Jesus* when He was on the cross. As we take this food out, it will be for our spirits. When we put this food out, some people are afraid of this, about feeding the spirits. They are afraid of doing this. But this is going to do us good if we do it this way. By doing this, those of us who are without jobs, it will be possible that you will receive work.)"

She then took the spiritual food out to bury it in the ground near the tipi. After she returned, the roadman stopped the staff to announce the main smoke: "There is a time that the sponsors of the meeting have the main smoke, and it is at that time now. The sponsor is given the main smoke, and she prays while the singing continues." So his wife prayed in a low tone while the singing continued.

The staff was stopped one more time before the morning water call for a man to say the following. "(I want to thank God the Father for bringing us through this night and taking us to a new day. And I want to thank God for the earth and all that He does on this earth and that our sorrow will be light, those of us who are in sorrow. And I ask God to protect and to take care of all these common men. In the near future some common men are going to offer prayers at the Crazy Horse Monument at Custer, South Dakota. At that time there will be the face of an Indian on that mountain [being presently carved]. And we pray that this will turn out good and it will be a blessing from God. We pray that the heads of households will be healthy and bodily able to take care of their homes and families. We pray that You will take care of our daughters-in-law, also anybody in mourning. We want God to watch over them at this hour and at this time. I want to ask people to pray for me here at this time. Some of you know that I work up there on the hill [i.e., at the hospital]. There, where I work, some half-breeds are against me. This woman that I am married to, she was brought up in a good way. And my in-laws over there heard a lot of talk and they felt bad about this whole thing. I am a minister, and I carry my Bible with me at all times. I know that I make quite a few mistakes, but I am still here at this time and place, and I want to pray, and I do know that the half-breeds are against me. This will be all I have to say.)"

The singing continued without any interruptions until the morning water time. The roadman's wife brought in the water and the three other ceremonial breakfast foods (meat, corn, and fruit) and made the following talk. "Before I pray, I want to thank each and every one of you for coming for this blessing. I sure like the singing, and I sure like the medicine, and I sure like to sing, too. But last night I was busy and I was working. I want you people to eat good this morning. I wanted you to have a good meeting, so I stayed out and got everything ready. Just as I came in, my boy was singing. When there is a meeting, I like to be there and stay the whole night. But still I want to thank each and every one of you who prayed for me and my family. I want to thank the woman who came all the way over here from Washington [State] and I want her to know that this is the last meeting for my daughter. Sometimes we pray from our hearts and sometimes it seems I hate to say good by to her [crying]. It seems like we keep trying to hang on to her. It seems like I want to pray. I thank each and every one of you for praying for my family. And I would like to pray in my own language and pray to the Almighty.

"(God the Father, I want to pray and I want to talk to You. I want to pray that You will watch over my family and my children. I want to pray that You will bless these ministers. That way we will pray and we will all pray together. I want to pray that there will be no hardship. I want to pray that those of us who are in mourning will have a blessing. God, I want to pray that everything in the future will be for the good. I want to pray for my daughter. Four years ago I prayed this way. I want to pray for my aunt, and I want God to take care of her. And one day we will all be together. I want to ask God to take care of my family and that there will be no more hardship. We want to remember God and pray together.

"We want to pray that all things and everything will be better for all the people and the *Native American Church*. I pray that all the Lakota people will be together. I want my sister to have a good home. As we live from day to day, You will have pity on the Lakota people. You will help the Lakota people. As I pray to God and this is happening, I want to be good. I pray, God, that the people will be happy and that we will love one another. And I pray that You will help my son. I pray that he will have a good home. All his life he has lived a man's life. I also pray that You will take care of my grandchildren and my husband. And I pray that You will take care of my daughter-in-law and keep her safe.

"I also pray that God will take care of Francis Richards. I pray that You will always keep him safe and protect him. I pray that You will take care of my uncles and grandchildren. I want you to take care of Josephine and also John. I want You to take care of my daughter-in-law and take care of my grandchildren. O God the Father, I want You to take care of my sons-in-law. I pray that they will have a good home and get an education. I pray that just in a matter of time, just in a few days, that You will take care of my home and watch over us. There is a young man who sometimes stays at my home. There were a lot of things that happened to him while he was here. You will watch over him. I pray that You will take care of my son and that You will always protect him. I pray almost every day, and I pray that You will watch my brother-in-law. I want to pray this way [crying]. I pray that some day I will be with my mother and that I will see my brother and . . . [a series of names]. God give them help.

"God bless this altar. I want You to watch over my mother-in-law and give her good health. I want You to watch the *State of South Dakota*. I want to ask You to give good health to all the people who are here this morning. I want You to watch over those in-laws of mine in the *State of Wyoming*. At this hour I want You to give them good health, my daughters-in-law and my sons-in-law. I want You to have pity on them. And I want You to watch over the children, my son's child. I want You to watch my daughter-in-law and I want You to protect her wherever she travels, on the highways or wherever. God, I want You to watch over my son when he prays here. And these people who are here now, I want You to have pity on them. And I also want You to have pity on my mother. God the Father, in the Name of *Jesus*, I thank you.)"

The ceremonial breakfast followed.

This meeting verified the Jungian analysis John Laney made of a Peyote meeting he attended:

The peyote meeting, which is at once intensely individual and intensively collective . . . [creates] in the presence of a living symbol, a tremendous charge of libido. . . . It teaches just as reflection upon the meaning of dreams and active imagination teaches, and as the consideration of one's behavior and attitudes teaches. The teaching may be a creative process, e.g., a song that is "caught"; it may provide a person with an understanding of his grief or his illness. . . . On the other hand, peyote also teaches collectively. It teaches the peyote ethic: kinship, brotherhood, moral reponsibility. The peyoter searches for an understanding of those things as personal and individual realizations. Throughout, there is an absolute conviction that we do not invent what we learn and know, that those things come from God through peyote. In psychological terms, this means an appreciation of the unconsious not only as the source of our collective values, but also as an individual wellspring of understanding within each of us (1971:128–29).

3

THE BODY OF CHRIST
INDEPENDENT CHURCH

The Body of Christ is a small independent church that broke off from the traditional Christian churches. Members are typical Pentecostals who conduct prayer meetings including preaching, singing, clapping hands, spontaneous prayer, witnessing, and the laying on of hands for healing. Eugene Rowland, the principal minister, and Garfield Good Plume tell its history and beliefs.

HISTORY AND BELIEFS

Eugene Rowland gives us our first information. "Eddie Rich from the Rosebud Reservation came to Pine Ridge in 1958 to preach Christ. He had a vision while fasting on a hill that Christ was calling him towards Pine Ridge. I was not ready to listen to him then. I had been in the service in Japan when the Korean War broke out. Our duty was extended and we were the first ones to go to Korea. After about a month, I was captured by the Communists, who forced us to march through the mountains in winter during the month of December about 350 miles to the border of China. Many soldiers died in this march. In the months that followed, the camp swelled to over 3,000. We ate once a day. We were not clothed for the cold weather. Only about 500 survived the ordeal. Some died of malnutrition, the cold, and disease. The Communists tried to brainwash me and told me there was no God, but they did not succeed. I prayed and promised the Lord that if I survived, I would serve Him in some capacity.

"When I got back to Pine Ridge, I forgot about the promise and started to drink. When Eddie Rich talked to me the first time in 1958, I still didn't listen. I then started to think about it. I was a Catholic, but in order to become a preacher, one had to be educated. I didn't get beyond the sixth grade. And so when Rich came back in 1959, I decided to become a preacher in his church. Rich got a charter, studied the Bible, and began to give teachings about Christ. We went into Canada and North Dakota, and we have churches there. The service consists of what the Lord wants us to do that particular night. Sometimes the healing doesn't take place right away, but gradually—the next day or later. Our Church is based on Acts 3:19, 'Therefore repent and turn to God.' Therefore, we have no infant baptism. But the Lord directs the meetings. My wife was sick with gallstones, and the doctor said she would have to be operated on. So she went to one of our services, and we laid hands on her and prayed, and she felt better. The next day at the hospital, the doctors X-rayed her seven times and were unable to find anything. That was a miracle healing. At another meeting we prayed for a young woman with a goiter on her neck. The growth went down right before our eyes.

"The American Indian Movement is telling people that Christianity is a white man's religion and that the Indian people should go back to their Indian religion. Sometimes when I preach, people mock me and make fun of me. Some Indian people still believe in yuwipi meetings and talking to the spirits, which is wrong, and Christ doesn't want it."

Garfield Good Plume gives us some more details. "Rich was a Congregational minister. His father, Fred Ashly, was a prominent yuwipi man, and he was his helper. However, Rich fasted in the Black Hills and saw a vision that the destruction of Jerusalem meant the destruction of yuwipi as a sign of Christ's coming. At this conversion he turned his back on the old ways and gave himself to Christ. His father, Fred Ashly, asked Rich to take over his yuwipi practice. But Rich believed it was the work of the devil. He believed that the devil could speak even through the voices of loved ones. After his conversion, his father said that if Rich left the yuwipi religion, the yuwipi spirits would kill himself. But the father died a natural death. Although Rich rejected the Pipe for his own church, he never criticized anyone for using it in non-yuwipi ceremonies. However, he was also dissatisfied with the Congregational Church becuase he saw discrimination against the Indians, and he decided to preach the "full Gospel" himself. His church was Indian in membership, language, and sharing food.

"Rich preached baptism in spirit and water as Christ told Nicodemus in the Gospel of John. They baptized in the Name of Jesus in Acts 2:38. They do this by immersion in Wolf Creek, which is near the church building. Rich also taught that the Indian people are part of the lost tribe of Israel. Rich's service followed a Pentecostal pattern: clapping of hands, spiritual songs similar to Negro religions. Rich attended a service of A. Allen, a Pentecostal minister from California, which was being conducted in Miracle Valley, Arizona. Rich went down there after his fast. Rich taught that the people must be in the twentieth-century age, have music that they enjoy. He used bread and grape juice in the service, reciting the words of institution from Matthew and St. Paul and explaining them. The Pentecostal music was derived from Arizona. Rich claimed that he found his Bible in a trash pile by accident. Rich believed in prophecy, tongues, and interpretation of tongues based on the Scriptural account of Miriam, Aaron's sister.

"Divine healings took place during his service. An arthritic man who has been in a wheelchair for eighteen years was healed. He also cast out devils. He prayed over people. In one case he asked a man to touch his jacket, like the woman who touched the hem of Christ's cloak in the Gospel. It is reported that he raised a person from the dead in Norris, South Dakota. A full-blood Indian with only a third-grade education was able to read in the English language.

"Visions occur in church services. They see clouds, a dove, and feel a rushing wind. This is both experience of an individual and the whole congregation. Sometimes members fast on a hill from three to seven days to solve a problem, to get over sickness, or to see visions. They don't tell their visions, since the Bible says that we should not take advantage of them. The visions of men and animals are an illusion which precedes the trance of angels and spiritual things, such as a Bible verse or prophecies. Just as the devil tempted Christ in the desert, so a man fasting is tempted by the devil in the first visions of men and animals. In one case, a coyote came and talked to a man. The devil was trying to scare him. At another time two prophets talked with each other, one at Wolf Creek and the other at Cherry

Creek on the Cheyenne River Reservation, many miles north. However, there is need to discern false prophecies. The minister does this from the Bible.

"A meeting consists of prayers, testimonials, song requests and singing, preaching by either the minister or someone filled with the Spirit (spiritual refilling if one is low in the spirit or slothful), laying on of hands and anointing with oil as James did in Acts. Rich instructed people to tell what God did for them in order to get His blessings, as well as to make an offering, even a penny. The baptism of water is only for adults fourteen years or older. There is a child blessing for those who are younger than that, after Christ being presented in the temple and Jesus having little children come to Him. Revivals are important in the Body of Christ Church. They go to other reservations as far as Canada. They also have revivals right at Wolf Creek."

There are a number of Lakota who preach conversion to Christ and sing gospel songs with guitar accompaniment at wakes and memorial dinners. Although the presence of the Body of Christ Church has encouraged this type of Pentecostal activity, these ministers are not necessarily associated with the Wolf Creek group. I met Pedro, Rowland's brother, singing gospel songs at a memorial dinner. He told me he was an independent, not a member of the Body of Christ Church, although he goes to Wolf Creek to help them at times. Add to this the divisions within the Church (Good Plume claims he has started his own church, called the Church of the Holy Ghost), and we see how difficult it is to determine to what extent the Body of Christ Church at Wolf Creek has extended its activity to other parts of the reservation.

TESTIMONY OF THE PRINCIPAL MINISTER

Better than any discussion about the Body of Christ is the personal witness of Eugene Rowland, delivered at one of the church services. It contains important insights.

"I will give my testimony before we begin this meeting. At one time it seemed I did not know the Lord. I did not know how to pray. One day I was a soldier in North Korea. And I was captured by the Communists. In 1950, February 18, I was a prisoner for three years. Behind the Bamboo Curtain I was there. During that time all I knew was the Lord's Prayer and the Hail Mary. That's all I knew. All my relatives are strong Catholics. My great-grandfather was in the battle at Custer's last stand. I was baptized a Catholic.

"When I was in Korea, I was captured and my outfit was annihilated. We were behind enemy lines. We tried to get back to our lines, and there was no way. We marched thirty-five miles to the north. Then in a few days they took us forty more miles behind the Bamboo Curtain. And now I know there is an anti-Christ. There is an anti-Christ on the reservation, in the U.S., in the schools, in the churches. This I know: there is an anti-Christ. The Lord has given me a revelation. He has given me dreams, visions when I was in the Communist concentration camp. I walked three hundred miles towards the north when the Communists captured us. And we walked all the way, and the Lord gave me a vision. And the Bible says where there is no vision, the people will perish. There is no vision among our people on the reservation. This is what I see: that there is no vision here. There is violence, jealously, crime, murder, adultery, fornication. This is what is happening on our reservations. There is no one to go out and teach and preach to them, to our people. And the Lord had given me this vision to talk to our people.

"I had a dream in the concentration camp. The dream was as I looked down the valley, our people were marching towards a hill. And I could see our people walking, riding horseback, and in old-time wagons. Some kids were walking. And as I looked towards the hill, I saw the cross and my grandfather, Chief Red Cloud, and my aunt in my dream. He had a costume on, his Indian costume, a war bonnet. That is what I saw in the dream. Towards the hill I saw a cross. And here in the Bible it says Jesus was crucified on Calvary hill. And he was buried on the third day, and He arose again. Before He went into heaven, He told His apostles: 'I am going to send the Paraclete back in my Name.' And we receive the Spirit. He is that Spirit that dwells in the midst of us. The Bible says where two or three are gathered in my Name, there I am.

"I went through that death march in 1950 right during December. Many soldiers were killed, but the hand of the Lord was upon me. The only prayer that saved me was the Lord's Prayer. In the battlefield the enemy was killing us all around. I was saying the Lord's Prayer. They were hitting us all around pretty hard. And the 1st Calvary Di-

vision, the 8th Battalion, was wiped out, and this is when I found
the Lord. This is when He had His hand upon me. And I was ready
to die. I was scared. I didn't know what to do. All my friends were
killed all around me. This is when I knelt down and prayed. I said the
Lord's Prayer. This I knew. I prayed: 'Abba God,' and this is when the
Spirit of the Lord rested upon me. And all fear went out. He cast out
the fear of death. This is when joy and peace came into my heart. I
felt the presence of God. When I was in the concentration camp, I
prayed day and night. Through the death march, I prayed. Soldiers
were killed right and left. This is when the Lord led me all the way.
It is a great testimony I will never forget, the testimony that the Lord
was with me always. He had His hands upon me. He took care of me.
So when I was in that Communist concentration camp, they told us
that there was no God. The Communist doctrine was taught. Many
of them were brainwashed, the ones that didn't pray, but I stayed with
the Lord all the way. And I want you to know I wasn't brainwashed
the Communist way. God led me all the way.

"So, when I came back, I could do nothing because I didn't have
enough education to do something in the Catholic Church. I didn't
have enough education to be a servant of God, a priest or anything
like that. So, I put everything down and started drinking and running
around. But one day a man came and introduced me to Jesus, to the
Gospels, the Bible. And in the Bible I read that Jesus was walking
along the shores of Galilee and he met fishermen. He said to them:
'Follow me and I will make you fishers of men.' The fishermen were
ignorant and unlearned. This is what I am, ignorant and unlearned.
But the Lord has given me wisdom, knowledge, understanding, revelations, dreams, visions because He is so merciful. He is a great God
that we are serving today. He is a God that answers prayers. He is a
God that died for us on the cross, for you and me. After that, I knew
I did not have to be educated to serve God in the world. The Bible
said that His message shall be preached in all the world, to all nations until the end of time. And we agree that the end of time is near.
The reason we preach the end of time is near is because there is no
vision, and the Bible says where there is no vision, the people shall
perish. And that is why I see in the life of my people that there is
no vision. They are perishing. They practice rape. It is up to us to
walk out and preach to our people. This is the Christian message we

have for the world. I almost died many times back in the concentration camp. The Lord put me there for a reason, for a purpose, that I might see and learn the vision of the anti-Christ.

"The Lord brought me out for a purpose, a testimony. This is why I am standing here preaching to my people. I believe the Lord is coming back soon, according to the Bible. He said: 'I am the Alpha and the Omega, the Beginning and the End.' And Jesus comes, the Almighty, the Lord of hosts. Amen. He is the God of Moses, of Isaac, of Jacob. He is the God of the world. He has called up Moses in the wilderness. He led God's people to cross the Red Sea. When he raised up the rod, the Red Sea split wide open. God's people walked across the Red Sea on dry land. During the day he directed the people by a cloud and at nighttime by fire. This is the vision the Lord has given us. It is that we should serve God every day, not only on Sunday, but every day. We are teaching the people to follow the Lord, to take up His cross and follow Him daily. He said that I am the Light of the world. He who follows Me shall not walk in darkness. 'I am the Light of the world.' These are the very words that Jesus said. This is the great testimony I have for the Lord. He brought me out of the bondage from Egypt. I was in captivity, but He brought me out from Egypt and he brought me to the Promised Land. Moses brought the people to the Promised Land. The Lord let him see the Promised Land, and God took him upon that hill and showed him the Promised Land and he died. And Joshua took over and crossed over to the Promised Land. This is what we are doing, taking our people to the Promised Land.

"In the Bible it is written: 'Man shall not live on bread alone but on every word that proceeds from the mouth of God.' The word of God is the Bible. Jesus was born in Bethlehem. He was born in a manger. He was born where they kept animals. He wasn't born in a mansion or a palace. When Mary and Joseph came to Bethlehem, they said: 'Go to other places; there is no room for You.' Today there is no room in the hearts of the people. They don't want to accept the Lord. There is no room. Therefore, they went to the manger, and that's where Jesus was born. The wise men came with their gifts—gold, frankincense and myrrh. Gold represents Jesus Christ because He paid all. He has paid a price for you and me. Frankincense because He was crucified and He died for you and me. The myrrh was what Mary Magdalene poured on the feet of Jesus, on his head and feet, and wiped them with her hair. She was a whore woman. She was a sinner. Yet, Jesus accepted her. This is why we are preaching to our Indian people that they may know that there is a great God and we can live forever into eternity.

"But there is eternal damnation also, the hellfire. But the Lord has brought me out, hand in hand, across the Red Sea through dry land. He walked through the wilderness for forty years. They went to Mount Sinai, where God spoke to Moses. He fasted forty days and forty nights, and God gave him the Ten Commandments. As Moses was up there talking to God, the people were playing around. They were making gods of gold. The great wrath of God came upon them. When the flood came, God's wrath came upon the people of this world. He will destroy the world by fire, since they were worshipping idols. The idols today that people are worshipping—the Sun Dancers are worshipping the sun. There is a word in Deuteronomy; I cannot worship the sun. People are idolatrous—the witchcraft. We are against witchcraft. This means Sun Dance and yuwipi. These are the sorcerers. These are an abomination to God. It is a fearful thing to be caught in the hands of the living God. God's wrath will come upon the people as it did in those days. People were playing around. They were drinking; they were marrying and giving in marriage; they were committing fornication.

"Today we can see that. Today the Son of Man is coming. He is coming after a Church without spot, without wrinkle, without blemish, and we are the Church. We are the true Church because Jesus said that we are the temples of the living God. Amen. The great and wonderful testimony the Lord has given me. We believe that Jesus Christ is the way, the truth, and the life. 'No man comes to the Father but by Me,' He says. Praise God. He did not say this is a true Church, but Jesus said, 'I am the way,' which is the Gospel to the kingdom, the Gospel which is the good tidings, the Bible which is the Gospel. Amen. He said that when you see the abomination, any desolation foretold by Daniel the prophet, He said stand in a holy place. He didn't say stand in a certain church with a checkbook. He said stand in a holy place. Where is the holy place? When you give yourself all to God and keep His commandments, this is the holy place. When you obey God's commandments, the Ten Commandments which He has brought down from Mount Sinai, that is why we are serving the

Lord today. God is terrible. God is a just God. God is a merciful God. This is why we are serving a great God, the Almighty. This is why 'I am the First and the Last, I am the Beginning and the End.' He says: 'which is, which was, and which is to come.' Almighty, the Lord of hosts.

"The gross conditions which we see today on our reservations— hatred, jealousy, anger, lust, malice, murder, fornication, adultery. There is a spiritual adultery, serving other gods (Amen), serving the Peace Pipe, just like they did when Moses was up on Mount Sinai, they made a god of gold. They made a calf of gold. The Indian people had a calf, the Peace Pipe, the calf—they are worshipping that. And it is an abomination unto God that we are serving other gods. There is only one God, who created heaven and earth, which is the one God Almighty. He is the only One. That is why it is a terrible thing to fall unto the hands of the living God. Praise God. He is a terrible God. In the last days He will destroy again (Amen). His great glory will shake the earth, will shake the heavens. He will shake the seas. Every creature on this earth in the waters will flee the presence of God. Praise God. While we are preaching, we will pray for our Indian people that they may live. Amen. The exhortation that the Lord has given us: walk along the straight and narrow path. Broad is the way that leads to destruction and death. People upon this earth are walking this broad way that enters unto death. Praise God. He is the great God. We can perceive the Spirit of His. It is moving upon us. His Spirit will be upon all flesh. Amen. Praise God.

"This great testimony I have, I can't forget. I tell it over and over. People are tired of hearing this testimony, but yet, God has put that in my mind so that I will never forget it. Because the Lord put my body in a Communist country behind the Bamboo Curtain that I might see, that I might know what is going to take place, what will come to pass, how we live, what the Communists will do. You know China is one of the biggest countries in the world, 600 million strong. Part of India is Communist; that is the second biggest country in the world. The third is Russia. And these are anti-Christ. In the Bible it tells us, in the Book of Revelations, the man that is not upright, the mark of this man is six, six, six [666], the mark of the beast. His head is fine gold; his arms and breasts are silver; his belly and thighs are brass; his legs are iron; his feet are iron and clay. We see the mark of the beast already (Yes). In Revelations what God has given us is coming to pass today. In the world today man is different; the people are different. Many years ago they had the love of God. But today it is different. This is the scene in the world. The stars will fall from heaven, and the waters will turn into blood. All this we will see. We know the great God. The wrath of God is coming upon us. Amen. Amen. This is why we should have the fear of God, not men. Amen. Praise God."

4

THE OGLALA LAKOTA
RELIGIOUS IDENTITY

In searching for an approach to understand the meaning of the Pipe, Bible, and Peyote among the Oglala Lakota, I discovered that, although the generalizations contained in the various theories of acculturation contain some valuable insights, they were of no value as a comprehensive model (cf. Dozier 1962; Linton 1943; Voget 1956; Wallace 1956). Instead, I looked to see the most important dynamic of their religious activity. What clearly stood out was the search for and acceptance of Lakota identity.

Erikson had discussed the place of identity among the Oglala Lakota:

It is said that when the buffalo died, the Sioux died, ethnically and spiritually. The buffalo's body had provided not only food and material for clothing, covering and shelter, but such utilities as bags and boats, strings for bows and for sewing, cups and spoons. Medicine and ornaments were made of buffalo parts; his droppings, sun dried, served as fuel in winter. Societies and season, ceremonies and dances, mythology and children's play extolled his name and image" (1945:320).

This observation led many to predict the complete demise of Lakota culture and tradition. However, Erikson reminds us that "in the remnants of the Sioux Indian's identity, prehistoric past is a powerful psychological reality" (1946:361).

THE NATURE OF THIS IDENTITY

To have a proper understanding of this identity, it is necessary to recognize that although the prehistoric past persists on a deep psychological level, it is still modified by contemporary influences. In other words, Lakota identity is not static but is itself changing from the process of defending its own identity in a rapidly changing environment. Lakota identity, therefore, is modern and complex despite the fanciful desire of some anthropologists that it remain in a "pure native state."

Hallowell, for example, emphasizes the importance of the primal influence among the Ojibwa in claiming that

a persistent core of psychological constellations, aboriginal in nature . . . is clearly discernable through all levels of acculturation yet studied. For this reason all the Ojibwa referred to are still Indians in a psychological sense, whatever clothes they wear, whatever their occupation, whether they speak English or not, and regardless of race mixture. While, culturally speaking, they appear more and more like whites at "higher" levels of acculturation, there is no evidence at all for a basic psychological shift in a parallel direction. . . . From a psychological point of view they are not *acculturated enough*, in the sense that, while contact with the version of Western civilization available has enabled them to acquire innumerable culture traits, so far at least it has not provided the psychological means that might implement a satisfactory basis for personal adjustment (1952: 110, 112).

However, Bernard James draws attention to the contemporary modifications by criticizing Hallowell's evaluation for giving too much attention to unimportant surviving remnants of Ojibwa culture and thereby distracting him from more important contemporary social functions. James, nonetheless, points out that Hallowell himself modified his position on the psychological persistence of Ojibwa values: "the fact of psychological continuity must not be taken to imply that no modifications in the psychic structure . . . has taken place. The nature of these modifications will direct attention to what is perhaps the most important conclusion that can be drawn from our data" (Hallowell 1955:351, quoted in James 1970:437). James claims that because these modifications have been neglected, "the persistency

theory is a simplistic notion, at least as it has thus far been stated"
(1970:438).

It is nonsense to try to understand modern personality without taking
into account modern cultural factors as major determinants. The formation of reservation personality has appeared baffling and elusive in the
Ojibwa case because we have relied too heavily on the inferences drawn
from projective methods, from analysis, historical reconstruction, and so
on, instead of placing proper weight on the point-blank probities of direct
observation. . . . But there is nothing inherently unique about the formation of personality on the reservations. It is formed there in the same
way that it is formed anywhere else (James 1970:439, 440).

Without attempting to settle this dispute, we should note that actually psychological persistence and acculturational modifications must
be recognized as aspects of identity, as examples can be cited for
both. We will discover that these same issues are involved with the
Lakota as we examine this identity from within and from without.

Within this identity there are three religious traditions — symbolized by the Pipe, the Bible, and Peyote — resulting in six religious
groups, with the interdynamic taking place between them. These
groups will be treated in the model of Lakota religious identity.

Another complexity from within is the tension between the full-
blood and the mixed-blood. Since there are very few racial full-bloods
left, the distinction between the sociological full-blood and mixed-
blood is of greater importance (MacGregor 1946:25). The tension between these two groups produces a confrontation in cultural values:
sharing vs. accumulation, Indian time (taking off for celebrations) vs.
white man's time (punctuality and regularity), extended family vs.
nuclear family, political consensus vs. majority vote, tribal owner-
ship of land vs. allotment. This tension has been the source of most
of the tribal politics on the reservation.

From my experience on the Pine Ridge Reservation, I believe that
some of the mixed-bloods have acquired sufficient acculturation for
a satisfactory personal adjustment without losing their Indian identity.
These are the ones who are anti–American Indian Movement, pro–
Tribal Government, and generally pro–Bureau of Indians Affairs. However, other mixed-bloods have not achieved this degree of accultura-

tion; that explains why, due in part to the influence of AIM, some mixed-bloods are discovering, or attempting to discover, their Lakota identity—moving away from the values of the white man and becoming sociological full-bloods. But this reverse acculturation is frequently more difficult than anticipated. Although they are insufficiently acculturated for a satisfactory adjustment in white society, they are sufficiently acculturated to make the return to full-blood values difficult, a fact that brings out the contemporary modifications rather than the psychological persistence. One full-blood told me that a few years ago this group was ashamed of being Indian and now they are ashamed of being white.

There is a complexity of the Lakota identity from without, the first factor being the relation between Lakota and pan-Indian identities. Hazel Hertzberg (1971), James Howard (1955), W. W. Newcomb, Jr. (1956), Margaret Sanford (1971), and Robert Thomas (1965) have useful treatments of pan-Indianism. However, we will examine more specifically its relation to the Lakota identity. Royal B. Hassrick wrote that "the Sioux had such faith in their national destiny that they haughtily dominated the heartland of the Northern Plains for nearly a century. . . . They were proud of their superiority and were vigilant in defending it" (1964:57). Let us examine the acculturation that has taken place in this identity as it has unfolded in history.

The use of the Pipe as a means of peace is probably the first pan-Indian movement among the North American Indians. Even the Sioux formed some alliances with other tribes, which gave them a sense of identity beyond themselves. Densmore brings out in a dramatic way the power of the Pipe in overcoming deep animosities in a vivid description of a peace council between the Chippewa, or Ojibwa, and the Sioux (1913:127–29). The Sun Dance also brought together different tribes, according to Bushotter. He states that "messages were sent to all the neighboring tribes, i.e., the Omaha, Pawnee Loup, Cheyenne, Cree, Hidatsa, Nez Perce, Winnebago, Yankton, and Santee. . . . The visitors from the different nations begin to come together in the spring, each visiting tribe forming its separate camp. Though some of the visitors were hereditary enemies, it matters not during the sun-dance; they visit one another, they shake hands and form alliances" (Dorsey:1894:452).

The Ghost Dance was another pan-Indian movement. The tree in the center and the woman standing there with the Pipe were Lakota adaptations from the Sun Dance (Mooney 1896: 915). However, as Powers indicates, the Ghost Dance was foreign to Oglala religious ideology: "Although the ghost dance was prematurely aborted with the massacre at Wounded Knee, it is unlikely that it would have survived much longer in its particular form" (1977:202). Here we see an unsuccessful interaction between Lakota and pan-Indian identity.

The next pan-Indian movement was Peyote, which followed the Ghost Dance by only fourteen years on the Pine Ridge Reservation. It should be noted in passing that Omer Stewart is critical of any causal relation between the spread of Peyote and the Ghost Dance (1972). From one viewpoint, what later became the Native American Church was very successful on the reservation. The Lakota put their own traditional stamp on the Half Moon fireplace in Red Bear's use of the Pipe at the time of origin on the reservation and throughout the years with Hawkins, Gap, and now Solomon Red Bear, Jr., the great-grandson of the first Red Bear. In addition, the four smokes with the ceremonial cigarette standing for the Pipe, the four water calls, the roadman going out of the tipi to pray in the four directions—all show how elements of the Half Moon fireplace had a strong continuity with traditional Lakota identity. The result is that the Native American Church acquired a Lakota identity without losing its pan-Indian one. But this very presence of a strong traditional identity has also influenced most Lakota to be satisfied with their Lakota religion. In a 1968 Baseline Study among those surveyed, only 7.5 percent said that they had attended Peyote meetings (10 percent full-bloods and 6 percent mixed-bloods) and only 0.8 percent claimed the Native American Church as their primary religious affiliation (Pine Ridge Research Bulletin 1969:5). I would estimate that the active members on the reservation never exceeded 350 in number.

Social dancing, called powwow celebrations, are events which bring many different tribes together. Although not religious, these events bring a sense of pan-Indianism to more tribes throughout the country than any other movement or activity.

The most recent pan-Indian movement is the American Indian Movement [AIM]. It is one that brings conflict and tension. These include national goals vs. reservation ones, anti-Christian vs. Christian attitudes in Lakota religion, tribal sovereignty vs. tribal government, the Sun Dance as a pan-Indian ceremony vs. a tribal one, and the deepening of full-blood and mixed-blood conflicts. Occupying Wounded Knee in 1973 for 71 days may have been good for national goals but, in my opinion, it lost the tribal election for Russell Means, one of the Lakota AIM leaders. AIM was an outside force called in to remove the mixed-blood Tribal President and even to abolish the entire system of Tribal Government. There is also confrontation between AIM members and the established medicine men over the presence of Christianity in traditional Lakota religion, which will be developed below. The presence of AIM has produced conflict within the Lakota identity which must be worked out in the years to come. Despite this, the Lakota have influenced AIM through the Pipe and the Sun Dance. I think that the Sacred Pipe as a religious symbol and the Sun Dance as a religious ceremony have regained their importance as a source of pan-Indian unity, an importance which may at one time have been eclipsed by Peyote.

Howard's study of pan-Indianism among the Oklahoma tribes helps our understanding. According to him, pan-Indianism among these tribes resulted from the loss of tribal identity and a failure to achieve sufficient acculturation into white society: "rather than becoming nondistinctive members of the dominant culture, many Indians have instead become members of a super tribal culture which we term pan-Indian" (1955:215). The main social expression of this new identity was the powwow and the main religious one was Peyote. Howard concludes: "Pan-Indianism is, in my opinion, one of the final stages of progressive acculturation, just prior to complete assimilation. It may be explained as a final attempt to preserve aboriginal culture patterns through intertribal unity" (1955:220). On the Pine Ridge Reservation, some Lakota fear AIM may be a force weakening the strong tribal identity rather than a help in preserving it due to an overemphasis on pan-Indianism and nativism.

The second complexity from without comes from the Lakota relating to the white man's world. Powers correctly states that there is a continuum between the Lakota and the white man's world. He comments:

The majority of the people living in the mid range move back and forth along the continuum situationally. At the white man's end of the scale they observe technology and change. But at the Oglala end they see ideology and continuity. There they find a connection with the past expressed in the concept of *wakan*, that which is sacred, but also that which is old. The continuity extends back into time long before the European arrived. Those who wish to be part of this continuous stream will move towards the Oglala end, consciously or unconsciously. Sometimes it is mere curiosity which brings an Oglala back to his traditions; sometimes it is illness of a sort, a symbolic illness for which no medical practitioner has a remedy at the white man's end of the continuum (1977: 205–6).

I quote this partly because it expresses so beautifully the Lakota identity which is the basis of their religious life, but also to point out an oversimplification. Powers is also stressing the psychological persistence to the detriment of the acculturational modifications. There are times when a Lakota goes back to his end of the continuum and finds it lacking. The spirits involved in traditional Lakota religion today, as in the past, are at one time a source of strength and at another time one of fear. According to McGee, their "adoration expressed fear of the evil rather than love of the good" (1897:1840). And Mooney states that Black Coyote had to obey a voice "somewhat resembling the cry of an owl or the subdued bark of a dog, demanding" that he cut out seventy pieces of his flesh to appease "an overruling spirit" so that more of his children would not continue to die (1896:898). Another deficiency was the vague and unconvincing belief in life after death in the Lakota tradition, which was treated above. The Lakota Christian who believes in the Resurrection of Christ has a greater sense of continuity with his basic human needs and desires in the traditional Christian church on the white man's end of the continuum than he does in his own Lakota tradition. People famous in Indian religion, such as Black Elk and all the present-day medicine men, receive their Christian sacraments and burials. I think it is more correct to say that the Lakota identity, just like anyone else's, is frequently ambivalent—containing both feelings of continuity and discontinuity with basic human needs, of security and insecurity, of strength and fear.

And when a Lakota does go back to his end of the continuum, he does not always go back to a pure Lakota identity but to one that has been modified by Christianity. And when he selectively returns to the white man's end, he returns to a Christianity that has been modified by Lakota tradition, so that in fact the distance between the two ends becomes shorter. The Oglala Lakota identity is indeed complex, but it is the only solid foundation upon which their religious life can be based.

A MODEL OF OGLALA RELIGIOUS IDENTITY

The following model relates the mutual dynamics of the three religious traditions — represented by Pipe, Bible, and Peyote — which are a part of the contemporary Lakota identity. These three traditions result in six religious groups. *Group* is a general and perhaps vague word; here it is used in the sense of "an assembly of persons who are considered as one or acting as one" because a more appropriate word cannot be found. The American Indian Movement is considered a movement; the Body of Christ Church and Native American Church, Cross Fire fireplace, are definitely churches; the Half Moon fireplace can be considered a church but more vaguely than the Cross Fire; Ecumenist I and II are traditional Lakota people sharing a common attitude towards Christianity. In the field these groups have clearly determined boundaries even though they defy classifications.

These identities will be summarized here. However, they will become clearer in the discussion that follows.

The Pipe alone represents a Lakota identity as conceived primarily but not exclusively by AIM: that is, based upon traditional Lakota symbols having acquired a nativistic value.

The Bible alone represents a Lakota Christian identity as conceived by the Body of Christ Church: that is, based upon a rejection of Lakota religious symbols. This apparent contradiction will be treated below. The Bible alone does not represent the identity of the traditional Christian churches, since in this study this identity is associated with the Pipe or Peyote or both.

The Pipe and the Bible represent a unified Lakota Christian identity as conceived by those in the Ecumenist II, based upon Lakota religious symbols that have acquired a Christian value. The Ecumenist I group is considered an imperfect stage of the Ecumenist II one. Those in this position have a split Lakota/Christian identity, which results in

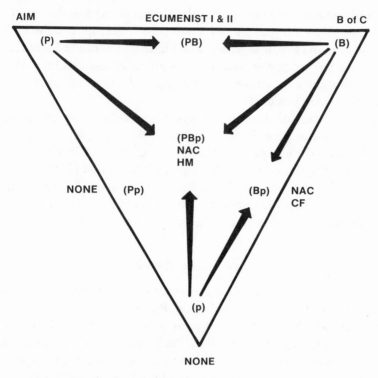

AIM = American Indian Movement
B of C = Body of Christ Independent Church
NAC, CF = Native American Church, Cross Fire Fireplace
NAC, HM = Native American Church, Half Moon Fireplace
(P) = Pipe; (B) = Bible; (p) = Peyote

their moving back and forth on a religious continuum between Lakota and Christian ends.

The Bible and Peyote together represent a unified Lakota Christian identity as conceived by the Native American Church, Cross Fire: that is, based upon Peyote's receiving an explicit Christian value, the Bible being placed upon the Peyote altar.

Pipe, Bible, and Peyote together represent a unified Lakota Christian identity as conceived by the Native American Church, Half Moon: that is, based upon Peyote's acquiring a new value through both the traditional Lakota and Christian religious symbols. (This is true even though the Bible itself is not brought into the meeting.)

Peyote would have represented the Lakota identity as conceived by the Half Moon without any association with the Pipe and the Bible.

The Pipe and Peyote together would have represented a Lakota identity as conceived by the same group without an association with the Bible. But since conditions are not verified, there are no religious groups in these positions.

The members of these six groups discover their own characteristic meanings in Pipe, Bible, and Peyote. For example, among these groups, with the exception of the Body of Christ, the Pipe has a common meaning shared by all (developed in the second chapter). These values will not be repeated here but only the ones characteristic of each group. These characteristic values could be considered as configurations in Ruth Benedict's meaning of the word (1936).

The American Indian Movement

One characteristic value of AIM is militancy. This is in keeping with Lakota tradition, as the Pipe was the center of the warrior societies. Wissler describes each society as having a Pipe bearer (1912). McGee states that the Sioux had a tomahawk Pipe that stood for either war or peace; this was part of the Sioux mentality (1897:172). Kroeber brings out the purely symbolic nature of these Pipes. The tomahawk Pipe of the eastern Indians was a metal hatchet with a bowl and a wooden handle which was also a stem; accordingly, the hatchet could be used either to chop or to smoke. The pipestone imitations of the Sioux could not be actually used to chop, so that this aspect was only symbolic (1948:480). We can recall the warlike associations with the Sun Dance. This part of the Lakota tradition, which was suppressed in the acceptance of passive resistance, is being revived today. On some occasions the Pipe is not the Peace Pipe but the war Pipe, uniting the Lakota in militant activity.

Another characteristic value is tribalism. One resolution of an International Treaty Council, held at Kyle, South Dakota, during the summer of 1978, was to "discourage whites from trying to take our religion, not understanding it, playing with our pipe and our sacred things, and trying to put on their own sun dances" (*Rapid City Journal* 1978). In this regard, we can recall the Lakota woman complaining of my presence at Green Grass during the Calf Pipe ceremony. This

expresses the AIM viewpoint that Lakota religion is to be shared
with no one outside the tribe. Although secrecy is a traditional aspect of Indian religion, AIM members' understanding of the Pipe involves a "new ethnicity," a concept discussed at the 1973 conference
of the American Ethnological Society: "one dominant theme in these
papers on identity would appear to be boundary maintenance, or, at
any rate, the need to define ethnic self always in the context of some
outside group" (Bennett 1975:6).

Tribal sovereignty is yet another characteristic value. AIM members claim that, according to treaty, the Oglala Nation has absolute
sovereignty. Another resolution of the International Council held at
Kyle was to "discourage immigration to our reservation." This claim
was dramatized during the occupation of Wounded Knee by declaring
the little hamlet a sovereign nation before the television cameras.
This declaration is similar to the Ghost Dance expectations of complete sovereignty. One young medicine man believes in tribal sovereignty but not by violence, since in some way God will give sovereignty to the Indian people. At the Sioux Treaty Hearings held in
Lincoln, Nebraska, during December of 1974, the AIM lawyers unsuc-
cessfully attempted to dismiss the criminal charges against some of
the participants in the Wounded Knee occupation on the grounds
that the U.S. Government did not have jurisdiction on the Pine Ridge
Reservation because of tribal sovereignty (Ortiz 1977: 13).

The Pipe is also a symbol of pan-Indianism. This was very notice-
able on the Longest Walk from San Francisco to Washington, D.C.,
participated in by a large number of tribes from all parts of the U.S.
The Pipe was carried on foot over three thousand miles — even through
snowstorms in the southwestern mountains. Here we see the Lakota
tradition of always carrying the Calf Pipe used. One Lakota commented
that if the march accomplished nothing practical in Washington, it
did bring many different tribes together in a common venture and
created a sense of solidarity. The Indians were also allowed to swear
on the Pipe instead of the Bible in the treaty hearings just mentioned
(Ortiz 1977:10). Since the Pipe was shared by many tribes from all over
the country, its pan-Indian identity was again prominent.[1]

Another characteristic value of the Pipe is an anti-acculturation
and anti-Christian one. Vine Deloria raises some legitimate questions concerning the relation between Indian religion and Christian-

ity (1973); Vernon Malon and Clinton Jesser discuss the conflict in values which took place between these two religious traditions among the Lakota (1959). However, AIM members reject any integration of Lakota and Christian traditions, a relationship described by Jorgensen and Clemmer as "that old will of the wisp 'acculturation through syncretism' at work. We are led to believe that the Indian religion is moving toward the real (Primitive) Christianity through the inevitable acculturation process" (1978:43). The error in this attitude is the attempt to keep a traditional Lakota religion static, forgetting that all traditions must be changing. For the mature adult, even enculturation involves cultural change, as is reflected in the definition: "Enculturation is the learning process by which man, throughout his life, acquires his own culture. . . . Thus enculturation in infancy (usually on an unconscious level) is a mechanism favoring cultural stability, whereas enculturation in the mature individual (involving conscious acceptance or rejection of new forms of behavior) is important for cultural change" (Encyclopedia Britannica 1974, Micropedia: 887)

The final characteristic value is nativism in Linton's sense as "any conscious organized attempt on the part of society's members to revive or perpetuate selected aspects of its culture" (1943:230). This is seen primarily in reviving what was lost. An appeal to the now defunct societies of the past (Wissler 1912; Blish 1926: 1934) as a source of the ethical values needed to live a true Lakota life today is an example of revivalistic tendency. Perhaps, AIM could be classified primarily as a revivalistic and secondarily as a perpetuative nativism. In my opinion, nativism is the most basic characteristic value, of which the other values are expressions.

The Body of Christ Independent Church

As we have seen, the Body of Christ is a small Pentecostal Christian Independent Church. Their fundamental interpretation of the Bible influences their concept of Lakota identity. They do not consider their church a white man's church, and yet they reject all traditional Lakota religious symbols as a means to true Lakota identity. We gain an insight into their understanding of Lakota identity, although expressed in terms of Indian identity, from a sermon which a visiting Kiowa minister from Oklahoma delivered in one of their services at Wolf Creek. (Parentheses indicate reactions from the congregation.)

"People try to say: 'Brother Keith, I'm an Indian,' but, brother, you better get rid of that Indian way. You better get rid of that Indian. (Applause.) And you better let the love of God begin to come into existence in a way as the Lord says: 'there is neither Jew nor Greek nor slave.' There is only the children of God. I am proud to be an Indian, but when I repent of my sins, when Jesus came with the Holy Ghost, I became proud of the fact that I am a son of God, that I had lost my identity, that Jesus took on the identity in my life. Sure, when I hear that old tom-tom beating, the old Indian inside me resurrects again, but I have to put him down—keep him under subjection and say 'no' because it is of the world. (Yes, O Jesus.) When I listen to my uncles singing Peyote songs in the Kiowa language, that old Indian inside of me, that old Kiowa inside of me, tries to raise his head but, brother, I got to put him down. I have to say: 'get behind me, Satan,' because it is just the old natural man, the old carnal man trying to raise himself up again. (Yes, it is.)"

The applause which occurred when the preacher urged them to get rid of the Indian should be noted. The mentioning of the "old Kiowa" after the "old Indian" inside of him is an example of pan-Indian shifting to tribal identity. But most important is the fact that this is an expression of a transcultural religious identity which is neither traditional Lakota nor white: in their minds a newly conceived Lakota identity, divorced from any Lakota religious identity and rejecting all Lakota religious symbols. This is expressed through Biblical allusions. According to their viewpoint, yuwipi is the work of the devil. Visions of men and animals are an illusion. The Pipe is compared to the golden calf the Hebrews worshipped in the desert. When faced with the problem of the Lakota Christian's relation to his past religious tradition, their solution is one of rejection.

However, Lakota associations are part of their church. The main Body of Christ community is a Lakota *tiospaye*, or extended family—the Black Feathers and other families married into them. Other Lakota associations include healing through supernatural means; visions, but not derived from the Lakota world; and conversion through an experience of power. What attracts Lakota to the Body of Christ Church is their feeling that the power of Christ is superior to the power of the Pipe: but an experience very different from the one that Black Elk had in his conversion, as will be seen below.

There is also a pan-Indian identity. The members have an evangelical spirit that leads to missionary activity among other Indian tribes. They go out from Wolf Creek to North Dakota, Canada, and other places to conduct revival meetings. This activity develops a strong awareness that their commitment to Christ is not just Lakota but for all tribes.

I feel there is no need to point out the features common to any evangelical Pentecostal-type Church. The Body of Christ Church fulfills the needs of its members through a deep religious experience of commitment to Christ. It has an important contribution to make to the study of acculturation, since it is an example of Christianity being a dynamic force in the life of full-blooded Lakota who are unacculturated in all areas of their life except religious symbolism. Although their rejection of Lakota religious identity is bound to have adverse psychological effects, it is possible that the Bible as a power in the traditional Lakota sense (as Densmore's informants and Sword experienced it), may be a sufficient mediating symbol between their Lakota and Christian identities. Their traditional understanding of power did make the Lakota open to new religious influences. However, we shall see that the Lakota Ecumenist II acceptance of traditional Lakota religious symbols would seem to be a much more appropriate solution, avoiding the misunderstandings of the Body of Christ's fundamentalism. But the fact that they are deeply dedicated and not superficial Christians runs contrary to the experience of Hallowell's "superficially acquired Christianity" among the Ojibwa (1955:112).

The Lakota Ecumenist II Group

Thomas W. Overholt in his article on the Ghost Dance states that "the phenomena of Indian conversion to Christianity and of Christian elements in native ceremonies are complex and interesting, and can't be discussed in detail here" (1978:193, n. 25). The detailed discussion below will be a critical attempt to fill in this gap in scholarly research. It will perhaps help clarify "a certain ambiguity in Black Elk's feelings about his power and the fate of his people" (Overholt 1978:180).

Sun Dancer walking between the dancing.

Frank Fools Crow piercing a dancer.

Frank Fools Crow taking a pierced dancer to his dancing position.

Pierced dancers.

George Plenty Wolf bringing
in ceremonial food after the
Sun Dance ceremony.

The people thank the Sun Dancers at the conclusion of the ceremony.

Benjamin Black Elk at the grave of his father, Nicholas Black Elk, at Manderson, S.D.

Benjamin Black Elk offers the Sacred Pipe in Our Lady of the
Sioux Catholic Church at Oglala, S.D.

Jake Herman and Edgar Red Cloud

Frank Fools Crow praying with the Sacred Pipe at the dedication
of St. Isaac Jogues Catholic Church in Rapid City, S.D. (Courtesy
of the Archives of the Diocese of Rapid City, S.D.)

Father Paul Manhart, S.J., making the Sacred Pipe a symbol of death.

The author praying with the Sacred Pipe in Sacred Heart Church,
Pine Ridge, S.D.

The contribution of the Ecumenist II group is in showing us how Christian religious symbols were implied and dimly grasped in the earlier Lakota ones. Eliade gives us an example in the Cross taking the place of the Cosmic Tree, being "conditioned by the very structure of the symbol of the Cosmic Tree" at the same time it "extends and perfects the idea of cosmic *renovatio* symbolized by the World Tree."

All this could be formulated in another manner. Symbols are capable of being understood on more and more "elevated" planes of reference. The symbolism of darkness allows us to grasp its meaning not only in its cosmological and initiatory contexts (cosmic night, prenatal darkness, etc.), but also in the mystical experiences of the "dark night of the soul" of St. John of the Cross. . . . But then one may ask if these "elevated" meanings were not in some manner implied in the other meanings, and if, as a consequence, they were, if not plainly understood, at least vaguely felt by men living on archaic levels of culture. . . . The difficulty of the problem rests on the fact that symbols address themselves not only to the awakened consciousness, but to the totality of the psychic life. . . . This admitted, two important consequences follow:

1. If at a certain moment in history a religious symbol has been able to express clearly a transcendent meaning, one is justified in supposing that this meaning might have been already grasped dimly at an earlier epoch.

2. In order to decipher a religious symbol not only is it necessary to take into consideration all of its contexts, but one must above all reflect on the meaning that the symbol has had in what we might call its "maturity" (1959:106–7).

From the Lakota Christian viewpoint in the Ecumenist II group, this maturity is Christ. However, those Lakota in the Ecumenist I position simply see common religious forms in the two religious traditions. In answer to Bruce Forbes' criticism that I am moving "beyond description and interpretation to an advocacy of the Ecumenist II position" (1985:86), I feel that I am discovering the Ecumenist II viewpoint in their religious imagination and not projecting my own onto it, even though I did advocate this viewpoint in my work among them.

Powers claims that seeing the Sacred Pipe as a foreshadowing of

Christ "is more about religious imperialism than empirical reality" (1986:118). The truth is that Power's rejection of this concept is a form of anthropological imperialism in which an anti-Christian bias does not allow him to see the empirial fact that Christianity had a significant influence on Lakota religion. Plenty Wolf accepted me as a Catholic priest praying with the Sacred Pipe. At least one time he believed that the power of the priest was stronger than his own power as a yuwipi man. In the late 1960s his granddaughter had an epilepsy attack. When the young girl was brought to him, he said that he did not have power over this and that she should be taken to the priest to be prayed over. There is no doubt that his respect for me as a priest increased when I prayed with the Sacred Pipe and that it, in turn, received a special meaning. The ample documentation below will show that some Lakota did have the faith to believe that Christ was the fulfillment of the Sacred Pipe.

In another place Powers makes unfounded assertions and prejudges the motives of a priest:

Historically and traditionally we would tend to interpret this use of native materials [offering up a sacred pipe and wearing beaded vestments] by a Catholic priest as strategy designed to win converts through a kind of moral deception, one deemed acceptable because the stratagem would ultimately lead to a civilized revelation rather than a primitive vision. But would we ever be willing to admit that the priest believed in the efficacy of the pipe? Were the trappings of native religion now part of his religious system?
Historically we must answer no. . . . We would agree, I think, to accept the priestly overtures as a stratagem of the Catholic Church, which, in the words of the Jesuits, "uses the best of any culture for its own advantages (Holy Rosary Mission 1963:20)" (1987:99).

Powers is talking about my praying with the Sacred Pipe, beginning in 1965. He had no way of knowing my intentions. My intention was to establish the Sacred Pipe as a sacramental in Catholic ceremonies. Although this gives the Pipe a new meaning, it in no way destroys its Lakota one. I certainly believe in the efficacy of the Pipe derived from both the Lakota spirits and Christ. I certainly never considered the Sacred Pipe as "the trappings of native religions." Powers simply assumes I have this negative attitude. We can recall Emerson Spider defending my praying with the Pipe in the Native American Church meeting. Below, we will see how many Lakota medicine men accepted this practice of mine. I wrote that the Catholic Church "uses the best of any culture for its own advantage" a quarter of a century ago, before my thought had matured. I would qualify this statement today, although there is a sense in which it is still true since, through the inculturation of the best of Lakota religion, the Catholic Church is better off. None of the medicine men, including George Plenty Wolf (whom Powers regards very highly) accused, or even suspected, me of moral deception. Powers is treating the whole process of inculturation very superficially, without any understanding.

Powers also shows his lack of understanding about the presence of Christianity among the Lakota in viewing its effects as restricted to its social functions. It is true that "as a means of survival and adaptation to the unalterability of the white man's dominance, Christianity has been used in such a way that old cultural institutions and their associated values may persist under new labels" (1987:124). But to claim that Lakota religion satisfies religious needs and Christianity social ones is simply being blind to the facts (1987:123). It is Christianity and not Lakota religion that at times of death is the primary source of strength for the vast majority of Lakota people. Lakota meditate on the Bible and receive the sacraments for religious needs and not social ones. But, of course, Powers is unfamiliar with these matters, for he has not spent any time serving the Lakota people in religious ministry.

Kaiser shares the same anti-Christian bias in making the old worn-out accusation that "Holy Men and traditional Lakotas practiced Christianity to please their conquerors" (1984:19). As we will see below, there was genuine conversion in the lives of Black Elk, Plenty Wolf, and other Lakotas on the Pine Ridge Reservation. Kaiser becomes very judgmental in stating that "some Catholic priests began feeling the need to make Christianity more relevant to the Lakotas, perhaps because they thought that more relevance would finally loosen the Lakotas' retention of old beliefs" (1984:19). I enhanced the Sacred Pipe in the eyes of the Lakota Christian by making it a sacramental sign of Christ not to suppress the Lakota religious tradition but to make it a permanent expression of Christianity. For a Christian to do this is to recognize the validity of Lakota religion.

The best starting point for an understanding of this relationship is

Black Elk's Messiah vision, which he received while participating in the Ghost Dance. I will quote from the Neihardt fieldnotes, published by Raymond DeMallie, since they contain material left out of his *Black Elk Speaks*—material which is essential in my discussion.

"As I landed there, I saw twelve men coming toward me and they stood before me and said: 'Our Father, the two-legged chief, you shall see.' Then I went to the center of the circle with these men and there again I saw the tree in full bloom. Against the tree I saw a man standing with outstretched arms. As we stood close to him these twelve men said: 'Behold him!' The man with outstretched arms looked at me and I didn't know whether he was a white or an Indian. He did not resemble Christ. He looked like an Indian, but I was not sure of it. He had long hair which was hanging down loose. On the left side of his head was an eagle feather. His body was painted red. (At that time I had never seen any picture of Christ.)

"This man said to me: 'My life is such that all earthly beings that grow belong to me. My Father has said this. You must say this.' I stood there gazing at him and tried to recognize him. I could not make him out. He was a nice-looking man. As I looked at him, his body began to transform. His body changed into all colors and it was very beautiful. All around him there was light. Then he disappeared all at once. It seemed as though there were wounds in the palms of his hands (DeMallie 1984:263).

"It seems to me on thinking it over that I have seen the son of the Great Spirit himself. All through this I depended on my Messiah vision whereas perhaps I should have depended on my great vision which had more power and this might have been where I made my great mistake" (266).

My first observation is that Black Elk is reflecting on his vision as a Lakota Christian, having been a Catholic catechist for close to twenty-eight years. His reflections involve an explicit knowledge of Christ. Secondly, the man in the vision was initially the Ghost Dance *Wanekia* ("savior") and not the Christ of his Catholic faith since Black Elk had nothing to do with the white man's religion at the time. He seemed to have acquired little knowledge of Christianity on his European trip in the Buffalo Bill show. The Christian message was not an explicit one for Black Elk but rather an intimation. Although the

Ghost Dance is a syncretism of Indian and Christian elements, Black Elk did not recognize it as such. On the level of phenomenology, Black Elk experienced a Messiah manifestation, but it was only later— after his conversion—that the Ghost Dance Wanekia would be recognized as the Son of the Great Spirit Himself in the sense of Christ. This discovery was the result of Black Elk's groping toward the Messiah's identity after his conversion to Christianity. At first he said that the man "did not resemble Christ. He looked like an Indian." And here Black Elk received his first lesson as a Lakota Ecumenist. For in later reflection he came to the conclusion that this man was the Son of the Great Spirit, proving that his preconceived assumption about Christ—that He could not be an Indian—was wrong. And to Black Elk, who knew Christ as a catechist, the signs must have been so obvious, reminding him of Christ in the transfiguration on Mount Tabor and the risen Christ showing the wounds of the nails in the palms of His hands.

In *Black Elk Speaks* Neihardt is misleading when he has Black Elk saying: "I heard the gossip that was everywhere now, and people said it was really the son of the Great Spirit who was out there; that when he came to the Wasichus [white man] a long time ago, they had killed him; but he was coming to the Indians this time" (1961:239). Black Elk actually told Neihardt: "From the rumors and gossips I heard this Messiah was the son of the Great Spirit that had come out there" (DeMallie 1984:258). But this is simply the name and title given to the man Wovoka (256–57), and there is no indication in the field notes that Black Elk identified the Ghost Dance Messiah with Christ at this point in time. The first mention of Christ in the field notes is when Black Elk reflects upon his Messiah vision after he had become a Catholic catechist.

And so the man he first recognized as the Ghost Dance Wanekia was now identified as the Christ of his Catholic faith. Black Elk then expresses a doubt. He is not sure whether following the Messiah vision instead of his first vision of the flowering tree was a mistake or not. And in my mind another question arises. Does his statement "all through this I depended upon my Messiah vision" refer to before or after the recognition of the Ghost Dance Messiah as Christ? Which vision is it that lacked power—the one in which the man was recognized only as the Ghost Dance Messiah or the one in which he was recognized as Christ? One thing is certain: a Lakota Christ has come to Black Elk in a Lakota vision.

I believe that Black Elk's vision dramatizes the starting point for the Ecumenist II position. Black Elk had an intimation of the presence of Christ of which he was only vaguely aware yet which produced an intense fascination. Only after Black Elk had explicitly known Christ could he realize that he had actually seen Him without knowing it. And this is what the Lakota Ecumenist does—discovering the presence of the unknown Christ in his Lakota tradition, since he is reflecting on this tradition from the viewpoint of his Christian faith.

A young medicine man relates what a man around ninety-one years old and living at Green Grass told him. The man said that after the White Buffalo Woman brought the Pipe, a white man came dressed in a buffalo robe. He spoke Lakota and blessed the Pipe. This was Christ Who came in the spirit before the white man brought Him. The young medicine man comments: "At the time that Christ died, the woman brought the Calf Pipe. When the Pipe was brought, there was a vision of a white man before they ever saw one. He was Christ coming in spirit to the Indian people at the same time that He was born among the white man. This is the reason the Indian respected the white man when he first came. This is the reason why I respect all the Christian Churches."

The association of additional symbols will give us a deeper understanding. The red pipestone is the blood of the Indian people. Catlin gave the reason for the Indian's alarm at the white man's discovering the Pipestone quarry in Minnesota: "As this red stone was part of their flesh, it would be sacrilegious for the white man to touch or take it away. . . . a hole would be made in their flesh and the blood could never be made to stop running" (1844:126). According to Sword, the shaman filled the Pipe and said, "Spirit Pipe, we smoke this pipe to you" (Walker 1917:126). Eagle Feather gives the Spirit Pipe of Sword a meaning that corresponds to the Ghost Dance Messiah of Black Elk before he recognized Him as Christ: "The Peace Pipe or Sacred Pipe is a very important part of the [Sun Dance] ritual and is used because the Traditional Sioux of modern times sincerely believe that it is our Jesus Christ, or our Saviour, and that He is still here on earth in the person of the Pipe. The non-Indians have killed and crucified their

Saviour. This is why traditional people do not celebrate Easter at all"
(Mails 1978:88). On the level of phenomenology, Eagle Feather is recognizing the same religious meaning of saviour in the Lakota Pipe and
in Christ, which is the Ecumenist I position. Black Elk went beyond
this in recognizing the Ghost Dance Messiah as Jesus Christ Himself.

I would like to return to Black Elk's conversion to Christianity, because in it there is yet another example of the Lakota religious experience of power. Black Elk experienced power in the traditional Lakota
world. John Lone Goose, who was the Catholic organist at Manderson and worked with Black Elk as a catechist, states:

"I first met Nick around 1900, when I was a young boy and he was
not a Catholic. I don't know what they call him in English, but in
Indian they call him 'yuwipi' man. Sam Kills Brave, he's a Catholic,
lived close to him. And before Nick converted, Kills Brave would say:
'Why don't you give up your yuwipi and join the Catholic Church?
You may think it best, but the way I look at it, it isn't right for you
to do that yuwipi.' Kills Brave kept talking to him that way and I
guess Nick got those words in his mind. He said that after Kills Brave
spoke to him, he wanted to change" (Steltenkamp, n.d.).

This information is confirmed by a Lakota man in his sixties who
grew up as a boy in Manderson. He told me that people expressed surprise when Black Elk became a Catholic catechist, since he had been
a yuwipi man. These same people described the yuwipi meetings
Black Elk had conducted. Although Neihardt does not describe any
of Black Elk's curing ceremonies as yuwipi, neither does he do so for
Chips, who was certainly yuwipi (1961:77).

It is against this background that we can appreciate the following
testimony of Lucy Looks Twice. "That's when in 1904 my father was
called to doctor a little boy in Payabya, seven miles north of Holy
Rosary Mission. The boy's family wanted my father to doctor their
son because they heard he was good at it. So my father walked over
there carrying his medicine and everything he needed for the ceremony. At that time they walked those long trails if they didn't have
a horse.

"When he got there, he found the sick boy lying in a tent. So right
away, he prepared to doctor him. My father took his shirt off, put tobacco offerings in the sacred place, and started pounding on his drum.
He called on the spirits to heal the boy in a very strong action. Dogs

were there and they were barking. My father was really singing away, beating his drum and using his rattle when along came one of the Blackrobes, Fr. Lindebner, Ate Ptecela (short Father). At that time the priests usually traveled by team and buggy throughout the reservation. That's what Ate Ptecela was driving.

"So he went into the tent and saw what my father was doing. Fr. Lindebner had already baptized the boy and had come to give him the last rites. Anyway, he took whatever my father had prepared on the ground and threw it all into the stove. He took the drum and rattle and threw them outside the tent. Then he took my father by the neck and said: 'Satan, get out!' My father had been in the 101 [Wild West] show and knew a little English so he walked out. Ate Ptecela then administered the boy communion and the last rites. He also cleaned up the tent and prayed with the boy.

"After he got through, he came out and saw my father sitting there downhearted and lonely, as though he lost all his powers. Next thing Fr. Lindebner said was "come on and get in the buggy with me." My father was willing to go along and so he got in and the two of them went back to Holy Rosary Mission. . . . My father never talked [i.e., normally] about that incident but he felt it was Our Lord that appointed or selected him to do the work of the Blackrobes. You might think he was angry, but he wasn't bitter at all.

"He stayed at Holy Rosary two weeks preparing for baptism and at the end of those two weeks he wanted to be baptized. He gladly accepted the faith on December 6, 1904, which was the feast of St. Nicholas. So they called him Nicholas Black Elk. After he became a convert and started working for the missionaries, he put all his medicine practice away. He never took it up again.

"My father said that what he was doing before he met Ate Ptecela was the work of the Great Spirit but that he suffered a lot in doing it. As a matter of fact, he had ulcers and had to be treated for them shortly after he started his missionary work. The Jesuits sent him to a hospital in Omaha and he was on a diet for two or three months until his ulcers cleared up. When he converted, knowing about Christ was very important to him and receiving communion was what he really held sacred.

"People who used to be treated by him when he was a medicine man started coming to him. They asked him about the new church he belonged to and he explained to them what it meant. Many followed his example and he instructed them in the new faith.

"[Steltenkamp continues] Stated most simply, according to Lucy, the only factors pertinent to her father were that (1) a holy man was present, (2) the holy man's power was known to be very strong, (3) resistance to such powers was unthinkable, and (4) Black Elk regarded his power as negligible by comparison. Her father had 'suffered a lot' while practicing as a medicine man and had experienced what might be called 'spiritual restlessness.' Lucy further mentioned that once her father undertook the work of a catechist, his ulcers were never again bothersome. Black Elk clearly felt that the 'Son of God had called him to lead a new life.' The Christian Lord Black Elk heard spoken of during the Ghost Dance times had 'selected him' to do his work.

"John Lone Goose adds one further comment: 'he never talked about the old ways [i.e., in his days as an active catechist]. All he talked about was the Bible and Christ. I was with him most of the time and I remember what he taught'" (Steltenkamp, n.d.).

Looks Twice's last remark is contrary to the Neihardt manuscript. It is certainly possible that she is projecting a later Christian meaning back to that time.

Black Elk's life as a Catholic catechist did require him to suppress traditional Lakota religion much of the time into his unconscious, which surfaced in the Neihardt and Brown interviews. It was the personal image of Christ in his Messiah vision that was a mediating symbol, in a Jungian sense, resulting in an integration of the two religious traditions on a deep emotional level.

Yet, it was by no means a total suppression. Black Elk did consciously integrate the two religious traditions in a remarkable way. The image of the Ghost Dance Messiah did surface into consciousness. According to Frank Fools Crow, "Black Elk was very interested in the teachings of the Roman Catholic Church, and spent many hours talking to priests about it. When he and I were discussing it one day, Black Elk told me he had decided that the Sioux religious way of life was pretty much the same as that of the Christian Churches. . . . We could pick up some of the Christian ways and teachings, and just work them in with our own, so in the end both would be better" (Mails 1979:45). Fools Crow's remark brings out both sides of Black Elk's life. When he "spent many long hours talking to the priest," he suppressed his Lakota religion. However, in private conversations, he consciously brought the two together. Fools Crow believes in Black Elk's position and in the mutual benefits both religions receive from each other. I don't question which religion was superior in Fools Crow's mind. When he became sick during the 1980 tribal Sun Dance and retired to his tent, he asked me to give him the Sacrament of the Annointing of the Sick and Holy Communion on the Sun Dance grounds. He did not ask for one of the Lakota medicine men to pray over him.

DeMallie brings out the same conscious inculturation. Commenting on Black Elk's teaching on the Sacred Pipe, DeMallie says that "these teachings seem to represent the end point in Black Elk's synthesis of Lakota and Christian beliefs, for in them he structures Lakota rituals in parallel fashion to the Catholic sacraments. Perhaps this was Black Elk's final attempt to bridge the two religious traditions that his life had so intimately embodied" (1984:71).

This explains why the very expressions that Black Elk uses in *The Sacred Pipe* show a Christian influence.

Any man . . . who is attached to the senses and to the things of this world, is one who lives in ignorance and is being consumed by the snakes which represent his own passions (Brown 1953:4n). . . . It should also be a sacred day when a soul is released and returns to its home, *Wakan-Tanka* (8). . . . Further, my relatives, our Father, *Wanan-Tanka*, has made His will known to us here on earth, and we must always do that which he wishes if we should walk the sacred path (13). . . . and as the flames of the sun come to us in the morning, so comes the grace of *Wakan-Tanka*, by which all creatures are enlightened (71). . . . I think I should explain to you here, that the flesh represents ignorance and, thus as we dance [in the Sun Dance] and break the thong loose, it is as if we were being freed from the bonds of the flesh (85).

These expressions are paraphrases, and sometimes almost direct quotations from the Bible and Catholic catechism. In addition, all un-Christian viewpoints, such as not making peace with the enemies outside the tribe, found in Sword's remarks, are completely absent from Black Elk's account.

Clyde Holler continues the discussion. He calls attention to Black Elk's remark to Joseph Brown: that just as Christ is coming at the end of the world, so the White Buffalo Calf Woman comes with the Sacred Pipe. Holler understands this as an identification of the Pipe with Christ (1984:42). I believe this is a valid interpretation of Black Elk's symbolic thinking. Black Elk's explanation of the Sun Dance also brings out this same synthesis. Black Elk abandons the traditional purpose of individual vows "made in time of anxiety, usually on the warpath" (Densmore 1918:86, 88–91), for, instead, taking on the suffering of the people that they may live, a purpose which shows a Christian influence. But the Sun Dance symbols also acquire a Christian meaning. An armlet of rabbit skin represents humility "because he is quiet, soft and not self-asserting." Black Elk also removes most of the references to war and interprets the color black as representing ignorance and sin. And so Black Elk frees the Sun Dance from its association with the hunter warrior complex and gives it a new interpretation "in terms relevant to the radically changed conditions of reservation life," including the acceptance of Christianity. This is done in terms "commensurate with Christianity" (Holler 1984:44–48).

However, Holler's evaluation of Black Elk's relationship to Christianity needs examination. He places Black Elk in the Ecumenist I position and then states that he worked consciously to integrate the two traditions (1984:41). However, this is the Ecumenist II position, which Holler develops with such insight.

The first is that it is typical of Black Elk's way of thinking and speaking to read back into his great vision an insight that could only have occurred to him after his years as a catechist. The same "reading back" characterizes Black Elk's entire account of the seven rites of the Lakota. Second, there is no hint of substitution in Black Elk's statement. Christ does not replace the pipe; both have co-equal validity. Third, and most obviously, Black Elk is saying to the Sioux, in what was to be his last written statement, that Indians should "pray with the pipe," that is, not abandon traditional religious practices for Christianity (42).

Black Elk reads back into his Lakota tradition the insights he acquired as a Catholic catechist. This is exactly what the early Christian converts from Judaism did with the Old Testament, making it a foreshadowing of Christ which reaches its fulfillment in Him (Steinmetz 1970). And so, Black Elk does the same, making Lakota religious tradition an "Old Testament" foreshadowing of Christ and reaching its fulfillment in Him. Secondly, Christ does not replace the Pipe since the Pipe becomes a cultural expression of Christ in becoming symbolically identified with Him. Third, the Lakota should not abandon their traditional religion for Christianity, but neither should they abandon their Christianity for their Lakota religion. Black Elk seems to be telling them privately to practice a Lakota Christian religion, since Lakota religion has acquired a Christian value. However, as a Catholic catechist he was unable to preach this publicly.

My first reason for putting Black Elk in the Ecumenist II position was primarily because of the mediating symbol of the Ghost Dance Messiah, recognized as Christ. It was Black Elk's unconscious which gave him the primary bridge between the two religious traditions from which his conscious activity flowed. My second reason is Black Elk's conscious integration of the two traditions, which DeMallie and Holler bring out. In answering Holler's comment: "But Steinmetz' Black Elk does not seem truly to be an example of the Ecumenist II position, since on Steinmetz' reading, as suggested by the recollections of Lame Goose, Black Elk is decidedly more Christian than traditional" (1984:41), I would like to suggest the following. I believe that Black Elk fluctuated between the two positions, being in the Ecumenist I position when talking to the priests and being in the Ecumenist II one in talking to Fools Crow and others privately. This fluctuation explains why different people see Black Elk in such different light.

Holler also states that "Black Elk's 'conversion' was not what is normally considered a conversion—the substitution of one religion for another" (1984:47). However, Black Elk had made a total commitment to Christ, as was evident from his life as a catechist. During a retreat for catechists, Father Sialm, S.J., writes: "On the third day of that retreat, Nick Black Elk came to me with this very worthy resolution: 'We catechists resolve never to commit a mortal sin'" (1923:78). Conversion to Christianity does not mean giving up a religious tradition but rather giving it a Christian meaning, which Holler has so convincingly shown above. Although Black Elk may start on the level of phenomenology, recognizing common and equal religious forms in both religions (Christ and the Pipe are coequal), the fact still remains that for him all Lakota religion is to be practiced in a Christian context, that is, in a way compatible with Christianity. In Black Elk's mind his interpretation of the Sun Dance, influenced by Christian tradition, is the fulfillment of his Lakota tradition. To equate conversion with the substitution of one religion for another is an inaccurate notion which does no justice to the deep psychological relationship a person has with his or her past. And we must recall Black Elk's Ghost Dance vision in which the Lakota Messiah became Christ.

This discovery of Christ in Lakota Religion would be worked out in greater detail by the Lakota who followed him. It has taken place primarily in their religious imagination. The Shoshones and Northern Utes have accomplished the same inculturation in their Sun Dances, but Jorgensen has prejudged it as "pseudo-Christian" (1972:21).

For Plenty Wolf the rawhide effigy of the man hanging from the Sun Dance tree represented the return of Christ. Dorsey states that the rawhide effigy of the man was a phallic symbol of fertility (1894: 457), and this an apt symbol of the return of Christ, which will be a source of new life. In Densmore's account, this same effigy indicates that the enemy was conquered by supernatural help (1918:188) — also an apt symbol, since in His return Christ overcomes universal evil. But Plenty Wolf discovers other meanings. The rawhide effigy of the buffalo is the Old Testament and the one of the man is the New Testament. We can recall Erikson's comment that the buffalo represents the old Lakota way of life. So Plenty Wolf's identification of the buffalo with the Old Testament is a way of expressing the belief that the traditional Lakota religion is a preparation for Christ in a way similar to the Old Testament for the Jews. For Plenty Wolf this was an intuition on a symbolic level and not an articulated understanding on a reflective level.

Powers calls this claim "religious imperialism," saying it takes "raw faith" to see the Sacred Pipe as a foreshadowing of Christ. However, Powers is unable to see that Plenty Wolf had this "raw faith," which enabled him to see that the Lakota religious tradition, like the Old Testament, was a preparation of Christ. And this is not an "analytical imposition," as Powers claims (1986:118–19). It goes beyond the recognition on the level of phenomenology of the common religious forms that actually exist in both religious symbols. This symbolic identification can only mean that the Lakota religious tradition reaches its perfection in Christ. If it doesn't have this meaning, what meaning does it have? Jorgensen and Clemmer have the same difficulty as Powers (1978:43). The time is long overdue for anthropologists to realize that they cannot understand the traditional religion of a Native American Christian without understanding his Christian tradition.

Plenty Wolf has yet another Christian interpretation: "the piercing of the flesh in the Sun Dance is a reminder of the piercing of Jesus. When a man pierces his flesh, he is doing it in remembrance of Christ." And, according to Plenty Wolf, the man who brought the Sun Dance from Montana to the Lakota said that "he was doing something like Noah did, bringing his people on a certain boat. We are going through the Sun Dance and we are reaching our destination just like Noah reached his."

Fools Crow invited me to participate in the 1971 Sun Dance so as to express his own Christian understanding of this ceremony. He also compared the Sun Dance tree to the Christian cross (Mailes 1978: 200). We can also recall Cherry Seed's telling Fools Crow that in accepting the Pipe he was going into a house with many strings attached to it. On later reflection, Fools Crow thought that this house, the sacred place of the Pipe, was the Catholic Church.

As we noted earlier, Red Cloud sang a Sun Dance song with the Pipe during the communion part of the Mass on the Sun Dance grounds. Plenty Wolf also prayed with the Pipe in the church at Slim Butte. Iron Rope told Pete Fast Horse in my presence: "I am glad this Father is interested in the Pipe. He can use this Pipe at Mass. . . . I would like to have Father use the Pipe when he prays at Mass. In a mysterious way God will give him many privileges. I know what Father asks in the Mass, I know it will come true. That's certain. So he should take up his Pipe without any hesitation." Pete Catches also defended my praying with the Pipe on the grounds that as a priest I was the equivalent of a "holy man" in the traditional Lakota sense. When he put me on the hill for a two-day Pipe fast in 1974, he told me that some would criticize him for this but that this was one of the great honors of his life. Kills Ree, a yuwipi man, insisted that I pray with the Pipe at the burial of his grandson. I was really overwhelmed when I discovered that this Pipe had been in the Chips family for several generations.

Still other examples of Lakota Christian inculturation can be given. Edgar Red Cloud discovered a profound Christian meaning in Mother Earth, saying that "when the Indians knew Mother Earth, they knew the Blessed Virgin Mary but they did not know her by name." He also stated that the Woman who brought the Pipe is the Blessed Virgin Mary who brought Christ, an identification which another Lakota made to Kemnitzer (n.d.). Two Bulls tells how his grandfather translated the obligation of a Lakota dream into Christian terms: "He dreamt of the thunder. But he was a Christian man. So whenever it thundered, he took out his Bible and read it to fulfill his dream. Catches shares his own experience in saying that he prayed with his Pipe in memory of his vision "just as the priest changes bread and wine into the Body of Blood of Christ in memory of the Last Supper."

Finally, Benjamin Black Elk told me that during most of his life he was in doubt about the relation between the Pipe and Christ. When he believed in the Pipe, was he betraying himself as a Christian? But, now that he saw that the Pipe and Christ were really one, his conscience's doubts of many years were ended and he had a deep spiritual peace in his soul. And that night the vision of the Pipe leading the Lakota to Christ, which we shared in his log cabin, made a deep impression on both of us.

These Lakota courageously discovered the presence of Christ in their Lakota religious tradition at a time when most of the missionaries were condemning it as un-Christian. As Fools Crow told me: "I never talked about the Pipe to a Catholic priest in the early days, but I brought the two religions together on my own." It was the Lakota medicine men and not the Christian missionaries who had the insight, even though on a symbolic level, that the traditional Lakota religion was pre-Christian. I have the humility to admit with Powers that the medicine men were impressed that I had "finally seen the light" (1977:116). And I have the deepest respect for the Lakota holy men who in their own way professed that the meaning of the Pipe in its maturity is Christ. How far these few have come since the first intimation of Christ which Black Elk had in the Ghost Dance Messiah vision.

The Ecumenist I Group

The Ecumenist I group consists of those Lakota Christians who have both Lakota and Christian identities, or a split identity. Their Lakota identity is expressed through the traditional Pipe,

and their Christian one through the Bible as a white value in the traditional Christian Church. Although their primary identity may be
Lakota, it does not follow that their Christian one is superficial, as
has so often been claimed. The ambivalence towards Lakota spirits,
life after death, and other religious symbols show this viewpoint to
be an oversimplification. As Powers states, they move back and forth
situationally between the Lakota and Christian ends of the continuum.
Each religion fulfills their needs in particular circumstances and times.
There seems to be a certain dissatisfaction with both religious traditions, so that they see complementary values in both—as, for example, seeking healing through a yuwipi ceremony and seeking coun-
seling in personal problems from the Christian minister or priest.

But there is a continuum within their Christian identity. This identity can be considered a continuum between the Ecumenist II position on one end and a minimal participation in the Christian churches
on the other. Members of this group move towards the Ecumenist II
end by discovering common religious forms in both the Lakota and
the Christian symbols on the level of phenomenology. These common forms include the concept of power, of Messiah, of mediator,
and of spiritual healing. They mediate between the two religious traditions through a transfer of emotional energy which happens, for example, when the same sense of power is felt in both the Lakota and
Christian symbols. I believe that this mediation sometimes allows
their Christian tradition to form a continuity with the Lakota one
on both conscious and unconscious levels so that the Lakota avoids
the symbolic sickness that Powers describes (1977:206).

This mediation can be achieved even though it is an imperfect
stage of the Ecumenist II position. The Lakota in the Ecumenist I position recognizes common forms in both religions but not their Lakota
religion as explicitly Christian. It is the difference between the beliefs
of Eagle Feather and Black Elk. Eagle Feather, in saying "the Pipe is
our Christ," saw the religious form of saviour in both the Lakota and
Christian. Black Elk made his Lakota religion explicitly Christian in
saying this Lakota "wanekia is the Son of the Great Spirit Himself."
It is the comparison of form on the level of phenomenology as compared to inculturation. But if the recognition of common religious
forms is sufficiently deep, then the Ecumenist I position achieves
some stability.

If, on the other hand, the awareness of common religious forms in both the Lakota and the Christian tradition is not present, then there is usually a movement towards the other end of the continuum within the Christian identity, that is toward minimal participation in the traditional churches with the indifference it involves. In other words, a split personal identity can result in an unstable psychological state. For some Lakota at this end of the continuum, the American Indian Movement gave them the opportunity to discover their latent Lakota identity. It is very unlikely for a person in the Ecumenist II group to move into another one. This we observed in the opposition of the medicine men to the anti-Christian attitude of AIM despite their sympathy towards its social and political goals.

Beyond doubt, the Ecumenist I group contains the majority of the Lakota people. Thus, the analysis of this group offers a contribution to the theory of religious acculturation by giving new insights into the shifting patterns of religious affiliations among the Oglala Lakota.

The Native American Church, Cross Fire Fireplace

The importance of the Native American church among the Oglala Lakota to the theory of religious acculturation resides particularly in its intimate connection with both the Bible and the Pipe. LaBarre lists several pages of Christian elements in Peyote and yet comes to the conclusion "that the layer of Christianity on peyotism is very thin and superficial indeed" (1975:166). He further states that "the Mission of El Santo Nombre de Jesus Peyotes [venerated in the region of Villa Union in Coah, Mexico since 1690] is so called merely from the abundance of the plant thereabouts" (162). However, what LaBarre is apparently unaware of is that a prayer to this Jesus of Peyote has the official approbation of a Catholic bishop, His Excellency Dr. Don Luis Guizar Barragan, and was distributed on printed holy cards (one is in the possession of Emerson Spider). The local bishop, at least, took the devotion seriously. LaBarre also mentions that the "Delaware followers of Wilson call the corn husk cigarette the 'pipe of Jesus'" (163). This designation is highly significant since, as we shall see, it integrates the same three religious traditions which the Lakota Half Moon members do. (I think LaBarre lacks an appreciation of symbolic signification.) Finally, Mooney wrote back in 1892:

"It may be proper to state that many of the mescal [Peyote] eaters wear crucifixes, which they regard as sacred emblems of the rite, the cross representing the cross of scented leaves upon which the consecrated mescal rests during the ceremony, while the Christ is the mescal goddess" (1892:65). Stewart's comment is relevant here: "I believe Peyotism was strongly influenced from Mexico when it was first introduced into the United States and that a number of Christian elements were already present when the fully established Peyote ritual was first observed by Mooney in 1892" (1977:931). But Opler, too, had a bias similar to LaBarre's: "Indeed, far from becoming a weakened and Christianized version of native beliefs, the Mescalero Apache acceptance of peyote resulted instead in an intensification of the aboriginal religious values and concepts at many points" (1936:144). He implies that in this case a Christian version must be a weakened one and that the intensification of aboriginal values is incompatible with Christianity. We will see just how wrong these assumptions are, at least with the Oglala Lakota.

The Cross Fire fireplace among the Oglala Lakota leaves no doubt of the strong Christian identity of Peyote. Emerson Spider clearly states that when he believes in Christ and reads the Bible, he is not a white man but a 100 percent Indian. And, at the State Convention in the summer of 1978, he told the members that neither the Cross Fire nor the Half Moon fireplaces are of any value unless they lead to Christ. The Bible has replaced the ceremonial cigarette in practice, even though Spider urges his members to respect the Half Moon tradition and if they attend a Half Moon meeting, they must do it their way and take part in the ceremonial smoke. Baptism is necessary to be a member of the Cross Fire. The Bible is always on the altar beneath the chief Peyote. The midnight water talk is always from the Bible. Cross Fire ministers are ordained. A member has even been appointed to the position of Bible teacher. Gospel singing has been introduced into some Peyote meetings. Spider's intense evangelical spirit is very obvious from an interview he had with Raymond DeMallie in August of 1982. (Spider 1987:20, 189–209). Some of the members are born-again Christians (197). As a fifteen-year-old boy, Spider took Peyote and was healed by Christ (198). And so they don't give large quantities of medicine as they did in the old days, since they are now relying on the healing of Jesus Christ (205). These are just a few of Spider's statements indicating a strong Christian identity.

Recently the Christian basis of the church has been made even more explicit. In October of 1979, Emerson Spider, Sr., Rev. William Richards, Rene Mills, Wilson Crow, and Mrs. Verolo Spider-Mills filed Articles of Incorporation for the Native American Church of Jesus Christ. Article III contains the purpose: "To promulgate the Christian Doctrine set forth by the scriptures of the HOLY BIBLE. To proclaim the teachings of JESUS CHRIST in an Indian way of worship to all AMERICAN INDIANS who may reside in the STATE OF SOUTH DAKOTA and within the UNITED STATES OF AMERICA. Moreover, to specifically promulgate the teaching of JESUS CHRIST to the AMERICAN INDIANS who customarily utilize the GOD GIVEN HERB (PEYOTE) in their Indian ways of worship of almighty GOD." This is perhaps the first Native American Church charter that explicitly mentions Peyote and has the Name of Jesus Christ in its official charter. Although the Cross Fire fireplace is not mentioned in the Articles of Incorporation, the incorporators presently intend to make this the exclusive fireplace in the bylaws when they are written. Rene Mills considers the Half Moon fireplace as an imperfect expression of Christ, as the Old Testament is.

The Native American Church, Cross Fire, is one alternative to a Lakota Christian church. The identity that is in consciousness most frequently is the Lakota one rather than the pan-Indian one. In fact, the Cross Fire has a weak pan-Indian identity on a national American level. They have obtained only state charters. During the summer of 1978, a proposal was made to sponsor a national convention on the Pine Ridge Reservation. The State Chairman showed no interest on the grounds that the national people have never helped the Native American Church in South Dakota. The Cross Fire represents a Lakota Christian identity that neither rejects traditional Lakota religious symbols as the Body of Christ Independent Church nor inculturates them as the Ecumenist II. Instead, there is the same inculturation of Christ in the Peyote among them as the Ecumenist II have achieved in the Pipe. In Spider's viewpoint, Christ is the real center of the Native American Church. Certainly, for the Cross Fire fireplace of the Native American Church among the Oglala Lakota, Christianity is no thin and superficial layer over peyotism.

The Native American Church, Half Moon Fireplace

The Half Moon fireplace represents a Lakota Christian identity which is expressed through three religious traditions. The Half Moon has a Lakota identity because it integrates traditional Lakota religious symbols, especially the Pipe, into their ceremonies. The old man Red Bear always prayed with the Pipe at his meetings. The practice was subsequently followed by Hawkins, Gap, and on occasion by Red Bear's great-grandson, Solomon. In addition, the Lakota word *Cannunpa* ("Pipe") is used for the ceremonial cigarette, creating a strong awareness of the cigarette standing for the Pipe. The symbol of the Pipe is as closely associated with the Half Moon as the Bible is with the Cross Fire, even though the actual Pipe is rarely brought into a Peyote meeting. In the Half Moon fireplace there is a whole range of traditional symbols: the roadman goes outside to pray in the four directions; there are four smokes and four water calls; sage is used to rub oneself with as protection against the evil spirits. Many members move back and forth between traditional Lakota ceremonies and Peyote meetings according to what best fulfills their needs at the time.

The Half Moon fireplace also has a strong Christian identity, even though the Bible is not actually present during the meeting. The Name of Jesus is included in both song and prayer. But the depth of feeling with which John Weasel Bear talked about the Sacred Heart of Jesus and Mary beneath the cross during a Peyote meeting at the midnight water call brings out more than any comments the depth of Christian commitment. The following prayer excerpt is from a Mother's Day meeting.

"This evening we have the heart [the ash formation in the fireplace], the Sacred Heart of Jesus. This heart means a lot of things to this religion, to the Native American Church. It has a lot of concern in there. Coming to Mother's Day. Even the Lord when He was crucified, He looked down upon His mother. His mother was standing below Him there. He didn't say anything to her. All He could do was to shed tears; He cried. That's all He could do. So His mother was standing below and looking up at Him. There was nothing she could do. So the Lord gave Himself for the people that are here on this earth. Not only across the ocean but over here too, for the Indian people.

He gave His life for you. The Great Spirit so loved the world that He died for you. From that time on, that is the way this Sacred Heart of Jesus came about. If any person believes in God, the Great Spirit, He said thou shall love thy neighbor as thyself. That's what the teaching of the Native American Church is."

Half Moon members do not have the same intense evangelical spirit as some of the Cross Fire ones, but they do have a definite Christian identity today, admitting an historical development.

The Half Moon fireplace is a remarkable example of religious acculturation in that it integrates the three religious traditions of Pipe, Bible, and Peyote. (A comparative study with other reservations would be of great value to determine how unique the Native American Church among the Oglala Lakota may be.) The Half Moon members have a greater sense of pan-Indian identity than the Cross Fire, as is reflected in their obtaining a National Charter from Oklahoma and renewing it three times. And yet, at the same time, they have a stronger Lakota identity. That both the pan-Indian and Lakota identities are stronger than the Cross Fire's is a remarkable phenomenon, showing that they are compatible. Finally, there is an inculturation of both the traditional Lakota and Christian symbols in the Peyote ceremonies. The celebration of this inculturation took place in the Peyote meeting described earlier, in which the Papal Blessing, the Pipe, and the Peyote were present on the Half Moon altar.

CONCLUSIONS

We are able now to make some concluding observations from the model of religious identity.

First, there are mutual influences between Pipe, Bible, and Peyote in the process of religious acculturation. When some Lakota identify the Calf Pipe Woman who brought the Pipe with the Blessed Virgin Mary who brought Christ, both religious traditions acquire a new meaning. Through their association with each other, both symbols are understood in a new light. We should not overlook the emotional associations which may be involved.

Secondly, the Pipe and Peyote both become mediating symbols. The Ecumenist II's understanding of the Pipe makes it a mediating symbol between the traditional Lakota and Christian religions. Spider's understanding of Peyote as leading to Christ makes it, also, a mediating symbol between those two traditions. The Half Moon members' perception of the ceremonial cigarette as a substitute for the Pipe makes smoking the cigarette a mediating symbol between the Native American Church and traditional Lakota Religion.

Third, the same attitude towards one of the religious symbols can result in a different practice. The American Indian Movement, considering the Bible as a white man's value, rejects it for "pure Lakota Religion." Those who take the Ecumenist I position have the same attitude towards the Bible but consider it an alternative to Lakota religion under certain circumstances.

Fourth, an attitude towards a religious symbol can be distinguished by whether a symbol is for oneself or others. Both Ecumenist I Lakota and Native American Church Cross Fire members perceive the Pipe as an alternate to the Bible. But the Ecumenist I persons consider this as an actual choice and participate in traditional ceremonies, while Cross Fire members do not (while nevertheless respecting those who do).

Fifth, there is both continuity and discontinuity between the Pipe and the Bible. We saw how the rawhide effigy of the man on the Sun Dance tree perceived both as a fertility symbol and as the enemy overcome by supernatural means in the past showed both continuity and discontinuity with Plenty Wolf's perception of it as a symbol of the return of Christ.

Sixth, Pipe, Bible, and Peyote represent dynamic states, not static ones. There are alternating states of consciousness between pan-Indian and Lakota identities. There are shifting relationships which result from an Ecumenist I Lakota moving back and forth on the continuum between traditional Lakota and traditional Christian religions as well as on the continuum between Ecumenist II and superficial Christianity within his Christian identity. There are shifting relationships of the Half Moon members, moving back and forth between traditional Lakota ceremonies and Peyote meetings. Finally, a Lakota may embrace several positions at the same time in regard to different aspects of his beliefs. He may be in the Ecumenist II position in his basic understanding of the Pipe and move to the Ecumenist I position in the practice of yuwipi. All the various continuums discussed above are simply ways of conceptualizing the various alternating states of religious experience. Alternations between the conscious and the unconscious would add yet another dimension to the model.

This by no means exhausts the opportunities for future field studies in religious identity, but it does indicate a method of approach in the complex shifting religious patterns, both within each religious group and between them, which are a part of the Oglala Lakota identity.

Finally, it seems that the above evidence establishes an important conclusion. One cannot understand the traditional religion of a Native American Christian without understanding his or her Christian religion. And the reverse is true. One cannot understand the Christian religion of this same person without understanding the traditional religion. I think both the missionary and the anthropologist have misunderstood the religious situation of the Native Americans. The Native Americans did not embrace a Christianity divorced from their traditional religions, as the missionary assumed, nor did they practice a traditional religion unaffected by their Christianity, as the anthropologist assumed. And whether a religion is practiced wholeheartedly or superficially depends upon the person. Black Elk practiced his Lakota religion with complete dedication, and he did the same with his Christian religion. And in some instances the Native American who is superficial in Christian religion is also superficial in the traditional religion.

EPILOGUE

Religious acculturation among the Oglala Lakota on the Pine Ridge Reservation can be compared to a tapestry woven from the rich religious experience of Pipe, Bible, and Peyote. It is impossible to unravel the threads of contemporary Oglala Lakota religion. Each religious group has contributed. The American Indian Movement helped young Lakota get in touch with the religious symbols deep in their psyches, through a revival of traditional Lakota Religion. The Body of Christ Church is a witness of conversion and commitment to Christ among the Lakota. The Native American Church offers the opportunity of another approach to religious experience in harmony with Lakota identity. Ecumenist I and Ecumenist II add a new Christian dimension to traditional Lakota religion, making up for some of its deficiencies and in turn being enriched by it. Pipe, Bible, and Peyote are all part of the search for a new religious identity.

Densmore had already noticed this acculturation process when she observed the "repent, repent" exhortation of the Sun Dance intercessor. Sword accepted the same religious form of power in both the Lakota Wakantanka and the white man's God. Black Elk recognized the Ghost Dance Messiah as the Lakota Christ. Ecumenist II Lakota recognized the presence of Christ in their religious symbols. Lakota religion has enriched the Christian churches with its own living symbols, and the Christian churches, in turn, have given Lakota religion an intimacy found in a personal relationship with Jesus Christ, the Son of the Great Spirit. Is it possible, perhaps, that the Lakota Christ of Black Elk's Messiah vision becoming fully conscious in a newly revived Lakota Christian Religion may be the flowering tree in the center of the nation's hoop? (DeMallie 1984:240, 259).

APPENDICES

APPENDIX A
The Homily at the Funeral of Benjamin Black Elk

This homily is included because of its importance in helping us understand those parts of the Black Elk tradition which have been neglected. It is a contribution to the well-balanced view which Raymond DeMallie developed in The Sixth Grandfather.

We come here today as a faith community to celebrate the eternal life of Benjamin Black Elk. We know his soul lives on and enters into the spirit world. Benjamin came from a great tradition. He had a father who was very important in the life of the Oglala Lakota. His father, Nicholas Black Elk, was perhaps the greatest Lakota mystic in the history of the Lakota people. He was the St. John of the Cross of the Oglala Lakota people. And from his vision he derived from God a gift of prophecy and a gift of healing which were very great. In these visions as a Lakota holy man the seeds of Christ were planted. He not only was converted to the Catholic Church but he was the greatest Catholic catechist on the reservation. Probably no man is more responsible for the planting of the Catholic Church at Manderson than Nicholas Black Elk. Perhaps this is the part of his life that is not well enough known. I can remember Ben telling me that his was the chapter in *Black Elk Speaks* that is not yet written. It is wonderful that this book, a great gift to the Indian people and to mankind, reveals to us the visions of this holy man. Yet Ben said that this book was incomplete, that someday he would have to write the last chapter, of his father as a Catholic catechist establishing the church here in Manderson. And he said that this would be the greatest and most important chapter of his father's life. And so it is fitting then that Ben had this spiritual training from his father, a training in two religious traditions. It would be a preparation then for a very unusual life.

Many years ago now, Ben Black Elk rode through the Black Hills seeking the spirit of his son, Benjamin Jr., who had passed into the other world. And it was this search that eventually led to his involvement at Mount Rushmore. And I think here we have an example of a proud Indian who literally greeted millions of people for a quarter of a century. I remember seeing him being so wonderful and being so open with small children. He had a winning way with the little children. And I would reflect on the story in the Gospel, of Christ calling the little children to Himself and He would not have them turned away. Ben Black Elk won the hearts of the American people. He certainly was an ambassador of good will. He captured the hearts of America.

But I think there is a much more important side of Ben Black Elk. There is his religious side. I can remember talking to him in his home about his religious searching, about his seeking to understand his own religious traditions, seeking to understand more deeply the life experience of his father as interpreted to the world through *Black Elk Speaks* and the *Sacred Pipe.* He was not satisfied with the understanding he had. He was seeking for a deeper and deeper understanding. Ben Black Elk was also a very strong Catholic. Ben, along with all mankind, with all of us, sinned and failed against almighty God. From my own personal experience I know he had a deep faith in the sacrament of confession. He knew there was a sacred power in the absolution of the priest. He knew he had a religious ceremony of purification to which he could go whenever it was needed. I saw Ben Black Elk receive this sacrament with great sincerity, with great faith and with great feeling.

This particular night we were talking together about the relationship of the vision of his father, of the Lakota religion, and his Catholic faith. We talked about this because both of these traditions meant very much to him. And we began to talk about the fact that there was no conflict between the two. And we talked about how the Sacred Pipe could lead a person to Christ and how the Sacred Pipe was a foreshadowing of Christ in His great office of mediator, of bringing man back to the Great Spirit. We talked, then, of how Christ fulfilled the traditions of the Sacred Pipe and how Christ is the living and eternal Pipe. And then Ben made a very startling confession to me. He said that through most of his life there was a conflict between these two traditions. He did have doubts of conscience. When he lectured on the Sacred Pipe and had a belief in the Sacred Pipe, was he betraying himself as a Christian? He said that now that he sees that the Sacred Pipe and Christ really are one, that they fulfill each other, the doubts of conscience of many years have ended. Now he had real spiritual peace in his soul. And this shared vision of the Sacred Pipe leading the Lakota people to Christ as the Living and Eternal Pipe made a deep impression on both of us. And this is what I would like to call the vision of Benjamin Black Elk.

In a way this vision was much more powerful and much more needed than even the visions of his father, Nicholas Black Elk. I think it is a vision that it would be well for all of us, as we look up now to the traditions of our fathers, to take to heart, a vision that we could pray over and explore. It is Christ, the God man, then, that gathers from the four directions the entire universe and carries it back to the Great Spirit in a way that fulfills the Sacred Pipe and does not destroy it. I think that this acceptance of Christ was a very important thing in the life of Benjamin Black Elk. It will be this vision that is going to help as we bring a living culture to the Oglala Lakota people today. I believe this vision is an important foundation of two cultures that are beginning to come to life on this reservation.

And so now we gather together to celebrate the eternal life of this great man. A man who holds out to us the hope of a better life, the hope of a more spiritual life.

Reading from the prophet Isaiah, what a wonderful picture it is, life in heaven. On this mountain the Lord of hosts will provide to all peoples; He will prepare a banquet, a banquet in which we will have a great deal of joy. For God will wipe away the tears of all peoples. He will take away our shame and our reproach. And so this is the heavenly banquet to which Benjamin has been called. And this is the heavenly banquet in which all of us someday will share. This is the heavenly banquet of which the Mass is but the sign or foreshadowing. We gather at the Eucharistic meal which will lead someday to the heavenly banquet to which Ben Black Elk has been called. And it is very evident in the early Church that the Christians were called to accept Jesus Christ as their Savior and Lord and to receive His power. And with this they were anointed with the Holy Spirit and with power. This is what Nicholas Black Elk certainly had, power as a holy man and power as a Catholic catechist. I think this is what Benjamin inherited, an influence and a power with people, one in which his memory and name will go on for a very long time.

Ben was very much impressed with the ceremony of the Sacred Pipe at the graveside which he saw performed for his friends. In this ceremony Ben made this great act of faith, that Christ is the Resurrection and the Life. Any man that believes in me, he will not die forever, he will not die spiritually. If he believes in Me, the Resurrection and the Life, his life goes on. And our Lord asked Benjamin the very same question He asked Martha: "Do you believe this?" And, along with Martha, Ben said "Yes, Lord, I believe You are the Messiah, the one who is to come and save the world." And then in that cabin that night, when he could see that Christ is the Living and Eternal Pipe, this act of faith, this vision, brought both of his religious traditions together. And I feel deep in my heart that this is the greatest achievement of Benjamin Black Elk. This is the crown of his spiritual life, of his spiritual groping. This vision in which we are all welcome to share in, this is his heritage to the Oglala Lakota.

And so we open our hearts and we turn now to the relatives, to those close and near to him, to those who will miss him so much, to the countless people who have such a deep love and affection for Ben Black Elk. We turn to them and we ask all these people to open up their hearts to the Holy Spirit, to let the spirit of Christ come in with peace, with understanding, with acceptance of God's will, to believe that God is a loving Father, that he does direct the lives of each one of us, including the life of Ben, according to His best plan to lead us to salvation. We open our hearts up to the hope for the resurrection. We open our hearts up to the peace of Christ, the same peace that Ben had that night in his cabin. Let the Holy Spirit come into our lives. May the blessing of almighty God descend upon each and everyone of us. Amen.

APPENDIX B

Homily at the Funeral of George Plenty Wolf

This homily is included as a tribute to a medicine man who bridged two religious worlds, at times in opposition to the Catholic Church which he so dearly loved. It is a contribution to understanding the developing relationship between the Christian Church and the Lakota people.

I chose to wear red vestments this morning because red is the sacred color of power. And we are celebrating this morning the life of a man who experienced power. He knew what power was, not only the power of the Sacred Pipe but also the power of Jesus Christ. He knew both powers in his life. And he really believed in both powers. And so we celebrate the ceremony with red vestments, with the sacred color of power.

The first time I laid the Sacred Pipe on a coffin was at the funeral of Rex Long Visitor at Slim Butte. I don't do that often. I feel a man has to really be worthy for me to lay the Sacred Pipe on his coffin. And I felt very strongly that this was the case with George. At that funeral of Rex Long Visitor about eleven years ago, George was there. And I remember George praying with the Sacred Pipe before the dinner, praying and blessing the food. And so George was with me since that very first day. We were very close because of this.

George Plenty Wolf was a deeply spiritual man. God called him in his early days to the work of a catechist at Manderson and around Holy Rosary. And then He called him to another work. God called George up to the hill to fast with the Pipe and to acquire a vision. And through this vision to acquire a power through one of God's greatest gifts, the Sacred Pipe. And George really believed in the Sacred Pipe. He believed there was power there and that his prayers would be answered. George also believed in Jesus Christ. I remember George walking into Pine Ridge all the way from the Red Cloud community as an old man, walking to attend Mass on Sunday. I remember giving him Holy Communion. And he had a great and a deep faith in the death and resurrection of Jesus Christ. And he also had a great faith that there was power in the sacraments containing the Presence of Christ. The first day he was in the hospital, about two weeks before his death, I anointed him with the anointing of the sick and I brought him Holy Communion and he blessed himself very reverently with great devotion. I could really see in his face, in his eyes, that he really believed in the sacraments, in Jesus Christ's Body.

I think George Plenty Wolf was an important man for the Lakota people. He was a man who walked in the traditional way, a man who prayed for people and carried the burdens of people because he was a "Pipe man." Yet he was also a man who recognized that the Sacred Pipe had a place in the Christian Church. George accepted my praying with the Sacred Pipe. And this meant something very much to me. I was very deeply grateful, since he was a medicine man and a "Pipe man." But it was something much more than simply personal. I feel that what George was doing was accepting the Pipe into the Christian Church. And I think that this is a very important thing he did in his life. And this is going to become more and more important now as the Lakota people go back to their roots and tradition. Here was the vision of a man who saw the Sacred Pipe as one of God's great gifts that should be brought to the feet of Jesus Christ and laid there since Jesus Christ is the Son of God. And I really believe in my heart that this is a most important vision and this is one of the greatest things George ever did in his life and to become more important as the years go on.

I feel that perhaps the life of George can be summarized in kind of a double vision. George was the man who was looking towards the hill. On the hill he saw a man with the Sacred Pipe fasting and receiving a vision and as he looked, he kept on looking up on that hill and that man with the Sacred Pipe changed into Jesus Christ hanging on the cross. This is the double image I feel summarized his life more than anything else.

What kind of man was George Plenty Wolf? He was a very kind man, a very gentle man. Someone who knew George for a long time told me that he never saw George angry. And this has been my own experience. He was a very humble man. He knew where his power came from. His powers came from the Great Spirit. He was simply the instrument of God. And George knew his limitations. I remember very clearly when one of his grandchildren had an epileptic fit, he told the people that he did not have the power to heal this, that she should be taken up to the hospital and that the priest should be called, that the priest should anoint her with the sacrament of healing. This is really genuine humility before Almighty God. I think George was a very patient man.

George carried the burdens of many people. Many people came to him for prayers. Carrying the Sacred Pipe meant he had to respond to these requests. Throughout his life George carried the burdens of many people. George healed people. There is no doubt in my mind that when the spirit of George left this world there were countless spirits whom he helped in this life waiting to receive him. What a reception that must have been. The spirits of all these people through all those years waiting now to receive the spirit of George.

I think George was a very understanding man. He had a calling from God and had a vision that made him walk the path of the Sacred Pipe, and he had a great love of Jesus Christ. And yet there were times that he was misunderstood, misunderstood by the Church he loved so much. And yet George had the patience and the understanding to accept this and to work in his own life to bring the two traditions together. I feel that this is very remarkable. And so we celebrate today the eternal life of a truly remarkable man. We celebrate the eternal life of one the people are going to miss, the community, the Lakota nation.

The Lord looked down and the Lord said: "The life of George is now completed. His work is finished. The spiritual work I gave George to do is now accomplished, and I will call George back to Myself." And, in words of Isaiah, on this mountain God will remove the mourning veil; on this mountain the Lord of hosts will provide for all people; on this mountain He will destroy death forever. The mountain is a holy, a sacred place. And on the hill George came into very close contact with God, his Father. And it is on this mountain that God will wipe away the tears from our faces. And we are going to say: "Behold our God to Whom we are going to look to save us." And this is done according to the words of Isaiah on the holy mountain.

And, in the Acts of the Apostles, St. Peter said: "I know it is true now that God is not going to show partiality, that God sent His Son, Jesus Christ, for all peoples and for all nations to proclaim the good news of peace and to lead people to accept that Jesus Christ is Lord." Jesus Christ is Lord of all nations, all peoples, of all continents. Jesus Christ is Lord of the Lakota People. And this is the great act of faith that George Plenty Wolf made. And then St. Peter continues, and he tells the way that in the baptism of John God anointed Christ with the Holy Spirit and power. And I thought that this is George Plenty Wolf. He too was anointed with the Holy Spirit and with power. And how Christ went around doing good works and healing all who were in the grip of the devil. I really feel that this is a description of the life of George in his work of prayer and in his work of being a man who carried the Sacred Pipe.

They finally killed Christ, hanging Him on a tree, only to have God raise Him up on the third day. And so we come to this great mystery of the death and resurrection of Christ. It is a mystery that doesn't contradict the mystery of the Sacred Pipe. But it brings us deeper into the mystery of the Great Spirit. He sent not only His great gift, the Sacred Pipe, to the Lakota People, but He sent His own Son, Jesus Christ also. In the Gospel, Christ said: "Whoever eats my flesh and drinks my blood will have everlasting life." He told the people that their fathers ate the manna in the desert when they were coming out of Egypt and died. But whoever eats His flesh will live forever. We know with certitude that these words apply to George Plenty Wolf. Our Lord speaks these words to him.

Midakuase. For the sake of my relatives. This is what George said so often as he concluded his ceremonies with the Sacred Pipe. And this is the way we conclude our thoughts, for the sake of our relatives. We offer up the Sacrifice of the Mass for the spirit of George praying for all the relatives. We ask God to bless his children and his grandchildren, to bless all those who are related to him, all those who are close to him, to pour the Holy Spirit into their hearts, to give them strength and courage, to bless them with the vision of the death and resurrection of Christ, that we are all living this great mystery and with the assurance that God has called George back to Himself, to eternal happiness. May the Holy Spirit be poured into their hearts with His peace and His joy, His consolation and hope and love. That the Holy Spirit may be with them now at this time.

NOTES

INTRODUCTION

1. More detailed information can be obtained from P. Beckwith (1886), DeLand (1904/1906), William Forbes (1894), Hayden (1863), Hyde (1937, 1956), Mekeel (1943), Robinson (1904), and Yarrow (1882).
2. Anyone wishing to pursue further the relationship between Eliade and Jung should also consult Mac Linscott Ricketts. (1970:221–34).
3. There is a growing literature on Red Power and Indian activism, including Burnette (1974), and Steiner (1969).
4. The Native Americans are using the term *ecumenism* in an annual pan-Indian Ecumenical Conference which unites Native American spiritual leaders of the United States and Canada from all religious faiths, indigenous and Christian.

CHAPTER ONE

1. John Smith has an excellent historical background (1967) and indicates its contemporary effect, including its use in the Catholic Church (1970). Wilbur Reigert interviewed one of its previous keepers, Martha Bad Warrior, on its history (1975:71–94).
2. However, the bundle was opened for Reigert, a Chippewa Indian, in 1936 (1975:73) and for an anthropologist, Sidney Thomas, in 1941. Sidney J. Thomas gives a detailed description of the bundle contents, including the Pipe regarded as the Calf Pipe (1941); Smith describes a related ceremony for the preparation of the offering cloths (1964).
3. Kenneth Philip has a complete evaluation of Collier's relation to the American Indian (1977).
4. Mails had additional information on Fools Crow (1979:49–53).
5. Fletcher (1882), Schwatka (1890) and Webb (MS. 1894) also describe the Sun Dance during the 1880s.
6. A memorial give-away is usually associated with the memorial feast

conducted one year after a person's death. At that time a meal is prepared for relatives and friends. After the meal, many possessions are given away to honor the deceased person. These gifts include star quilts and dancing shawls, which relatives make during the course of the year, and suitcases, dinnerware, and other practical items bought at stores. During the Sun Dance, only the giving away of possessions takes place.

7. The entire homily is found in Appendix A.

8. William Stolzman, S.J., has excellent original ethnographic material on the spirits which supplements the material obtained from the Lakota here (1986:104–15).

9. Kemnitzer (1976:261–80) and Powers (1982) both have excellent treatments of yuwipi as a modern healing ceremony among the Lakota.

10. A winter count is the recording of historical events by means of pictures painted on a buffalo hide. One of the most important Sioux winter counts is the one recorded by Baptiste Good in the first part of last century. For a complete description consult Mallery (1893: 287–328).

11. Frederick Streng discusses the sacred/profane dichotomy in some detail (1980 16:122–26).

12. The coup stick was used by a warrior to touch the enemy, either dead or alive. To touch an alive enemy and escape brought even more honor than touching the dead body. The expression "counting coup" developed from this practice.

13. Christoph von Fürer-Haimendorf in a cross-cultural study brings out just how diverse this concept can be (1974).

CHAPTER TWO

1. Blue Bird told Stewart (n.d.) that he went to Oklahoma in 1902. This confirms the statement of Bernard Red Cloud.

2. This corrects the diffusion charts of Shonle, LaBarre, Driver, and Massey referred to above.

3. The sponsor is the person responsible for the meeting taking place and for its purpose. The water woman is the person who brings in the ceremonial water and blesses it at the conclusion of the meeting.

4. It is reminiscent of the Shaking Tent rite among the Algonquian and Blackfoot.

CHAPTER FOUR

1. For an understanding of the Pipe among all the North American tribes, see Steinmetz 1984:27–80.
2. Although Kemnitzer reported a frequent use of Lakota in a 1966 revival meeting at Wolf Creek (personal notes), the service I attended in the summer of 1978 was entirely in English.

BIBLIOGRAPHY

Aberle, David F.
   1966   *The Peyote Religion among the Navaho.* Chicago: Aldine.
Albers, Patricia, and Seymour Parker
   1971   The Plains Vision Experience: A Study of Power and Privilege. *Southwestern Journal of Anthropology* 27:203-33.
Allen, Douglas
   1978   *Structure and Creativity in Religious Hermeneutics in Mircea Eliade's Phenomenology and New Directions.* The Hague: Mouton.
Altizer, Thomas J.
   1975   *Mircea Eliade and the Dialectic of the Sacred.* Westport, Conn.: Greenwood.
Amiotte, Arthur
   1976   Eagles Fly Over. *Parabola* 1, no. 3: 28-41.
Beckwith, Martha Warren
   1930   Mythology of the Oglala Dakota. *Journal of American Folklore* 43: 339-442.
Beckwith, P.
   1886   Notes on Customs of the Dakotahs. *Smithsonian Institution, Annual Reports of the Board of Regents:* 245-57.
Benedict, Ruth F.
   1922   Visions in Plains Culture. *American Anthropologist* 24:2-23.
   1923   *The Concept of the Guardian Spirit in North America.* Memoirs of the American Anthropological Association, no. 29.
   1936   Configurations of Culture. *American Anthropologist* 34:1-27.
Bennett, J. W., ed.
   1975   The New Ethnicity: Perspectives from Ethnology. *1973 Proceedings of the American Ethnological Society.* St. Paul: West.
Berndt, R. M.
   1962   *An Adjustment Movement in Arnhem Land, North Territory of Australia.* Paris and The Hague: Mouton.

Blish, Helen

1926   Ethical Conceptions of the Oglala Dakota. *University of Nebraska Studies* 26:1–47.

1934   The Ceremony of the Sacred Bow of the Oglala Dakota. *American Anthropologist* 36:180–87.

Blumensohn, Jules

1933   The Fast among North American Indians. *American Anthropologist* 35:451–69.

Brown, Joseph Epes

1953   *The Sacred Pipe: Black Elk's Account of the Seven Rites of the Oglala Sioux.* Norman: Univ. of Oklahoma Press.

Buechel, Eugene, S. J.

1970   *A Lakota-English Dictionary.* Ed. Paul Manhart, S.J. Pine Ridge, S.D.: Red Cloud Indian School.

Burnette, Robert

1974   *The Road to Wounded Knee.* New York: Bantam.

Catlin, George

1844   *Letters and Notes on Manners, Customs and Conditions of the North American Indian.* 2 vols. Rpt. New York: Dover, 1973.

Charles, Lucille Hoerr

1945   The Clown's Function. *Journal of American Folklore* 58:25–34.

Collier, Donald

1944   Conjuring Among the Kiowa. *Primitive Man* 17:45–49.

Collins, Dabney Otis

1969   A Happening at Oglala. *The American West* 6:15–19.

Cooper, John M.

1944   The Shaking Tent among Plains and Forest Algonquians. *Primitive Man* 17:60–84.

DeLand, C.E.

1904/   Aborigines of South Dakota. *South Dakota Historical Collections*
1906   3:269–86.

Deloria, Ella

1929   The Sun Dance of the Oglala Sioux. *Journal of American Folklore* 42:354–413.

1932   Dakota Texts. *American Ethnological Society Publications* 14:1–279.

*1937a   MS. Dakota commentary on the Walker texts. *Library of the American Philosophical Society* 30(X8a.50):27–47

*1937b   MS. Teton Sioux Folklore and Ethnology. Translations of the 259 Bushotter texts in the national Anthropological Archives. Smithsonian Institution, Washington, D.C. *Library of the American Philosophical Society* 30(X8c.3)

*1938 MS. Story of the Woman from the Sky. pp. 20–24 in Dakota texts from the Sword manuscript. Library of the American Philosophical Society 30(X8a.18)

Deloria, Vine, Sr.

1987 The Establishment of Christianity among the Sioux. In *Sioux Indian Religion: Tradition and Innovation*, ed. Raymond J. DeMallie and Douglas R. Parks, 91–112. Norman: Univ. of Oklahoma Press.

Deloria, Vine, Jr.

1973 *God is Red.* New York: Grosset and Dunlap.

DeMallie, Raymond J., ed.

1984 *The Sixth Grandfather: Black Elk's Teachings Given to John G. Neihardt.* Lincoln: Univ. of Nebraska Press.

DeMallie, Raymond J., and Robert H. Lavenda

1977 Wakan: Plains Siouan Concepts of Power. In *Anthropology of Power*, ed. Raymond Fogelson and R. Adams, 153–65. New York: Academic Press.

Densmore, Frances

1913 *Chippewa Music II. Bureau of American Ethnology Bulletin* 53.

1918 *Teton Sioux Music. Bureau of American Ethnology Bulletin* 61.

1931 "Lakota Fieldnotes." Manuscript, personal files of Omer Stewart.

1953 The Belief of the Indian in a Connection between Song and the Supernatural. *Bureau of American Ethnology Bulletin* 151:217–23.

Dorsey, George

1906 Legend of the Teton Sioux Medicine Pipe. *Journal of American Folklore* 19:326–29.

Dorsey, James Owen

1889a Teton Folk Lore. *American Anthropologist* 2:143–58.

1889b Teton Folk Lore Notes. *Journal of American Folklore* 2:133–39.

1894 A Study of Siouan Cults. *11th Annual Report of the Bureau of American Ethnology:* 351–544.

1897 Siouan Sociology. *15th Annual Report of the Bureau of American Ethnology:* 205–44.

Dozier, Edward P.

1962 Differing Reactions to Religious Contacts among North American Indian Societies. *Proceedings of the* 34th International Congress of Americanists. Vienna (1960): 161–171

---

*The reference notations are from John Freeman, *A Guide to Manuscripts Relating to the American Indian in the Library of the American Philosophical Society* Philadelphia: American Philosophical Society, 1966.

Driver, Harold E., and William C. Massey
  1957   Comparative Studies of North American Indians. *Transactions of the American Philosophical Society* 47, pt. 2
Dudley, Guilford, III
  1977   *Religion on Trial: Mircea Eliade and His Critics.* Philadelphia: Temple Univ. Press.
Duratschek, M. Claudia, O.S.B.
  1943   The Beginnings of Catholicism in South Dakota. Ph.D diss., Catholic University of America, Washington, D.C.
  1947   *Crusading Along the Sioux Trails.* Yankton, S.D.: Grail Publications.
Dusenberry, Verne
  1962   The Montana Cree: A Study in Religious Persistence. Stockholm Studies in Comparative Religion, no. 3
Eliade, Mircea
  1958   *Patterns in Comparative Religion* New York: Sheed and Ward.
  1959   Methodological Remarks on the Study of Religious Symbolism. In *History of Religions: Essays in Methodology,* ed. Mircea Eliade and Joseph Kitagawa, 86–107. Chicago: Univ. of Chicago Press.
  1964   *Shamanism: Archaic Techniques of Ecstasy.* New York: Pantheon.
  1973   *Australian Religions: An Introduction.* Ithaca, N.Y.: Cornell Univ. Press.
Erdoes, Richard
  1972   *The Sun Dance People.* New York: Random House.
Erikson, Erik
  1945   Childhood and Tradition in Two American Indian Tribes. *The Psychoanalytic Study of the Child* 1:319–50. Rev. in *Personality in Nature, Society and Culture,* ed. C. Kluckhohn and H. Murray, 176–203. New York.
  1946   Ego Development and Historical Change: Clinical Notes. *The Psychoanalytic Study of the Child* 2:359–96.
  1959   Identity and the Life Cycle. *Psychological Issues* 1, no. 1 Monograph 1
  1963   Hunters Across the Prairie. In *Childhood and Society,* 114–65. 2nd ed. New York: Norton.
Feraca, Stephen
  1961   The Yuwipi Cult of the Oglala and Sicangu Teton Sioux. *Plains Anthropologist* 6:155–63.
  1963   Wankinyan: Contemporary Teton Dakota Religion. Studies in Plains Anthropology and History, no. 2. Browning, Mont: Museum of the Plains Indians.

Feraca, Stephen, and James H. Howard
1963   The Identity and Demography of the Dakota or Sioux Tribe. *Plains Anthropologist* 8:80–84.

Fletcher, Alice
1882   The Sun Dance of the Sioux. *Proceedings of the American Association for the Advancement of Science* 31:580–84.
1883a   The Elk Mystery or Festival. *Peabody Museum of American Archaeology and Ethnology Reports* 16/17:276–88.
1883b   The Shadow or Ghost Lodge. *Peabody Museum of American Archaeology and Ethnology Reports* 16/17:296–307.
1883c   The White Buffalo Festival of the Uncpapas. *Peabody Museum of American Archaeology and Ethnology Reports* 16/17:260–75.
1896   The Emblematic Use of the Tree in a Dakota Group. *Proceedings of the American Association for the Advancement of Science* 45:191–209.

Forbes, Bruce David
1985   Rev. of Pipe, Bible and Peyote among the Oglala Lakota, by Paul B. Steinmetz, S.J. *The American Indian Quarterly* 9:84–87.

Forbes, William H.
1894   Traditions of the Sioux Indians. *Collections of the Minnesota Historical Society* 6:413–16.

Fowler, Loretta
1978   Wind River Reservation Political Process: An Analysis of Symbols of Consensus. *American Ethnologist* 5:748–69.

Fugle, Eugene
1966   The Nature and Function of the Lakota Night Cults. *University of South Dakota Museum News* 27, nos. 3 and 4.

Fürer-Haimendorf, Christoph von
1974   The Sense of Sin in Cross Cultural Perspective. *Man: Journal of the Royal Anthropological Institute* 9:539–56.

Gilmore, M. R.
1932   The Dakota Ceremony of Presenting a Pipe to Marshall Foch and Conferring a Name Upon Him. *Papers of the Michigan Academy of Science, Arts and Letters* 18:15–21.

Girardot, Norman J. and Mac Linscott Ricketts, eds.
1982   *Imagination and Meaning: The Scholarly and Literary Worlds of Mircea Eliade.* New York: Seabury.

Grobsmith, Elizabeth S.
1974   Wakinza: Uses of Yuwipi Medicine Power in Contemporary Teton Dakota Culture. *Plains Anthropologist* 19:129–33.

Haines, Francis
    1938   The Northward Spread of Horses Among the Plains Indians. *American Anthropologist* 40:429–37.
Hallencreutz, Carl F.
    1979   "Christ is the Mountain": Some observations on the Religious Functions of Symbols in the Encounter of Christianity and Other Religions. In *Religious Symbols and their functions*, ed. Harald Biezais, Stockholm: Almqvist and Wiksell.
Hallowell, A. Irving
    1942   *The Role of Conjuring in Saulteaux Society.* Philadelphia Anthropological Society Publications 2.
    1952   Ojibwa Personality and Acculturation. In *Selected Papers of the XXIXth International Congress of Americanists*, ed. Sol Tex, 105–12. Chicago: Univ. of Chicago Press.
    1955   *Culture and Experience.* Philadelphia: Univ. of Pennsylvania Press.
Hassrick, Royal B.
    1964   *The Sioux: Life and Custom of a Warrior Society.* Norman: Univ. of Oklahoma Press.
Hayden, F. V.
    1863   Contributions to the Ethnography and Philology of the Indian Tribes of the Missouri Valley. *Transactions of the American Philosophical Society* 12:364–78.
Hertzberg, Hazel W.
    1971   *The Search for an American Indian Identity: Modern Pan-Indian Movements.* Syracuse, N.Y.: Syracuse Univ. Press.
Hodge, Frederick W., ed.
    1907/   Handbook of American Indians North of Mexico. *Bureau of Amer-*
    1910   *ican Ethnology Bulletin* 30.
Holler, Clyde
    1984   Black Elk's Relationship to Christianity. *The American Indian Quarterly* 8:37–49.
Holy Rosary Mission
    1963   *Red Cloud's Dream.* Pine Ridge, S.D.: Red Cloud Indian School.
Horton, Robin
    1971   Ritual Man in Africa. In *Reader in Comparative Religion: An Anthropological Approach*, ed. William A. Lessa and Evon Z. Vogt. New York: Harper and Row.
Howard, James
    1954   The Dakota Heyoka Cult. *Scientific Monthly* 78:254–58.
    1955   Pan-Indian Culture of Oklahoma. *Scientific Monthly* 81:215–20.

1967   Half Moon Way: The Peyote Ritual of Chief White Bear. *University of South Dakota Museum News* 28, nos. 1 and 2.

1976   Yanktonai Ethnohistory and the John K. Bear Winter Count. *Plains Anthropologist Memoir* 11.

Hultkrantz, Åke

1953   *Conceptions of the Soul among North American Indians.* Ethnographical Museum of Sweden Monograph Series 1.

1956   Configurations of Religious Belief among the Wind River Shoshone. *Ethnos* 21:194–205.

1961   Owners of the Animals in the Religion of the North American Indians. In *The Supernatural Owners of Nature,* ed. Åke Hultkrantz, 53–64. Stockholm Studies in Comparative Religion 1.

1967   Spirit Lodge: A North American Shamanistic Seance. In *Studies in Shamanism,* ed. Carl-Martin Edsman, 32–68. Stockholm: Almqvist and Wiksell.

1969   Pagan and Christian Elements in the Religious Syncretism among the Shoshoni Indians of Wyoming. In *Syncretism* ed. Sven S. Hartman, 15–40. Stockholm: Almqvist and Wiksell.

1970   The Phenomenology of Religion: Aims and Methods. *Temenos* 6: 68–88.

1971   The Structure of Theistic Beliefs among North American Plains Indians. *Temenos* 7:66–74.

1972   An Ideological Dichotomy: Myths and Folk Beliefs among the Shoshone Indians of Wyoming. *History of Religions* 11:339–53.

1974   Conditions for the Spread of the Peyote Cult in North America. In *New Religions,* ed. Harold Biezais, 70–83. Stockholm: Almqvist and Wiksell.

n.d.   The Development of the Plains Indian Sun Dance. In *Perennitas: Studi in Onore de Angelo Brelich,* 223–43. Rome: Edizioni dell' Ateneo.

Hurt, Wesley R.

1960a   Factors in the Persistence of Peyote in the Northern Plains. *Plains Anthropologist* 5:16–27.

1960b   A Yuwipi Ceremony at Pine Ridge. *Plains Anthropologist* 5:48–52.

Hurt, Wesley R., and James Howard

1952   A Dakota Conjuring Ceremony. *Southwestern Journal of Anthropology* 8:286–96.

Hyde, George

1937   *Red Cloud's Folk.* Norman: Univ. of Oklahoma Press.

1956   *A Sioux Chronicle.* Norman: Univ. of Oklahoma Press.

Jahner, Elaine
  1987   Lakota Genesis: The Oral Tradition. In *Sioux Indian Religion: Tradition and Innovation*, ed. Raymond J. DeMallie and Douglas R. Parks, 45–65. Norman: Univ. of Oklahoma Press.
James, Bernard
  1970   Continuity and Emergence in Indian Poverty Culture. *Current Anthropologist* 11:435–52.
Jorgensen, Joseph G.
  1972   *The Sun Dance Religion: Power for the Powerless.* Chicago: Univ. of Chicago Press.
Jorgensen, Joseph G., and Richard Clemmer
  1978   Rev. of *The Indian in America*, by Wilcomb E. Washburn. *The Indian Historian* 11:38–44.
Kaiser, Patricia L.
  1984   The Lakota Sacred Pipe: Its Tribal Use and Religious Philosophy. *American Indian Culture and Research Journal* 8:1–26.
Kemnitzer, Luis S.
  1970   Cultural Provenience of Objects Used in Yuwipi: A Modern Teton-Dakota Healing Ritual. *Ethnos* 35:40–75.
  1976   Structure, Content and Cultural Meaning of Yuwipi: A Modern Lakota Healing Ritual. *American Anthropologist* 3:261–80.
  n.d.   Manuscript notes, personal files of Luis S. Kemnitzer.
Kroeber, Alfred
  1933   Rev. of *Method and Theory of Ethnology*, by Paul Radin. *American Anthropologist* 35:765–66.
  1948   *Anthropology.* New York: Harcourt, Brace.
LaBarre, Weston
  1960   Twenty Years of Peyote Studies. *Current Anthropologist* 1:45–60.
  1975   *The Peyote Cult.* 4th ed. New York: Schocken.
Lame Deer, John
  1972   *Lame Deer, Seeker of Visions.* Ed. Richard Erdoes. New York: Simon and Schuster.
Laney, John
  1972   The Peyote Movement: An Introduction. *Annual of Archetypal Psychology and Jungian Thought:* 110–31.
Lanternari, Vittorio
  1965   *The Religions of the Oppressed: A Study of Modern Messianic Cults.* New York: New American Library.
Lewis, Thomas
  1970   Notes on the Heyoka, the Teton Dakota "Contrary" Cult. Pine Ridge

Research Bulletin II:7–19. Pine Ridge, S.D.: Public Health Service, Community Mental Health Program.

1972   The Oglala (Teton Dakota) Sun Dance: Vicissitudes of Its Structure and Function. *Plains Anthropologist* 17:44–49.

Linton, Ralph

1943   Nativistic Movements. *American Anthropologist* 45:230–40.

Lommel, Andreas

1967   *The World of the Early Hunters.* London: Evelyn, Adams and Mackay.

1970   Rev. of *Shamanism: The Beginning of Art. Current Anthropologist* II:39–48. [Seventeen book reviews of Lommel's study, plus his précis and reply]

Lurie, Nancy Oestreich

1961   *Mountain Wolf Woman, Sister of Crashing Thunder: The Autobiography of a Winnebago Woman.* Ann Arbor: Univ. of Michigan Press.

Lynd, James

1862   The Religion of the Dakota. *Collections of the Minnesota Historical Society* 2:150–74.

McAllestar, David P.

1959   Peyote Music. *Viking Fund Publication in Anthropology,* no. 13.

McGee. W. J.

1897   The Siouan Indians: A Preliminary Sketch. *15th Annual Report of the Bureau of American Ethnology:* 153–204.

MacGregor, Gordon H.

1946   *Warriors without Weapons.* Chicago: Univ. of Chicago Press.

McLaughlin, Marie L.

1916   *Myths and Legends of the Sioux.* Bismark, N.D: Bismark Tribune Co.

1973   *Native American Tribalism: Indian Survivals and Renewals.* New York: Oxford Univ. Press.

Mails, Thomas E.

1978   *Sundancing at Rosebud and Pine Ridge.* Sioux Falls, S.D. Augustana College.

1979   *Fools Crow.* New York: Doubleday.

Malan, V. D., and Clinton Jesser, Jr.

1959   The Dakota Indian Religion: A Study of Conflict of Values. Bulletin 473, South Dakota Agricultural Experimental Station, Brookings, S.D.

Mallery, Garrick

1893   Picture-writing of the American Indians. *10th Annual Report of the Bureau of American Ethnology.*

Marett, R. R.

  1934   Rev. of *The Method and Theory of Ethnology*, by Paul Radin. *American Anthropologist* 36:116–18.

Mekeel, Scudder

  1943   A Short History of the Teton-Dakota. *North Dakota Historical Quarterly* 10:137–205.

  n.d.   MS. "Lakota Fieldnotes," manuscript, personal files of Scudder Mekeel.

Melody, Michael Edward

  1978   Maka's Story: A Study of a Lakota Cosmogony. *Journal of American Folklore* 91:149–67.

Mooney, James

  1892   A Kiowa Mescal Rattle. *American Anthropologist*, o.s. 5:64–65.

  1896   The Ghost Dance Religion and the Sioux Outbreak. *14th Annual Report of the Bureau of American Ethnology*, pt. 2. Rpt. Chicago: University of Chicago Press, 1965.

  1897   The Kiowa Peyote Rite. *Der Urquell*, n.s. 1:329–33. Leyden.

Neihardt, John G.

  1961   *Black Elk Speaks: Being the Life Story of a Holy Man of the Oglala Sioux*. Lincoln: University of Nebraska Press.

Newcomb, W. W., Jr.

  1956   The Culture and Acculturation of the Delaware Indians. Papers of the Museum of Anthropology, no. 10. University of Michigan.

Nurge, Ethel

  1966   The Sioux Sun Dance in 1962. In *Proceedings of XXXVI International Congress of Americanists*, 102–14. Seville: Sevilla.

  1970   *The Modern Sioux: Social Systems and Reservation Culture*. Lincoln: Univ. of Nebraska Press.

Olson, Paul A.

  1982   *Black Elk Speaks* as Epic and Ritual Attempt to Revise History. In *Vision and Refuge: Essays on the Literature of the Great Plains*, ed. Virginia Faulkner and Frederick C. Luebke, 3–37 Lincoln: Univ. of Nebraska Press.

One Feather, Vivian, ed.

  1974   *Ehanni Ohunkakan: Myths from the Walker Collection*. Spearfish, S.D.: Black Hills State College.

Oosterwal, Gottfried

  1971   Comments (32–33), in Weston LaBarre, Materials for a History of Studies in Crisis Cults: A Bibliographical Essay, *Current Anthropology* 12: 3–44.

Opler, Morris E.

  1936   The Influence of Aboriginal Pattern and White Contact on a Recently Introduced Ceremony, the Mescalero Peyote Rite. *Journal of American Folklore* 49:143–66.

Ortiz, Roxanne Dunbar

1977   *The Great Sioux Nation Sitting in Judgment on America.* Berkeley, Calif.: Moon Books.

Overholt, Thomas W.

1974   The Ghost Dance of 1890 and the nature of the Prophetic Process. *Ethnohistory* 21:37–63.

1978   Short Bull, Black Elk, Sword and the "Meaning" of the Ghost Dance. *Religion* [Lancaster, Eng.]:171–95.

Paige, Harry W.

1970   *Songs of the Teton Sioux.* Los Angeles: Westernlore.

Pettazzoni, Raffaele

1956   *The All Knowing God: Researches into early Religion and Culture.* London: Methuen.

Philip, Kenneth

1977   *John Collier's Crusade for Indian Reform 1920–1954.* Tuscon: Univ. of Arizona Press.

Pine Ridge Research Bulletin

1969   Public Health Services, Indian Health Service, Mental Health Program. Pine Ridge, S.D. No. 10.

Pond, Gideon

1889   Dakota Superstitions. *Collections of the Minnesota Historical Society:* 215–55.

Powers, William K.

1977   *Oglala Religion.* Lincoln: Univ. of Nebraska Press.

1982   *Yuwipi: Vision and Experience in Oglala Ritual.* Lincoln: Univ. of Nebraska Press.

1986   *Sacred Language: The Nature of Supernatural Discourse in Lakota.* Norman: Univ. of Oklahoma Press.

1987   *Beyond the Vision: Essays on American Indian Culture.* Norman: Univ. of Oklahoma Press.

Radin, Paul

1923   The Winnebago Tribe. *37th Annual Report of the Bureau of American Ethnology.* Rpt. Lincoln: Univ. of Nebraska Press, 1973.

1924   *Monotheism Among Primitive Peoples* London: G. Allen and Unwin. Rpt. as *Special Publication of Bollingen Foundation* no. 4, Basel: Ethnographical Museum, 1954.

1933   *The Method and Theory of Ethnology.* New York: McGraw-Hill.

Ray, Verne

1941   Historical Backgrounds of the Conjuring Complex in the Plateau and the Plains. In *Language, Culture and Personality: Essays in Honor of Edward Sapir*, ed. Leslie Spier, 204–16. Menasha, Wis.: American Anthropological Association.

Reigert, Wilbur

　1975　*Quest for the Pipe of the Sioux: As Viewed from Wounded Knee.* Jean Fritze, Keystone Route 184, Rapid City, S.D.

Ricketts, Mac Linscott

　1970　The Nature and Extent of Eliade's "Jungianism." *Union Seminary Quarterly Review* 25:211–34.

Riggs, Stephen

　1869　*Tah-Koo Wakan: The Gospel among the Dakota.* Boston: Congregational Publishing Society.

　1880　The Theogony of the Sioux. *American Antiquarian* 2:265–70.

　1883　Mythology of the Dakota. *American Antiquarian* 5:147–49.

　1893　*Dakota Grammar, Texts and Ethnography.* Department of the Interior, U.S. Geographical and Geological Survey of the Rocky Mountain Region. Rpt. Blue Cloud Abbey, Marvin, S.D. 1977.

Robinson, Doane

　1904　A History of the Dakota or Sioux Indians *South Dakota Historical Collections* 2:1–523. Rpt. Ross and Haines, Minneapolis, 1967.

Ruby, Robert H.

　1955　*The Oglala Sioux.* New York: Vantage.

　1966　Yuwipi, Ancient Rite of the Sioux. *Magazine of Western History* 16:74–79.

Saler, Benson

　1977　Supernatural as a Western Category. *Ethos* 5:31–53.

Saliba, John A.

　1976　*"Homo Religious" in Mircea Eliade: An Anthropological Evaluation.* Leiden: E. J. Brill.

Sanford, Margaret

　1971　Pan-Indianism, Acculturation and the American Ideal. *Plains Anthropologist* 16:222–27.

Schaeffer, Claude E.

　1969　Blackfoot Shaking Tent. *Glenbow Alberta Institute Occasional Paper*, no. 5, Calgary, Alberta.

Schmidt, Wilhelm

　1933　*High Gods in North America.* Oxford: Clarendon Press.

　1935　*The Origin and Growth of Religion, Facts and Theories.* London: Methuen.

Schultes, Richard Evans

　1938　The Appeal of Peyote (Lophophora Williamsis) as a Medicine. *American Anthropologist* 40:698–715.

Schwatka, Frederich

    1890   The Sun Dance of the Sioux. *Century Magazine*, n.s. 17:753–59.

Shonle, Ruth

    1925   Peyote, the Giver of Visions. *American Anthropologist* 27:53–75.

Sialm, Placidus, S.J.

    1923   A Retreat to Catechists. *The Indian Sentinel* 3:78.

Silva, Antonio Barbosa da

    1982   *The Phenomenology of Religion as a Philosophical Problem: An Analysis of the Theoretical Background of the Phenomenology of Religion, in General, and of Mircea Eliade's Phenomenological Approach in Particular.* Uppsala: CWK Gleerup.

Slotkin, J. S.

    1952   Menomini Peyotism: A Study of Individual Variation in a Primary Group with Homogeneous Culture. *Transactions of the American Philosophical Society* 42, pt. 4.

    1956   *The Peyote Religion: A Study in Indian-White Relations.* Glencoe, Ill.: Free Press.

Smith, John L.

    1964   A Ceremony for the Preparation of the Offering Cloths for presentation to the Sacred Calf Pipe. *Plains Anthropologist* 9:190–96.

    1967   A Short History of the Sacred Calf Pipe of the Teton Dakota. *University of South Dakota Museum News* 28:1–37.

    1970   The Sacred Calf Pipe Bundle: Its Effect on the Present Teton Dakota. *Plains Anthropologist* 15:87–93.

Spider, Emerson

    1987   The Native American Church of Jesus Christ. In *Sioux Indian Religion: Tradition and Innovation*, ed. Raymond J. DeMallie and Douglas R. Parks, 189–209. Norman: Univ. of Oklahoma Press.

Spier, Leslie

    1921   The Sun Dance of the Plains Indians: Its Development and Diffusion. *Anthropological Papers of the American Museum of Natural History* 16:451–527.

Stanner, W. E. H.

    1960   On Aboriginal Religion. *Oceania* 30:245–78. Rpt. in *Oceania Monograph*, no. 11 (1966): 25–58.

Steiner, Stan

    1969   *The New Indian.* New York: Dell.

Steinmetz, Paul B., S.J.

    1970   The Relationship Between Plains Indian Religion and Christianity: A Priest's Viewpoint. *Plains Anthropologist* 15:83–86.

    1980   Pipe, Bible and Peyote Among the Oglala Lakota: A Study in Religious Identity. *Stockholm Studies in Comparative Religion* 19.

1984a *Meditations with Native Americans: Lakota Spirituality.* Santa Fe: Bear and Co.

1984b The Sacred Pipe in American Indian Religions. *American Indian Culture and Research Journal* 8:27–80.

Steltenkamp, Michael, S.J.

1982   *The Sacred Vision: Native American Religion and Its Practice Today.* New York: Paulist Press.

n.d.   "The Catholic Life of Black Elk." Manuscript, personal files of Michael Steltenkamp, S.J.

Stewart, Omer

1944   Washo-Northern Paiute Peyotism: A Study in Acculturation. *University of California Publications in American Archaeology and Ethnology* 40:63–141.

1948   Ute Peyotism: A Study of a Cultural Complex. *University of Colorado Studies, series in Anthropology,* no. 1 Rpt. New York: Kraus, 1972..

1956   Three Gods for Joe. *Tomorrow: Quarterly Review of Psychical Research* 4:71–76.

1976   The Peyote Religion and the Ghost Dance. *The Indian Historian* 5:27–30.

1977   Rev. of *The Peyote,* by Weston LaBarre. *American Anthropologist* 79:930–31.

n.d.   Manuscript notes, personal files of Omer Stewart.

Stolzman, William, S.J.

1986   *The Pipe and Christ: A Christian-Sioux Dialogue.* Chamberlain, S.D.: St. Joseph's Indian School.

Streng, Frederick J.

1980   Sacred or Holy, in *The New Encyclopaedia Britannica,* 15th ed. *Macropaedia* 16:122–26.

Tennelly, J. B.

1936   Letter to Adelbert Thunder Hawk, June 29, 1936. Marquette University Memorial Library. BCIM Box 235, Folder 12.

Thomas, Robert K.

1965   Pan-Indianism. *Midcontinent American Studies Journal* 6:75–83. Rpt. in *The Emergent Native Americans: A Reader in Culture Contact,* ed. Deward E. Walker, Jr., 739–46. Boston: Little Brown.

Thomas, Sidney J.

1941   A Sioux Medicine Bundle. *American Anthropologist* 43:605–9.

Turner, Harold

1980   New Tribal Religious Movements in *The New Encyclopaedia Britannica,* 15th ed. *Macropaedia* 18:697–705.

Tylor, Edward B.

1871   *Primitive Culture.* 2 vols. London: J. Murray. Rpt. New York: Harper Torchbooks, 1958.

U.S. Government

1883a   Teller to the Commissioner of Indian Affairs, Dec. 2, 1882, in *Report of the Secretary of the Interior* in serial 2190, pp. xi–xii.

1883b   Rules for the Courts of Indian Offenses, April 10, 1883. *Annual Report of the Commissioner of Indian Affairs.*

1916   U.S.A. v. Harry Black Bear. U.S. District Court for the District of South Dakota, Western Division No. 820, Sept. 7–8, 1916. Federal Records Center, General Service Administration, Kansas City, Mo.

1934a   John Collier, Circular No. 2970 on Indian Religious Freedom and Indian Culture, Jan. 3, 1934.

1934b   Letter of Rev. Lawler to the Superintendent of the Pine Ridge Reservation in File, "Sioux Indians, Indian Religion." Federal Records Center, General Service Administration, Kansas City, Mo.

1936   Letter of Pine Ridge Superintendent W. O. Roberts to Fred Daiher, assistant to the Commissioner, Sept. 26, 1936, 37805 OS. Federal Records Center, General Service Administration, Kansas City, Mo.

1978   American Indian Religious Freedom. Hearings before the U.S. Senate, Select Committee on Indian Affairs, 95th Congress on S.J. Res. 102, Feb. 24 and 27. [This bill was passed by both Houses of Congress.]

Vecsey, Christopher

1987   Sun Dances, Corn Pollen and the Cross: Native American Catholics Today. *Commonweal* 114 (June 5) 345–51.

Voget, Fred W.

1956   The American Indian in Transition, *American Anthropologist* 58:249–63.

von Franz, Marie Louise

1980   *Projection and Re-Collection in Jungian Psychology: Reflections of the Soul.* LaSalle: Open Court Publishing Co.

Wake, C. S.

1905–   Mythology of the Plains Indians. *American Antiquarian* 27:9–16;
06   73–80; 323–28; 28:205–12.

Walker, J. B.

1917   The Sun Dance and Other Ceremonies of the Oglala Division of the Teton-Dakota. *Anthropological Paper of the American Museum of Natural History* 16, pt 2.

1980   *Lakota Belief and Ritual.* Ed. Raymond J. DeMallie and Elaine A. Jahner. Lincoln: Univ. of Nebraska Press.

1982   *Lakota Society.* Ed. Raymond J. DeMallie. Lincoln: Univ. of Nebraska Press.

1983   *Lakota Myth.* Ed. Elaine A. Jahner. Lincoln: Univ. of Nebraska Press.

Wallace, Anthony F. C.

1956   Revitalization Movements. *American Anthropologist* 58:264–81.

Wallis, Ruth A., and Wilson D. Wallis

1953   The Sins of the Fathers; Concept of Disease Among the Canadian Dakota. *Southwestern Journal of Anthropology* 9:431–35.

Washburn, Wilcomb

1975   *The Indian in America.* New York: Harper and Row.

Webb, H. G.

1894   MS. *The Dakota Sun Dance of 1883,* MS. no. 1394a, National Anthropological Archives, Smithsonian Institution, Washington, D.C.

Wissler, Clark

1905   Whirlwind and the Elk in the Mythology of the Dakotas. *Journal of American Folklore* 18:267–68.

1907   Some Dakota. *Journal of American Folklore* 20:121–31.

1912   Societies and Ceremonial Associations in the Oglala Division of the Teton-Dakota. *Anthropological Papers of the American Museum of Natural History* 11:1–97.

1926   *The Relation of Nature to Man in Aboriginal America.* New York: Oxford Univ. Press.

Yarrow, H. C.

1882   Some Superstitions of Live Indians. *American Antiquarian* 4:136–44.

INDEX

Pipe, Bible, and Peyote was designed by Betty McDaniel, composed by Lithocraft, Inc., printed by Cushing-Malloy, Inc., and bound by John H. Dekker & Sons, Inc. The book is set in Trump Mediaeval and printed on 50-lb. Glatfelter Antique, B–16.